The Age of Doubt

The Age of Doubt

Tracing the Roots of
Our Religious Uncertainty

CHRISTOPHER LANE

Yale UNIVERSITY PRESS   *New Haven & London*

Published with assistance from the foundation established in memory of Calvin
Chapin of the Class of 1788, Yale College.

Yale University Press books may be purchased in quantity for educational,
business, or promotional use. For information, please e-mail sales.press@yale.edu
(U.S. office) or sales@yaleup.co.uk (U.K. office).

Designed by Mary Valencia.
Set in Minion type by The Composing Room of Michigan, Inc.
Printed in the United States of America.

Library of Congress Cataloging-in-Publication Data

Lane, Christopher, 1966–
The age of doubt : tracing the roots of our religious uncertainty /
Christopher Lane.
p.   cm.
Includes bibliographical references and index.
ISBN 978-0-300-14192-4 (clothbound : alk. paper)   1. Faith.   2. Theology,
Doctrinal—England—History—19th century.   3. Faith—History of
doctrines—19th century.   4. Belief and doubt.   I. Title.
BT771.3.L36 2011
234'.23094209034—dc22
2010037921

A catalogue record for this book is available from the British Library.
This paper meets the requirements of ANSI/NISO Z39.48-1992
(Permanence of Paper).

10 9 8 7 6 5 4 3 2 1

Doubt is uncertain belief.
—JAMES H. SNOWDEN, "The Place of Doubt in Religious Belief" (1916)

How much faith is involved in the workings of reason and how much reason lies in the assertions of faith?
—EDWARD ROTHSTEIN, "Reason and Faith, Eternally Bound" (2003)

CONTENTS

The Age of Doubt

Putting Faith in Doubt

"Why is it thought so very wicked to be an unbeliever?"[1] In Britain today, a question like this would probably generate surprise, even some confusion. With religious leaders debating whether Anglicanism should remain the country's state religion and church attendance falling to record lows (at 15 percent), doubt and unbelief are no longer exceptional qualities in the country. They have become national hallmarks. Far from conveying wickedness or sin, they suggest that one is open to debate, leery of dogma, and focused on change.

It wasn't always so. The novel containing the above question, *The Nemesis of Faith*, was burned as heretical at Oxford University in 1849. It sparked a furious row over whether the work was fiction or thinly veiled autobiography. Lawyers wrote lengthy briefs on whether its author, James Anthony Froude, had perjured himself by denouncing the Church's Thirty-Nine Articles, so breaking a contract both religious and legal. Forced to resign his fellowship at Oxford, Froude—who would go on to become one of the nation's best-known historians—found himself disinherited by his father. Friends also disowned him, either appalled by his stated doubts or wary of associating with an "infidel," a word still used at the time in the country's newspapers.

In nineteenth-century Britain, religious doubt became a serious, widespread concern. It also galvanized cultural debate and scientific inquiry. And it did so, significantly, just as the nation's empire was reaching political and administrative control of almost one quarter of the world. While Cecil Rhodes wrote in his "Confession of Faith" that he "would annex the planets if [he] could," Britain's leading intellectuals, battling the Church, struggled to absorb radical scientific discoveries in botany, biology, and geology.[2] Those upended almost everything the Bible had taught them about the world. Each discovery, more terrifying than the last, threw into crisis a book that for centuries had anchored their values and meaning. "It was the epoch of belief," Charles Dickens famously declared in *A Tale of Two Cities,* "it was the epoch of incredulity, . . . we had everything before us, we had nothing before us."[3]

Reeling in shock and often horrified by what they unearthed, many well-known intellectuals suffered a profound crisis over what they did and did not believe. John Henry Newman explained in his *Parochial and Plain Sermons,* "We are in a world of mystery, with one bright Light before us, sufficient for our proceeding forward through all difficulties. Take away this Light, and we are utterly wretched—we know not where we are, how we are sustained, what will become of us, and of all that is dear to us, what we are to believe, and why we are in being."[4]

While Newman himself recognized and briefly experienced "a perilous substratum of doubt," his beliefs endured, leading to his conversion to Roman Catholicism. For many others harboring similar doubts, however, the movement went in the other direction, away from Christianity, often due to nagging questions that, Newman explained, "rob . . . Certitude of its normal peacefulness."[5] Dejection was widespread. Some Victorians wrote books that asked frankly, *Is Life Worth Living?* Their despair grew so intense that it helped to define the era.[6]

That perspective has become something of a truism about nineteenth-century Britain. Yet not all Victorians thought that religious doubt was inherently sinful or tragic. In insisting that God was unknowable and unprovable, large numbers of others found a release from faith and dogma. They came to welcome the change, seeing doubt as less a matter to fear than a condition to prize. The results, not just their volume, are impressive. As one scholar notes, "Never has an age in history produced such a detailed literature of lost faith, or so many great men and women of religious temperament standing outside organized religion."[7]

One may not think that the Victorians have much to teach us about religious doubt and uncertainty. But they lived through tumultuous times, when their deity seemed to abandon them, traditions appeared to be losing their grip, and fundamental questions loomed about the well-being of the country and the future of the world. The stakes were high. Religious doubt ultimately involved questioning the fabric of British social and cultural life. As the country struggled to establish exactly what it believed and why, the very doctrines and beliefs that it had used to define itself imploded, under immense duress and opposition, leaving something approaching the secular culture we inhabit today.

It was, in hindsight, an extraordinary time when the nation came as close as it ever would to publicly debating its religious beliefs. Extraordinary, too, because the conversation eventually included whether belief in God was necessary, even possible, after scientists, philosophers, and a host of writers had argued otherwise. In short, though the Victorians are often perceived today as self-confident, even smug, they were given to vibrant disagreement about the fundamentals of religious belief. We still have much to learn from their debates.

The Age of Doubt shows how integral religious doubt became to large swaths of Victorian culture, from its most tightly scripted traditions to its most revolutionary arguments and discoveries, chief among them evolutionary theory. It also traces how Victorian literature and science affected each other, including through their shared use of doubt. While scientists reached for metaphors to make sense of vast conundrums, poets and novelists struggled to make sense of the most provocative scientific discoveries: the descent of man, the evolution of species by natural selection, and the dating and formation of the Earth as billions of years old.

The debates about religion and science that flared in nineteenth-century Britain predate by almost two centuries the "new" atheism that has evolved today, undermining many of its claims for originality. Indeed, the Victorians' crisis of faith generated a far more serious engagement with all facets of religious belief and doubt. More profoundly than any generation before them, the Victorians came to view doubt as inseparable from belief, thought, and debate, as well as a much-needed antidote to fanaticism and unbridled certainty.

That theirs was a century of religious doubt makes it a subject ripe for reinvestigation. Many of the questions that they encountered continue to recur—in the United States more intensively than in Britain—as fierce cultural battles over the status of faith and reason. In the States today, as Edward Rothstein noted recently, two of the most urgent questions driving cultural debate are "How much faith is involved in the workings of reason and how much reason lies in the assertions of faith?"[8] In using the Victorians to answer those searching questions, and transitioning accordingly from Victorian Britain to contemporary North America, I hope to demonstrate that we, too, cannot clarify our beliefs, religious and otherwise, until we have reckoned with religious uncertainty and the myriad questions that it poses.

This book tells the story of Victorian doubt by describing what it felt like to lose one's religious faith—as an individual and, more broadly, as a people and society. Armed with a rich variety of sources, including a large archive of neglected historical material that captures how the Victorians' thoughts about religious belief and doubt changed over the course of the century, we'll see the scope of their doubt massively expand, from the Creation story, the Flood, and the existence of miracles to the virgin birth, the resurrection of Christ, and, ultimately, the very existence of God. That expansion also makes clear why "doubt" sometimes surpassed the religious context of Victorian Britain, acquiring a strongly psychological inflection and joining forces more broadly with skepticism, a philosophical stance against credulity.

The Victorians' preoccupation with doubt makes our perception of them as pious, reserved, and self-confident look one-sided, even faulty. A large number of prominent Victorians challenged the zeal and dogma that, in several quarters, had hastened their loss of religious faith. After countless writers and worshippers found it impossible to uphold biblical explanations of creation, many tried to house their beliefs in society and culture, to make both agents of redemption.[9] "The replacement of *serve God* by *serve society* was," Owen Chadwick asserts, "intelligible to everyone."[10] Others looked for ways to harmonize their beliefs with new discoveries and responsibilities, including by developing an ethic of doubt—a philosophy of persistent uncertainty, where skepticism becomes welcome and creative, rather than obtrusive and disabling.

Like those questioning Victorians, this book advances an argument on behalf of doubt itself. It dwells on the advantages of religious and philosophic uncertainty as a creative stimulant and assesses the benefits of skepticism in a world that still tries to rid us of that quality.[11] Like Thomas Cooper, a colorful but little-known Victorian poet whose religious beliefs wavered, it takes not-knowing (including about the existence of God) as a valuable, necessary stance: "I say not that there is no God: but that / *I know not.* Dost *thou* know, or dost thou guess?"[12]

The Victorians' preoccupation with religious doubt is all the more striking because they lived through a religious revival "unmatched since the days of the Puritans."[13] In the first decades of the nineteenth century, religion was everywhere, and the Established Church was a commanding institution that, with Britain's Parliament, governed the population. The same bishop of Oxford who would vigorously challenge Darwin's theory of evolution in 1860 told worshippers, "Irreverence and doubt are the object of your greatest fear."[14]

Sermon after sermon warned congregations that doubt was not just sinful and immoral but a condition marred by emptiness and despair. "Consider the miseries of wives and mothers losing their faith in Scripture," urged Cardinal John Henry Newman, as some doubters tried to cling to their faith by focusing on the sorry plight of those who had lost theirs.[15]

Like that of so many other men of the cloth, Protestant and Catholic, Newman's strategy backfired and sent the Church into defensive retreat. As the scholar Joseph Altholz asked appropriately, "Could the rising generation, self-consciously devoted to truth but increasingly aware of disturbing facts, be expected indefinitely to contain their doubts and profess an assurance which was decreasingly real?"[16] Given the tension voiced at the time between reason and faith, the fervor that inspired the Victorians' Evangelical revival ironically hastened its decline and collapse. The Church was ill equipped to engage with scientific naturalism, rationalism, free thought, and growing interest in liberalism; it confronted internal rifts over the very nature of belief and found that evidence was not on its side. Having failed to reach the large number of workers who had migrated to Britain's industrializing cities in search of work, the Church splintered into factions. Many of the factions were peopled by nonconformists (chiefly dissenting Methodists and Evangelical Calvinists) who, in doubting and rejecting Anglicanism, claimed a more immediate relationship to God and a starker, more literal relation to scripture. Unlike their liberal, Broad Church counterparts, who were more open to science and to the "Higher Criticism" reshaping biblical scholarship, the Evangelicals put a premium on conversion—the experience of being "born again"—and stressed the importance of practical piety, including through social activism at home and missionary zeal abroad.

Religious doubt can look quite different to each of these groups, as I hope to convey, but overall it joined philosophical skepticism in asking what were felt to be increasingly urgent questions: Was the planet really created in one day, as Genesis stipulated, or over eons? Were the miracles described in the Bible credible or meant to be seen more as apocryphal?

When the history of Christianity was fully examined, did its monotheistic arguments blend imperceptibly with the "pagan" beliefs that had preceded it? And, a critical issue for many Victorian believers and scholars, by no means easy to settle: What was the precise ratio of God to man in Jesus of Nazareth?

Realizing that an increasingly literate and probing public wanted answers to these difficult questions, traditionalists and conservatives tried to fend off an onslaught of historical and philosophical studies that appeared in the 1840s and 1850s, including from liberal Anglicans trying to respond more constructively to the crisis, as we'll see in chapters 4 and 5.[17] But the conservative rejoinders were more flat-footed than convincing; and to growing numbers of worshippers, the dogmatism of many bishops, priests, and ministers lost its appeal. The erosion—indeed, rejection—of belief that followed was as fierce and passionate in the second half of the century as the embrace of it had been in the first. Indeed, by the century's end, doubt generally had acquired the merit of putting things in "balance," with legal scholars characterizing its legal doctrine as "reasonable."[18] Prominent theologians were calling doubt "highly useful" and a necessary "borderland between knowledge and ignorance."[19] The word "agnosticism" had become a much-discussed principle, and the saying that people should be given "the benefit of the doubt" was held up as an ideal, if not quite a universal practice.[20]

To some readers, this may sound like a relatively straightforward account of a country transitioning to secularism. But the consequences of religious uncertainty and eroding belief were, for many Victorians, complex and unsettling, a point with added significance given Britain's preeminence as a world power. Narrative portraits of Thomas Carlyle, Sir Charles Lyell, Anne and Branwell Brontë, Robert Chambers, Alfred, Lord Tennyson, Charles Darwin, George Eliot, Matthew Arnold, Herbert Spencer, Thomas Huxley, and Leslie Stephen—key figures in this book—help to convey why. Drawing also on accounts of several of their important forebears—David

Hume, William Nicholson, James Hutton, and Percy Bysshe Shelley—I show that for these writers, doubt was integral to the possibility of free thought and the culture they built around it.

For many of these writers and thinkers, it must also be said, their initial shock over religious disbelief was immense and far-reaching. As late as 1878, the author William Hurrell Mallock, trying to speak for his generation, wrote that their "hearts are aching for the God that they no longer can believe in." He continued, "One may almost say that with us one can hear faith decaying. . . . The causes of this decay have been maturing for three hundred years, and their effects prophesied for fifty."[21]

Is Life Worth Living? was the question Mallock asked earnestly in another of his books. His answer—that life is its own reward—came only after he described the impact that religious doubt was having on many around him: "Modern thought has not created a new doubt," he insisted; "it has [instead] made perfect an old one" about the validity of belief.[22]

Confronting a similar "cureless affliction" over religious uncertainty, Matthew Arnold for some years saw the universe as offering neither "certitude, nor peace, nor help for pain."[23] Indeed, because of that predicament, he and other intellectuals sought alternatives and partial remedies, including that culture itself could become a redemptive force. That revised perspective helped to change the course of philosophy, sociology, and political theory, as well as what was taught in schools. Its impact, contested then as now, was also felt across other, vastly different creative endeavors, from the novel to the canvas and the political stage. Shortly after Arnold declared, "The thing is, to recast religion," John Morley insisted, in his treatise *On Compromise,* "Both dogma and church must be slowly replaced by higher forms of faith."[24] As Bernard Lightman underscores, "many vestiges of traditional religious thought [are] embedded in Victorian agnosticism."[25]

The value of those secular "forms of faith" is worth revisiting, especially in light of the challenges they face around the world today. Although some of them—Utilitarianism and Marxism, to name just two—have since been challenged and found wanting, others, such as Herbert Spencer's concept of "the Unknowable" and George Eliot's model of secular fellowship, laid out profound ideas that are still with us, including ethical guidelines that blend freedom with responsibility.

Although today our understanding of doubt includes much besides religion, doubt's vexed relationship to faith can still fixate us. Consider the number of discussions generated by John Patrick Shanley's Pulitzer Prize–winning play *Doubt: A Parable,* the vast amount of press covering revelations of Mother Teresa's pervasive religious doubt, and even Antony Flew's apparent conversion to religion after a career spent as "the world's most notorious atheist."[26]

Books on religious faith and the "new" atheism now battle it out on the best-seller lists. Ready for a showdown, they routinely accuse each other of being dogmatic and of failing to heed each other's arguments. (A witty and intelligent novel, *Thirty-Six Arguments for the Existence of God,* captures the flavor of their furious dissent.)[27] Meanwhile, less than half of Britons believe in a God and two-thirds of the country (66 percent) have no connection to any religion or church.[28] In the United States, those percentages are much lower but trending upward, with 15–16 percent of the population now claiming "no religious affiliation" (up from 8 percent in 1990) and nearly a quarter of Americans in their twenties professing no organized religion. Yet the Victorians' battle over evolution still flares on both sides of the Atlantic, with more Americans (43 percent) believing in creationism than evolution, and "just under half of Britons accept[ing] the theory of evolution as the best description for the development of life."[29]

In other respects, our modern challenges are surprisingly comparable to those facing nineteenth-century Britons, a further reason to focus on that century of doubt. The Victorians were greatly concerned about the effects of their industrial revolution; today we are still trying to gauge the benefits and price of globalization. The Victorians witnessed—without always welcoming—breathtaking developments in geology, archaeology, and evolutionary theory. Today, we enjoy—and often fear—remarkable break-throughs in biomedicine, neurochemistry, and genetics. The Victorians pondered the many gains and drawbacks of mechanization; we ask what technology is doing to our lifestyles, communities, and relationships. And the Victorians debated intensively whether the Bible should be taken liter-ally. Today, science and religion are still widely perceived as antagonists, and large percentages of people, disbelieving science, insist that the Earth is relatively young (in the region of thousands—rather than billions—of years old). Looked at in this light, the dramatic, far-reaching effects of the human genome project can seem comparable in impact to Lyell's *Principles of Geology* (1830–33) and Darwin's *On the Origin of Species* (1859).

One sign that the Victorians still preoccupy us, nearly two centuries later, is that we're still arguing over the second of these books, as many of the issues that it raises are not limited to the field of education. While Lyell struggled to "free the science [of geology] from Moses" as he explained why the earth could not have been created in a single day, Darwin argued that the fittest species adapt and evolve by means of natural selection.[30] That process trumps "the old argument of design in nature," Darwin concluded, and thus argues against not only the infallible word of scripture, but also the necessity of viewing God as the divine creator. Yet Lyell remained deeply re-ligious throughout his life and suffered intense private anguish about the possibility of evolution, a theory he tried for decades to ignore, then refute. And Darwin, having weighed a life in the Church and married a deeply de-vout woman, wrote candidly that his hard-fought agnosticism left vast is-sues unexplained: "I gradually came to disbelieve in Christianity as a di-vine revelation," he recalled, years later, "but I was very unwilling to give up my belief." The solution, for him, was to remain in a state of open, au-thentic doubt: "The mystery of the beginning of all things is insoluble by us; and I for one must be content to remain an Agnostic."[31]

Like many of their peers, Darwin and Lyell remind us that doubt offers a productive, even hopeful way of "being in two minds"—a way of ultimately reaching hard-won conviction that permits dissent, sharpens insight, and inspires creativity in the place of dogma and rote learning. Among its other qualities, doubt tends to be progressive, forward-looking, and nonprose-lytizing, allowing the coexistence of contraries that the adamant reject in the search for quick fixes and yes-or-no answers. As Robert Baird explains, "Creative doubt stimulates the evaluation of beliefs." It encourages us to discard "beliefs found wanting" and reaffirm "those found adequate . . . with new vigor and life."[32]

Sadly, our own age has begun to repolarize over these concerns and to press for such black-and-white thinking that countless shades of gray are lost. The more strident our culture becomes—whether in response to the extremism of others or, ironically, as a partial cause of it—the more *belief* itself, in its connection to religion, becomes a word capable of evoking ela-tion and dread. We might prefer thinking that *our* religious beliefs, to the extent that we have them, foster only guidance and comfort. But when moderates scatter under duress and fundamentalists assert a monopoly on truth—even an endless war against "infidels and nonbelievers"—the dif-ferences among faiths, like those among believers and nonbelievers, can seem hopelessly unbridgeable.

After a trio of prominent best-sellers on atheism appeared between 2004 and 2007, drawing huge audiences on both sides of the Atlantic, it be-came commonplace for reviewers into split into two camps. One group cheered Sam Harris' *End of Faith,* Richard Dawkins' *God Delusion,* and Christopher Hitchens' *God Is Not Great* as a long-awaited debunking of re-ligious mysticism as well as a much-needed corrective to dogmatism, sanc-timony, and—in the case of the United States—the Christianizing of a sec-ular state.[33] (Harris, in particular, made the terrorist attacks on 9/11 central to his polemic against all forms of religion.) On the other side, with titles just as adamant—*God Is No Delusion, The Reason for God,* and *Answering the New Atheism*—devout critics in Britain and America not only vigor-ously defended their faith but roundly accused all three writers of a dif-ferent kind of dogmatism, along with arrogance, theological ignorance, and an uncompromising rationalism that left no room for doubt, flexibility, or error.[34]

Each side hunkered down and flung barbs without really engaging, much less conceding, the arguments of the other side. As Dawkins opined in the London *Times,* what was the point of parsing the finer theological subtleties of Aquinas or Duns Scotus (Terry Eagleton's prompt in the *London Review of Books*) when they amounted to a "celestial comfort blanket"?[35] When Hitchens, Harris, and Dawkins asserted that religion can foster division and extremism, an essential point that few today can afford to ignore, many devout reviewers insisted that moderates and fanatics have little in common than their beliefs and that it is insulting to lump them together.

Because Dawkins and Harris, in particular, likened faith to false consciousness (calling faith, respectively, a "delusion" and an "impostor"), their approach and guiding assumptions were more likely to harden resistance among the devout than pave the way for flexibility, much less secular enlightenment.[36] To that extent, Victorian unbelief and doubt achieved a far-more intensive engagement with theology, and Dawkins may have much less to teach us about certainty than he imagines. By contrast, Froude, Robert Chambers, and Thomas Huxley have a lot more to tell us than we currently give them credit for. Yet, oddly, Dawkins reserved particular scorn for skeptics such as Huxley (justly dubbed "Darwin's bulldog"), who coined the word *agnosticism* in 1869 but for complex personal and scientific reasons would not commit to full-blown atheism.

Dawkins insists that scientists cannot hedge on facts and absolutes: there are simply right answers and wrongheaded assumptions, even when the issues are generally considered metaphysical: "Either [God] exists or he doesn't. It is a scientific question."[37] But science is full of uncertainty, as Victorians such as Arthur James Balfour made clear in *A Defence of Philosophic Doubt.*[38] And scientists and secularists have made their fair share of mistakes. Besides, matters of faith do not always involve or require absolutes, and it would be naive to imagine otherwise.

In upholding philosophical and religious uncertainty as an ethical position, then, I hope to bring historical depth and perspective to today's contradictions, to let the Victorians pose questions to believers and nonbelievers that they might prefer to leave unasked. Their reasons for avoidance are not difficult to fathom. When faith or its absence is absolute, doubt of any kind can seem anathema. Whether as heresy or unwelcome prying, it can resemble a threat that the devout would prefer to banish, and the nonbeliever to eliminate completely. When the stakes are so high, no one wants a skeptic around questioning whether an assumption is plausible or a conviction untenable. Believers and nonbelievers alike want enough certainty to ensure that doubt is not an option. As this book shows, these responses are not unique to the twenty-first century.

While thus chiefly a study of the power and vast range of the Victorians' loss of religious faith, my book tries to gauge the consequences for us of failing to heed their most difficult lessons. In our own overheated climate, we give less credence to uncertainty; yet the crises that preoccupy us—including religious extremism—demand that we tolerate increasing amounts of it. The Victorians have more answers for us than we have realized.

ONE

Miracles and Skeptics

T he roots of Victorian doubt take us far into the eighteenth century, when scientists and philosophers began openly to question
biblical accounts of the Earth's creation. Geologists studying cliffs
and ravines publicly doubted whether a single flood could have covered
the entire planet, much less whether one man and his family could have
rescued every species of animal on Earth from it. Philosophers, too, openly
challenged the idea of the miraculous. In doing so, they also cast doubt on
the truth and reliability of the Gospels and Old Testament.

In 1781, after both lines of inquiry crossed, rattling the Established
Church, an anonymous pamphlet appeared bearing the startling title, *The
Doubts of Infidels; or, Queries Relative to Scriptural Inconsistencies and
Contradictions.* The author called himself "A Weak but Sincere Christian"
who was submitting his questions to "The Bench of Bishops for Elucidation." As a self-described infidel, however, the author captured both the
word's flavor of heresy and its suggestion of infidelity (*infidel* comes to us
via the Old French *infidèle*).[1] Bristling with anger, the author was doubtful of the bishops' ability to answer pages of well-documented concerns

about scriptural inconsistency, which he detailed for them chapter and verse.

The pamphlet has been attributed to William Nicholson, a renowned London chemist and philosopher, and its anger is best understood as responding to an act of Parliament passed the same year. After the bishop of Chester, Dr. Beilby Porteus, rallied in 1780 to stop freethinkers and doubters from meeting on Sundays, he helped to create a new law called "An Act for Preventing Certain Abuses and Profanations on the Lord's Day, Called Sunday." The law wasn't amended until 1932, when the Sunday Entertainment Act began to chip away at its broad powers, and it had a significant effect on British culture and society in the decades in-between. Public institutions such as museums, art galleries, libraries, and public gardens were required to stay closed on Sundays. Even public lectures were banned on such days. As the freethinking philosopher John Stuart Mill later complained in his influential treatise *On Liberty* (1859), the act also encouraged "repeated attempts to stop railway travelling on Sundays." What one sees in such attempts, he complained, is a form of "religious bigot[ry]" and "persecution": "The notion that it is one man's duty that another should be religious, . . . a belief that God not only abominates the act of the misbeliever, but will not hold us guiltless if we leave him unmolested."[2]

The 1781 act seemingly began with more limited powers, but they were easily misinterpreted. The law authorized the government to fine—even to imprison—landlords and proprietors who allowed "public entertainment or amusement upon the evening of the Lord's Day." According to the bishop, the chief concern was this: groups were meeting "under pretence of inquiring into religious doctrines, and explaining texts of holy Scripture" when they were "unlearned and incompetent to explain the same."[3]

If that sounds over the top, even a fraction paranoid, consider that Bishop Porteus, an avid reformer and abolitionist, with interests also in the Society for the Propagation of the Gospel in Foreign Parts, had sought the aid of Parliament to crack down on religious criticism in Britain. In the

Figure 1. Henry Meyer, portrait of the Right Reverend Beilby
Porteus, bishop of London, 1834, stipple engraving after a 1787
portrait by John Hoppner. © National Portrait Gallery, London.

bishop's own words, which his biographer uncovered a few years later, "The
beginning of the winter of 1780 was distinguished by the rise of a new
species of dissipation and profaneness."[4]

On Sundays, the bishop noted with dismay, groups across London
would assemble in public meeting rooms, using names such as "*Christian
Societies, Religious Societies, [and] Theological Societies*" (*LBP*, 72). "The *pro-
fessed* design of the former," writes the man later appointed bishop of the
capital, "was merely to walk about and converse . . . ; but the *real consequence*, and probably the *real purpose* of it, was to draw together dissolute

people of both sexes . . . [for] the *amusement* [of] discuss[ing] passages of Scripture" (72–73; emphasis in original).

The bishop insisted that these meetings "gave offence . . . to every man of gravity and seriousness . . . , several of whom I have heard speak of it with abhorrence." Foreigners apparently had been "shocked and scandalized . . . considering it a disgrace to any Christian country to tolerate so gross an insult on all decency and good order" (*LBP*, 72–73).

Anyone wondering what Bishop Porteus meant by "good order" should recall that, just a few decades earlier, Robert Walpole's regime had closed theaters it deemed critical of the Crown and Parliament. Nor was it easy to voice even mild doubt about Christianity.[5] A few decades earlier still, an eighteen-year-old university student named Thomas Aikenhead had been tried, convicted, and hanged in Edinburgh for blasphemy. His crime: "denying the Doctrine of the Trinity."[6]

In June 1780, just months before the bishop inveighed about moral decay, riots broke out in London after a huge crowd, numbering between forty and sixty thousand, marched to Parliament to protest the repeal of anti-Catholic legislation. Among other things, the laws had prevented Catholics from serving in Britain's military, a deficit felt strongly at the time, with the American colonies five years into a war of independence and war looming against France. Led by Lord George Gordon, head of the Protestant Association, the crowd descended on Westminster with banners warning "No Popery" and statements of concern that Catholics might band with Britain's European enemies rather than support their own army.

The rioters attacked numerous Catholic churches and homes, as well as a large number of other buildings in the city. But the bishop, obviously aware of the volatility of Protestant sentiment at the time, chose to focus instead on meetings that were allegedly sowing religious doubt. As he put it, the meetings were set up to be "a school for Metaphysics, Ethics, Pulpit Oratory, Church History, and Canon Law" (*LBP*, 73).

"It is easy to conceive what infinite mischief such debates as these must do to the younger part of the community," he railed, "who, being unemployed on this day, . . . would look upon every doubt and difficulty started there as an unanswerable argument against religion, and would go home absolute sceptics, if not confirmed unbelievers." Bishop Porteus didn't seem especially confident about the resilience of Anglicanism after even mild discussion. He also imagined that doubt stemmed entirely from these meetings. But nor was he happy about the rise of devout nonconformists and, a separate but related concern, the growing popularity of free thought. "The Theological Assemblies were calculated to extinguish every religious principle," he explained, and thus "threatened the worst consequences to public morals" (*LBP*, 74).

If one still doubts Bishop Porteus' panicked resolve, consider what he did next. "It was," he insists, "highly necessary to put a speedy and effectual stop to such alarming evils. I mentioned it early in the winter to several persons of rank and authority." But as "no one [seemed] inclined to take the matter up," the bishop turned to eminent lawyers and magistrates, all of whom assured him that "nothing but an Act of Parliament, framed on purpose, could effectually suppress" the meetings and the ideas they were propagating (*LBP*, 75). After hiring another lawyer to have "a proper Bill sketched out," the bishop approached various lords and, finally, the solicitor-general, who undertook to have it moved and seconded in the House of Commons.

The bill was "violently opposed" by several members of Parliament, Bishop Porteus recalls, "but it passed without a division" (*LBP*, 76). In the House of Lords, too, heated exchanges broke out over whether existing laws weren't sufficient. Yet there also the bill was finally approved, so passing into common law across the country. Wrote Robert Cox, Victorian author of *The Literature of the Sabbath Question*, "By the comprehensiveness of its enactments and the severity of its penalties, the statute was at once effectual. It is now," he added wryly, meaning in the mid-1860s, "the barrier which prevents the admission of the public on Sundays to the Crystal Palace at Sydenham—an institution very different in its character and tendencies from those which inflamed the zeal of Bishop Porteus."[7] But the act had far more sweeping effects on British culture. Because the law forbade the performance even of music in churches on such days, a National Federation of Sunday Societies was formed in Leeds in May 1894, seeking to "remove all [such] vexatious restrictions."[8] It would take almost four more decades before the 1781 law was amended and the British public was allowed to visit museums, zoos, and picture galleries on Sundays, and as recently as 1972, with the passing of the Sunday Theatre Act, for that freedom to extend to seeing theatrical performances on those days.[9]

According to the bishop, the new law was meant to take away "no other liberty but the liberty of burlesquing Scripture, and making religion a public amusement, and a public trade" (*LBP*, 82). But at a time when Catholics were barred from joining Britain's judiciary, civil service, and Parliament; when Methodists were harassed and persecuted for preaching "unofficially" in fields and schoolrooms, without the sanction of the Established Church; and when the moral climate in Britain would soon spawn groups like the Society for the Suppression of Vice, the bishop's notion that the magistrates and courts would not abuse the latitude that his act granted them seems naive or disingenuous.

That may help explain the vehemence of Nicholson's reaction in *The Doubts of Infidels,* which he addressed to every bishop because of their colleague's appeal to Parliament. Writing as a freethinker rather than a devout nonconformist (a position which reveals that many of the roots of unbelief reached far into the eighteenth century), Nicholson proved to be a rhetorical match for Bishop Porteus, not least because he was well versed in scripture and natural philosophy.[10] A chemist by training, he was also a journalist, publisher, scientist, and inventor who had briefly set up a law practice, then moved to Amsterdam to sell pottery. After returning to England a few years later, he turned his abundant energy to writing essays for light periodicals, translating Voltaire, and finishing *An Introduction to Natural Philosophy,* an impressive treatise that took off soon after it appeared in 1781. The same year, obviously incensed by the bishop's "Sunday Bill,"

Figure 2. T. Blood, portrait of William Nicholson, chemist, philosopher, journalist, and inventor, by 1812, stipple engraving after a portrait by Samuel Drummond. © National Portrait Gallery, London.

which he described as amounting to "zealous exertion against the infidels," he condemned the "prosecutions and pillory against infidel writers and publishers" that had occurred as a result.[11]

The anonymous pamphlet excoriates the suppression of religious discussion and dissent. "Your late zealous exertion," Nicholson charged, "must have convinced [you] that you are in earnest in your attempts to propagate and establish our holy faith. An act of parliament is an excellent engine for producing that kind of uniformity of opinions, which consists in holding the tongue. . . . It is carrying the notion of liberty too far, to suppose, because we are free-born Englishmen, that we may choose our own faith and go to heaven *our own way!*" (*DI*, v–vi).

Nicholson reminded the bishops of the excesses of "the holy inquisition," when zealots in southern Europe imprisoned, tortured, and burned alive tens of thousands who refused to vow allegiance to Catholicism. Representing himself as a "weak but sincere Christian," he stated: "It happens unfortunately for us, that these mechanical and persuasive arguments are unknown in *Britain*. Instead of that most strong and logical argument, called the torture, we are obliged to adopt plain reason, or, at most, when that fails us, the *prison, fine,* and *pillory*" (*DI*, vi–vii; emphasis in original). Nicholson's "Epistle Dedicatory" to the bishops, clergy, "and All Other Supporters of the Church Militant Here on Earth" turns out to be brilliantly controlled satire (v).

The rest of his pamphlet—the main body of its twenty-four-page argument—is a list of strong objections to taking the Bible as absolute truth. These too are presented as "The Doubts of Infidels," and so can appear as the valid concerns of a doubter wishing ardently to believe. The list of questions begins: "1. How can *the attributes* of God be vindicated, in having performed so great a number of miracles, for a long succession of very distant ages, and so few in *latter times?* (*DI*, 1).

Question 2 invites a thought experiment: "Suppose a book to be published, containing assertions of historical facts long past, which had no collateral testimony of other authors; suppose those facts in general to be improbable and incredible; suppose the book to be anonymous, or, which is worse, ushered into the world under the name of a person who, from the internal evidence of the thing, could not have written it; can it be imagined, that such a book would find credit among people, who have the least pretensions to reason or common sense?" (*DI*, 2). Question 3 is blunter still: "Is the account of the creation and fall of man, in the book of Genesis, physical or allegorical?" (3).

And so on, for twenty-one more pages. It is a relentless, rigorously precise list of anomalies and contradictions in the Bible. The experience of reading it is similar, one imagines, to auditing one of the best meetings that the bishop of Chester managed to make illegal: one's sense of Christian history is likely to shift dramatically as a result.

Nicholson's study of natural philosophy had brought him close to the ideas of David Hume, a key member of the Scottish Enlightenment who had written a remarkable essay on miracles four decades earlier. Hume was just twenty-six when he wrote it in 1737, the year Thomas Paine was born. Its impact upon publication eleven years later was swift and severe, leading to charges of atheism and suggestions of heresy. Allegedly, Hume was—as Nicholson had claimed to be—an infidel.

Hume's other work on religion and skepticism, including his *Natural History of Religion,* stirred such controversy that his *Dialogues Concerning Natural Religion* weren't published until three years after his death. Initially they bore no mention of his or even his publisher's name. Friends such as Adam Smith, the renowned philosopher and economist, had refused to go near it.

Ever since, Hume's religious position has been subject to much debate. He was reckoned to be an atheist, at least by the Church of Scotland, which considered bringing charges of heresy against him. Even so, as one present-day scholar points out, while Hume "did not believe in the God of standard theism . . . he did not rule out all concepts of deity."[12]

The Victorian biologist Thomas Huxley later dubbed Hume "that prince of agnostics," because he wrote, concerning religious principles: "doubt, uncertainty, suspence of judgment appear the only result of our most accurate scrutiny, concerning this subject."[13] Even so, many have called his position deist—a religious and philosophical belief that a supreme being created the universe and that the act can be known by reason and observation, without need for religion.[14]

One thing is clear: Hume recoiled from blind faith. He found its state of acceptance alarming, because it short-circuits discussion and doubt, a point where he and Bishop Porteus could almost agree. "A wise man . . .

proportions his belief to the evidence," Hume insists in the essay on miracles.[15] He inclines to hesitation and holds judgment until he is fully persuaded. Having reached that state by his midtwenties, Hume concluded: a miracle is a "violation of the laws of nature." It resembles an intervention by "some invisible agent" that cannot be confirmed or disproved but whose probability is highly unlikely ("M," 135, 121).

Hume's essay on miracles is fascinating for other reasons, too. In addition to his prevailing skepticism, he paid close attention to psychological factors that predispose us to believe in the incredible. Indeed, he sounded a wise note in describing our tendency to turn the unusual into an omen and good fortune into a sign of heavenly favor. From Hume's point of view, "the strong propensity of mankind to the extraordinary and the marvelous" ("M," 124) is a serious problem, given the number of people that it affects. "The Syrians worship[ped] . . . a fish," the Roman philosopher Cicero observed, in examples Hume later adapted, "and the Egyptians deif[ied] . . . almost every species of animal; nay, even in Greece they worship[ped] a number of deified human beings."[16]

Hume's examples were blunter, and his rhetoric less forgiving. "Battles, revolutions, pestilence, famine and death," from the perspective of the devout, "are never the effect of those natural causes which we experience." Rather, they are turned into "prodigies, omens, oracles, [and] judgments" that falsify cause and meaning ("M," 125). Equally troubling to Hume: the tendency of humans to exaggerate what portentous information they may have the opportunity to convey. "What greater temptation than to appear a missionary, a prophet, and ambassador from heaven?" (144).

Although Hume carefully removed the essay on miracles from his *Treatise of Human Nature* (1739–40), that work was still thought so antireligious that it caused, in his words, a "Clamour" of charges of "*Scepticism, Atheism,* &c." Pamphlets soon appeared, attacking him for "doubt[ing] every Thing," including by promoting "principles leading to downright Atheism, by denying the Doctrine of Causes and Effects."[17] Indeed, when

Hume received encouragement to apply for a chair of moral philosophy at the University of Edinburgh, his candidacy stirred such resentment from the clergy that, despite resolutely defending his positions in *A Letter from a Gentleman to His Friend in Edinburgh* (1745), he was denied the post.

Although the "Clamour" helped to ensure passage of Bishop Porteus' legislation several decades later, Hume was not one to back down. He included the essay on miracles in his *Enquiry Concerning Human Understanding* (1748), making clear that his doubt about organized religion had, if anything, hardened. "I flatter myself," he couldn't resist adding, "that I have discovered an argument" that should be "an everlasting check to all kinds of superstitious delusion" ("M," 115).

As the Church was still clamping down on dissenters and turning Sundays into days of worship, without music or science, it didn't take kindly to seeing its venerated God portrayed as "some invisible agent." Still, Hume faced the onslaught with courage. To the young philosopher at loggerheads with an ecclesiastical community as powerful as the one that Nicholson later railed against, his opponents' bid to view miracles as exceptions to normal standards of proof was exactly the problem. Suspending "sense and learning" made it look as if the Church encouraged blind assent ("M," 125).

There were, he noted, enough reasons to distrust accounts of the extraordinary—from the tendency of witnesses to exaggerate what they see to the susceptibility of listeners to trust all that they hear. Given our all-too-human biases, he concluded, miracles and prophecies should be judged on grounds of credibility, just like any other historical report.

Not surprisingly, the Church didn't see it that way. It continued to insist that miracles are a special case, exempt from investigation. According to their defenders, normal standards of proof simply do not apply. Nor, they add, do such standards have any hope of capturing the "meaning" of events labeled "miraculous."

Hume considered such moves evasive, even pernicious. The devout create legends to fit their beliefs, he argued, and in the process disregard more plausible explanations for the extraordinary. To that end, miracles are really a subset of broader religious beliefs. To investigate a miracle logically is to "put it to such a trial as it is, by no means, fitted to endure" ("M," 137).

"To make this [problem] more evident," Hume continued, making clear why he became such a powerful influence on Nicholson and other turn-of-the-century freethinkers:

> Let us examine those miracles, related in scripture. . . . Here then we are first to consider a book, presented to us by a barbarous and ignorant people, written in an age when they were still more barbarous, and in all probability long after the facts which it relates, corroborated by no concurring testimony, and resembling those fabulous accounts, which every nation gives of its origin. . . . It gives an account of a state of the world and of human nature entirely different from the present: Of our fall from that state: Of the age of man, extended to near a thousand years: Of the destruction of the world by a deluge: Of the arbitrary choice of one people, as the favourites of heaven; and that people the countrymen of the author: Of their deliverance from bondage by prodigies the most astonishing imaginable. ("M," 137)

Hume concluded his essay by asking whether "the falsehood of such a book, supported by such a testimony, would be more extraordinary and miraculous than all the miracles it relates." His incendiary conclusion must also be left in his own words, to avoid any risk of misstating it: "The *Christian Religion* not only was at first attended with miracles, but even at this day cannot be believed by any reasonable person without one" ("M," 138).

"What Hume" did, A. N. Wilson recently observed, "was remove any philosophical *necessity* for believing in God."[18] That's one reason his work on religion caused such a furor and threatened charges of heresy. In the Old Testament in particular, Hume observed, God exhibits a range of emotions—vehemence, jealousy, favoritism, and mercilessness—that are conspicuously absent from the New Testament. To that end, he implied, the differences between our Old Testament God and the capricious acts of Greek and Roman deities are less than we might suppose. When God speaks to Moses as a burning bush on Mount Horeb, for example, it seems doubtful that monotheism left paganism centuries behind.

"Were anyone inclined to revive the ancient pagan theology," one of Hume's characters explains in *Dialogues Concerning Natural Religion* (1779), he would learn from the poet Hesiod that the "globe was governed by 30,000 deities, who arose from the unknown powers of nature."[19] But thirty thousand gods was too many for humanity to appease. ("The Gods are hard to reconcile," one of Tennyson's Homeric choruses laments, with provocative capitalization.)[20] If humanity were to worship properly, it needed to satisfy fewer gods, which finally meant limiting its adoration and expectations of favor to just one. Conflict nonetheless erupted rapidly over how that one rather jealous and punitive god would be viewed and interpreted, especially by those who worshipped differently or not at all.

For Hume, the parallels between paganism and monotheism—stoked by the Greeks' skeptical tradition—opened a path to criticizing all forms of religious dogma, including, most provocatively, the existence of God. Nor did withholding judgment on that issue stop him from asking how others formed theirs. Still, if religion were indeed an emotional response to distress and uncertainty, as Hume insisted, then dismissing faith in miracles as excessive credulity would be incendiary but ultimately futile. For believers simply apply their own preferred criteria, calling the miraculous a nonnatural event. To them, as the writer of the Epistle to the Hebrews puts it in the Authorized King James Version of the Bible, "Faith is the substance of things hoped for, the evidence of things not seen" (Hebrews 11:1).

Even so, there are striking differences in how that celebrated statement has been rendered and translated. In 1881, the English Revised Version of the Bible changed two key words. Faith became "the *assurance* of things hoped for, the *proving* of things not seen," which dramatically lessened the contrast between hope and assurance, evidence and proof. In the 1901 American Standard Version, by contrast, the emphasis shifted from "substance" and "assurance" to "things" as a whole: "Faith is assurance of *things* hoped for, a conviction of things not seen." In 1973, the New International Version decided to render that idea even more conspicuously: "Faith is being sure of what we hope for and certain of what we do not see," a statement that thoroughly transforms the meaning of the King James Version, equating faith with certainty as if the two were identical.

Although to a skeptic these and other revisions cast doubt on what exactly one is putting one's faith in, the same is not always held true for believers, as the same epistle repeatedly underscores, however confusingly: "Through faith we understand that the worlds were framed by the *word* of God, so that *things which are seen were not made of things which do appear*" (Hebrews 11:2, King James; emphases mine). With such lines in mind, philosophy professor Robert Baird argued in 1980, "The very fact that faith can be misplaced, . . . that one can take as ultimate that which is not ultimate at all, is a reflection of the logical possibility that a person may be mistaken."[21] Groups, communities, and of course nations can be, too.

In eighteenth-century Britain, as among believers today, the devout argued that Hume's emphasis on reason disqualifies itself.[22] A deadlock ensued over the status of reason itself and whether it could be a yardstick for assessing what are, to believers, signs and evidence of God.[23] Hume's supporters have since wondered: Is it *excessively* rational to ask how beliefs are turned into explanatory forces? Should it also be off-limits to wonder how such beliefs comfort or reprimand the believer, depending on temperament, behavior, or cultural tradition?

For many believers, however, an attachment to religion is capable of withstanding doubt from others and from oneself. Indeed, faith commonly prizes the resilience needed to overcome such doubt, sometimes even before it can be registered as such. As Hume put it, people are largely motivated by "the ordinary affections of human life; the anxious concern for

happiness, the dread of future misery, the terror of death, the thirst for re-
venge, the appetite for food and other necessaries. Agitated by hopes and
fears of this nature, especially the latter, men scrutinize, with a trembling
curiosity, the course of future causes, and . . . in this disordered scene, with
eyes still more disordered and astonished, they see the first obscure traces
of divinity."[24] Although Hume considered such emotions entirely understandable, he let them rebound on theology by suggesting that the latter is,
at bottom, inseparable from human need. As a philosopher, moreover, he
wanted us to pay attention to that need. If "religion originates in our emotional responses to the uncertainties of life, in our feelings of insecurity and
vulnerability in a hostile world," as one of Hume's editors puts it, capturing his position, then emotion is not a viable or appropriate platform for
establishing whether God exists.[25]

Hume was certainly right about one point: miracles have been, and in
many cases still are, integral to theology. A foundation for intricate, far-
reaching religious structures, they are often so sacrosanct that it is considered anathema to scrutinize them. Even today, doubt about their probability is frequently deemed offensive to religion as a whole. Still, as Baird
reminds us, "Even if one refers to his ultimate concern as 'God,' humility insists upon the question: Does one's understanding of God corre-
spond to reality? Creative doubt encourages this question. Dogmatism
suppresses it."[26]

Despite the uproar that greeted Hume's work on religion, one of his
friends and literary executors, the influential geologist James Hutton, found
in it permission to challenge existing preconceptions about creation. Hutton did so also from a deist perspective. Unlike Hume, however, he detailed the religious implications of his findings with great reluctance.
Doubtless with Hume's fate in mind, he tried to preempt such criticism
over the reception of his own geological treatise, *Theory of the Earth*. His
concerns turned out to be justified. Since he "limited the role of Genesis to
a general celebration of divine creative power," scholars noted recently,

Hutton was—like Hume and Nicholson—charged with the "infidel purpose to subvert the credit of Scripture."[27]

Published in two parts in 1788, Hutton's treatise sparked passionate debate. Drawing from "principles of natural philosophy" that he had outlined in his earlier *System of the Earth* (1785), Hutton's *Theory* also changed the course of geology.[28] In offering a view of earth history without a clear beginning or end, it was "uniformitarian" in focus and comprehensive in a way that was breathtaking and provocative. Influential Victorian thinkers such as Charles Lyell were still praising the work far into the nineteenth century, and it is worth addressing why. "When we trace the parts of which this terrestrial system is composed," Hutton wrote carefully, "we perceive a fabric, erected in wisdom, to obtain a purpose worthy of the power that is apparent in the production of it."[29]

Every balanced phrase, here as throughout his argument, hits at key ideas circulating at the end of the eighteenth century, including that the world's intricate design reflects the glory of deliberate intention. Hutton doubted many things but not the existence of God. He viewed the Earth almost as an organism that operates in cycles. With ideas about soil erosion and deposition drawn from the English scientist Robert Hooke, who had devised them more than a century earlier, Hutton advanced a challenging thesis: the Earth could not have been created out of one enormous flood. Indeed, far more than just a few thousand years old, the planet has a history that recedes *infinitely*.

Hutton's theory was some twenty-five years in the making. As one of five sons by Edinburgh's city treasurer, he was almost as precocious as Hume, attending the city's prestigious university at the age of fourteen (Hume had been twelve, possibly younger) to be a "student of humanity." Instead of turning to law or philosophy, as his friend had, he opted for medicine, completing a dissertation on blood circulation at Leiden after several years of preliminary research in Paris. He returned to Scotland to look after the family estate, a lowland farm in remote Berwickshire. This responsibility gave him ample opportunity to study the winds, tides, and rugged landscape.

Hutton pointed to the minute, nearly invisible effect of deposited sand and shale, which the outgoing tide partly washes away before the incoming tide can deposit it anew. Over a considerable period, this endless motion slowly and unevenly raises the seabed, creating land. Yet the addition and erosion are so microscopic as to take eons to accomplish.[30]

Hutton's belief that geology was in no way concerned "with questions as to the origin of things" almost inevitably brought his interest in geological processes and unconformities into conflict with the opening verses of Genesis.[31] And though theological debates over free thought broke out toward the end of the eighteenth century, many of them inspired by Hume, most Christians accepted those verses literally, as confirmation that the world was no more than a few thousand years old. To the devout, after all, God had created the world rapidly, in just one day. The Bible said so, and weekly sermons told them to accept that postulate.

Hutton's ideas about cycles of erosion and deposition were threatening because they left the Earth with neither a strict sense of design nor a precise date stamp. Not that Hutton was reluctant to provide one; he discovered instead how difficult it would be to establish and measure one. The logical, somewhat terrifying conclusion of his *Theory of the Earth* was an infinite regression of minute patterns of soil elevation and erosion. "We find no vestige of a beginning," he declared poetically, and "no prospect of an end" (*TE*, 75).

Because of such statements, the geologist Richard Kirwan, then president of the Royal Irish Academy in Dublin, denounced Hutton as an atheist—indeed, an illogical one to boot. "Modern geological researches," he opined, had "proved too favourable to . . . various systems of atheism or infidelity."[32] "Dr. Hutton," he added, "suppos[es] . . . the world we now inhabit to have arisen from the ruins and fragments of an anterior, and that of another still prior, without pointing at any original. If we are thus to proceed *in infinitum* I shall not pretend to follow him."[33]

One year earlier, John Williams, a mineral surveyor from Wales, had similarly misrepresented Hutton's theory, accusing him of "warp[ing] and strain[ing] every thing to support an unaccountable system, viz. the eternity of the world." Hutton should be thought pernicious, he continued, because he wanted nothing less than to "depose the almighty Creator and Governor of the universe from his office."[34]

The attacks didn't stop there. The geologist was roundly derided for arguing that the inside of the Earth was scalding hot, even that molten lava was partly responsible for the fusion of scarp and rock. Experts at the time preferred Abraham Gottlob Werner's "Neptunist" belief that all rocks stemmed from a single, enormous flood. That was what scripture told them.

Werner's theory is now obsolete, but in the 1770s and 1780s, when the Prussian taught at the Freiberg Mining Academy, students from all over Europe would flock to his classes, then return to their respective countries almost disciples, to broadcast his theory. Werner published little but a textbook on fossils and minerals, but his brilliant teaching inspired his students to publish books of their own on related theories.[35]

Though he recognized different kinds of rock formation, Werner stuck rigidly to the idea that there was once an all-encompassing ocean, which receded, leaving land. The transition was for him relatively uncomplicated, and its details didn't concern him. But they greatly troubled Hutton, who devoted much time and energy in *Theory of the Earth* to speculating on its likely causes. Unlike Werner, he credited volcanic activity as a likely cause of such a flood. Hutton also joined Hume in using such activity to tackle a superstition that is still with us today: "A volcano is not made on purpose to frighten . . . people into fits of piety and devotion, nor to overwhelm devoted cities with destruction; a volcano should be considered as a spiracle to the subterranean furnace, in order to prevent the unnecessary elevation of land, and fatal effects of earthquakes" (*TE*, 55).

For Hutton, volcanoes were an "excellent contrivance" and a testament to nature's "amazing power" (*TE*, 56). In giving nature such power, however, he contradicted those who considered a volcano's unpredictable eruptions signs of disorder in the universe. The accusations of atheism were unfair and off the mark. Given his deism, Hutton wanted desperately to *reconcile* new scientific discoveries to theology, not oppose them. As he put it, "We . . . acknowledge an order, not unworthy of Divine wisdom, in a subject which, in another view, has appeared as the work of chance, or as absolute disorder and confusion" (12). The question haunting *Theory of the Earth* was whether he finally succeeded in *presenting* such order and thus in answering those who stressed the stronger likelihood of chance and random chaos.

An empiricist strongly committed to shaping his theory to the geological evidence before him, Hutton was convinced that the Neptunist argument about a cataclysmic flood was wrong. After all, if it takes the ocean millennia to create rock formations from minute deposits, then why would the creation of entire continents be entirely different? Hutton did not fully intuit the influence of shifting tectonic plates; their importance was not established until the mid-twentieth century. In the eighteenth century, the Earth's major features were generally assumed to be fixed. And even though his description of tides washing away much of what they leave behind complicated that idea, Hutton found himself wanting to imply that there is a guiding rationale for this movement that makes it all balance out.

So strong was that theological assumption that when a major earthquake struck Lisbon in November 1755, destroying half the city and with it hundreds of thousands of lives, writers and intellectuals from England's Henry Fielding to France's Voltaire found no religious justification for the quake and rapidly lost their faith. Like Hutton, they shared an Enlightenment belief that "the globe of this earth is evidently made for man. He alone, of all the beings which have life upon this body, enjoys the whole and every part" (*TE*, 16). The widespread destruction and loss of life in the earthquake shattered that belief, leaving notions of man's preeminence in doubt, if not yet in tatters.

Prior earthquakes had of course caused equal or greater devastation. In 1737, the year Hume wrote his essay on miracles, a major quake (9.3 magnitude) off Russia's eastern peninsula caused a tsunami in the Pacific that also killed tens of thousands. But the Portuguese were devout Catholics and eager explorers, with a culture strongly committed to the pursuit of empirical knowledge. With Lisbon that much closer to Paris, London, and Edinburgh, the impact on faith of its earthquake was greater in England than that of the earlier eruption.

Writing in the aftermath of the Lisbon crisis, Hutton learned that earthquakes and even simple land erosions raise large metaphysical questions: "Why make such a convulsion in the world in order to renew the land?" he wondered. "If, again, the land naturally decays, why employ so extraordinary a power, in order to hide a former continent of land, and puzzle man?" (*TE*, 49). The questions go to the heart of his difficulty in reconciling science and religion.

Having failed to dispel such unwanted doubt, Hutton's treatise repeatedly alights on it. "Although there be no doubt with regard to some power having been applied in order to produce the effect, yet we are left . . . to conjecture at the power" (*TE*, 52). Hutton also wonders, with notable use of the passive voice, whether the world has been "intentionally made imperfect, or has not been the work of infinite power and wisdom," a significant last query that intensified the charge of atheism. After all, it hides the creative agent and thus challenges the argument for design (15).

That is one reason John Williams, responding to Hutton's thesis, restated so ostentatiously his love for "the indulgent providence of Almighty God." He did so a few years before William Paley followed suit in *Natural Theology; or, Evidence of the Existence and Attributes of the Deity* (1802). "Almighty, wife and benevolent Creator!" Williams burst out in his second volume. "How excellent are thy works!—how convenient for needy man!—how suitable to answer the designs of thy providence!"[36] Even so, the devastation in Lisbon made it harder for other writers and thinkers to voice that sentiment with equal confidence.

Hutton tried in the end to follow Williams, pushing a thesis that his geological evidence flatly contradicted (that nature was systematic and thus ultimately beneficent to man). But it was his friend and fellow geologist

John Playfair who better caught the drift of Hutton's more vexing proposition. In contemplating his point about endless, bottomless time, Playfair conceded, "the mind seemed to grow giddy by looking so far into the abyss of time."[37] Planetary time was now an abyss, not a carefully ordered sequence of six days. The age and breadth of the universe, which skeptical perspectives on religion had broached but not resolved, grew almost sublime in scale.

Not all who studied that abyss came up empty. Later referencing Hutton, a young Percy Bysshe Shelley invoked it reverently as a pantheistic force in "Mont Blanc" (1817), his remarkable account of the strength and majesty of the Alpine peak. Shelley's poem opens in quasi-Huttonian language with an address to the Ravine of Arve, the cleft through which the Arve River cascades with impressive force:[38]

> The everlasting universe of things
> Flows through the mind, and rolls its rapid waves,
> Now dark—now glittering—now reflecting gloom—
> Now lending splendor.[39]

The lines, sharp and eloquent, draw on connective dashes to link the elements haphazardly. In Shelley's poem, such "glittering" combinations reenact the erratic movement of the tumultuous river. "Has some unknown omnipotence unfurled / The veil of life and death?" his speaker asks provocatively. Indeed, the poem departs radically from Hutton in its willingness to consider the mountain and the river tumbling off it as manifesting energies different from—even in competition with—the Old Testament God. That comes as less of a shock to modern readers, given knowledge today of Shelley's tract *The Necessity of Atheism,* which he published anonymously in 1811, an act that resulted in his immediate expulsion from Oxford University. ("God is an hypothesis," he had argued, "and, as such, stands in need of proof.")[40]

Shelley's poem was similarly provocative in referring less to monotheism than to the "heresy" of pantheism. Once there, he let readers contemplate why such a move "teaches awful doubt" about the history of the planet —doubt that Shelley renders the catalyst for a new relation to the natural world. That relation stems from his acknowledging that the planet's "scarr'd and riven" surface raises questions that man cannot answer and, indeed, is likely never to answer:

> None can reply—all seems eternal now.
> The wilderness has a mysterious tongue
> Which teaches awful doubt, or faith so mild,
> So solemn, so serene, that man may be,
> But for such faith, with Nature reconcil'd.[41]

"Instead of faith in God," comments Michael Erkelenz, glossing these lines, "the wilderness teaches faith in an uncreated and never-ending Nature." In Shelley's poem, Nature appears "self-sufficient and self-sustaining," and "therefore no god need be invented to explain its existence."[42]

For others, though, including some of his Victorian readers, Hutton's *Theory of the Earth*—combined with Hume's intense philosophical skepticism—helped to bring their beliefs to a crisis. What clinched it for many was Hutton's poetic conclusion, "We find no vestige of a beginning, no prospect of an end" (*TE*, 75). That alone raised urgent questions about scientific truth that clashed with almost everything the Victorians had been taught about the origins of the world.

TWO

Stunned Victorians Look Backward and Inward

In the old Ashmolean Museum at Oxford, near the university's some-what ramshackle collection of ancient coins, engravings, and zoolog-ical artifacts, crowds of boisterous undergraduates would gather to hear a local celebrity discuss fossils. The speaker was a vicar, but a most atypical one. A stout, balding man with a fondness for outlandish clothes, he was as renowned for his entertaining lectures as he was for keeping a hyena in his back garden. Even by Oxford standards, his reputation was hard to beat.

A powerful cleric with Broad Church sympathies, the Reverend William Buckland became reader in mineralogy at the university in 1813. He was de-scribed as a "wonderful" speaker whose lectures "overflow[ed] with witty illustrations."[1] As one student explained, he would "enforce an intricate point" with the "Samsonic wielding of a cave-bear jaw or a hyena thigh bone."[2] A portrait of the reverend lecturing in 1823 shows him holding up a hyena's skull and pointing intently to its ragged jawline. Strewn before him are an ammonite, the skull of an ichthyosaur, and other relics and specimens. Behind, a geological map of England and several sketches, including a depiction of two hyenas hunkered down over recently gnawed bones.

The lectures, which helped to establish Buckland's reputation at Oxford, showcased his relatively new emphasis on geohistory, which he stretched to include not only "the Composition and Structure of the Earth" but also "the Physical Revolutions that have affected its Surface, and the Changes in Animal and Vegetable Nature that have attended them."[3] With attendees ranging from the bishop of Oxford and various heads of colleges to a gaggle of excited undergraduates, the lectures accented Buckland's discovery of a large cache of fossil bones in Kirkdale Cave, Yorkshire. These he represented as the remnants of a den of hyenas, since extinct, which he claimed scavenged in northern England until the Flood had wiped them out just a few millennia earlier.

Buckland's knowledge of geology stemmed, as it did then for many amateur scientists, from frequent excursions on horseback across England to the far reaches of Wales, Scotland, and Ireland. His wife, Mary Moreland, an accomplished artist, would often accompany him. Back home in Oxford, they startled guests by serving such gastronomic delights as badger, beaver, crocodile, and even the odd mole and bluebottle fly.[4] The reverend's bemused colleagues and students greeted such idiosyncrasy with a tolerance unusual for the times, given the conservatism of the university and the controversies that had begun to flare over the still new science of geology.

In his inaugural address as reader of geology at Oxford, commemorating the new position, Buckland tried to reconcile the rift dividing Werner's and Hutton's readers. Those following Werner were still committed to arguing that the Flood was universal and relatively recent; they went by the name "catastrophists." Uniformitarians such as Hutton, on the other hand, focused more on small-scale changes that made the surface of the globe look closer to a "law-bound system of matter in motion."[5]

To downplay that rift, the reverend gave his lecture a bold, even hubris-

Figure 3. George Rowe, *William Buckland, Bachelor of Divinity, Fellow of the Royal Society, Professor [sic] of Mineralogy and Geology at Oxford,* 1823, lithograph. © National Portrait Gallery, London.

tic, title: *Vindiciæ Geologicæ; or, The Connexion of Geology with Religion Explained.* Science and religion were for him "inseparable," he explained in his dedication to the university's chancellor. Indeed, "the study of geology has a tendency to confirm the evidences of natural religion; and . . . the facts developed by it are consistent with the accounts of the creation and deluge recorded in the Mosaic writings."[6] Buckland's Irish contemporary William Henry Fitton described such claims as "scriptural geology," and not entirely unfairly.[7]

The Ashmolean Museum, where Buckland gave this particular lecture, has since moved to an impressive neoclassical building. The earlier location, on the city's Broad Street, was a cramped, slightly dingy two-story building. The first university museum in the world, it housed a number of quirky artifacts, including a stuffed dodo (already an emblem of extinction, and thus of the impermanence of species),[8] which by 1755 had become so motheaten that it had to be thrown away.[9]

In Buckland's day, the Ashmolean took its bearings from the sequence of topics that William Paley described in *Natural Theology* (1802), a treatise the lively and argumentative clergyman had submitted as "Evidence of the Existence and Attributes of the Deity, Collected from the Appearances of Nature."[10] In attempting to illustrate Paley's thesis, the museum made plain its reverence for still earlier forms of creationism, such as those developed by the seventeenth-century English naturalist John Ray, author of *The Wisdom of God Manifested in the Works of the Creation* (1691).[11] "By the Works of Creation," Ray explained in a later edition, "I mean the Works created by God at first, and by Him conserved to this Day in the same State and Condition in which they were first made."[12]

Writing in the aftermath of Humean and Huttonian skepticism (and of the French Revolution), Paley found himself under pressure to curb the religious and philosophical doubt that such work and events had kindled. So he modeled his argument for design on a now-famous analogy—if nature were like a watch, it needed a watchmaker to assemble and organize its intricate parts: "Every indication of contrivance, every manifestation of design, which existed in the watch, exists in the works of nature; with the difference, on the side of nature, of being greater or more, and that in a degree which exceeds all computation."[13]

While Paley's analogy invoked a long tradition of scholars who found design in complexity and took this intricacy as evidence of God's existence, complex artifacts do not in fact require a designer (Darwin's model of natural selection, overturning Paley's, was devastating for that reason). Still, as Paley believed that arguments for design extended beyond nature to include society, it was, by his reasoning, impious to question a social order that God had ordained. That is also one reason why the *philosophes,* or intellectuals of the eighteenth-century Enlightenment, were blamed for the Revolution in France. For Paley, seeking to overturn their influence, trust in the apparent order and logic of design was critical. "The consciousness of knowing little," he assured readers, "need not beget a distrust of that which he does know."[14] Faith in the existence of God—evident from the beauty and order of the natural world—would, he argued, take care of everything else.

Despite its reputation today as one of the world's leading universities, Oxford at the time was by Cambridge and Edinburgh standards distinctly parochial. "All the great intellectual currents of the eighteenth century had swept by" the university, Leonard Wilson notes, "leaving it undisturbed."[15] Edinburgh, like London and Paris, had been "shaken by a new revolution in chemistry, vibrant controversy in geology, [and] new economic, social, and political theories, but these had barely touched Oxford." At the time, history, economics, and political science "were neither taught nor studied" there. "Natural science had been established [only] in a very small way and was represented by short courses in lectures in chemistry and mineralogy."[16]

The establishment of a readership in geology was thus, for Oxford, a significant development—and the inaugural lecture of its first appointee a momentous occasion. The prince regent had endowed the chair, and many university and clerical luminaries had gathered to hear its designated speaker. The Reverend Buckland had to tread carefully, even if that meant backpedaling on difficult controversies and promising listeners that geology, in his hands, would advance Church doctrine, not undermine it.

As Buckland saw it, the study of rocks and the earth, now "exalted to the rank of sciences," should aim to "unite the highest attainments of abstract science and literature with the much more important purposes of Religious Truth" (*VG*, 2, 11). The latter would remain its yardstick and final proof. Accordingly, "any investigation of Natural Philosophy which shall not terminate in the Great First Cause will justly be deemed unsatisfactory" (*VG*, 11).

The purpose of making such pronouncements was largely to handcuff geology to scripture. That was no problem to Paley and like-minded Evangelicals, not least because, as the Victorian preacher and polemicist John Charles Ryle later explained, "The first leading feature in Evangelical Religion is the *absolute supremacy it assigns to Holy Scripture,* as the only rule of faith and practice, the only test of truth, the only judge of controversy."[17] Consequently, the doctrinal and scientific reach of Evangelical creationism was (and, for many such believers, remains) limited to confirming the veracity of Genesis, whose opening verses rank among the Bible's most poetic.

Buckland, evidently, was eager to compete with them. Although his argument and thinking were more sophisticated than Paley's, he garnished his lecture with comforting metaphors, including that nature's "new kingdom" (*VG*, 11) gives us "genial showers [that] scatter fertility over the earth" (he declined to mention the frosts and droughts that also harden it). The world gives us "never-failing reservoirs of . . . springs and rivers" to water our crops, Buckland added, ignoring the world's vast stretches of desert where rivers and rain are scarce. In these examples, he declared, "We find such undeniable proofs of a nicely balanced adaptation of means to ends, of wise foresight and benevolent intention and infinite power, that he must be blind indeed, who refuses to recognize in them proofs of the most exalted attributes of the Creator" (13).

The implication that skeptics and nonbelievers were blind pales beside Paley's tactic of openly questioning their sanity. To contend that "the present order of nature is insufficient to prove the existence of an intelligent Creator" is, Paley asserted, to advance "a doctrine, to which, I conceive, no sound mind can assent."[18]

Within a decade, such unfortunate rhetoric would backfire, leaving Paley and Buckland sounding a lot more self-satisfied than their arguments and research warranted. Regarding his own quite basic and tautological explanation for geological formations, for instance, Paley insisted that he was not "under the smallest doubt in forming our opinion."[19]

It was of doubt precisely that Paley hoped to rid the world. So he turned the tables on skeptics and secularists, distorting their arguments by claiming that if God were not involved at every stage of creation, then we must somehow revert to the "opposite conclusion . . . that no art or skill whatever has been concerned in the business." Asking rhetorically, "Can this be maintained without absurdity?" he replied, "Yet this is atheism."[20]

In hopes of countering the deist argument that God created the world once, then retired to let nature take its own course, Buckland ended up skating on thin ice: "When therefore we perceive that the secondary causes producing [the earth's] convulsions have operated at successive periods, not blindly and at random, but with a direction to beneficial ends, we see at once the proofs of an overruling Intelligence continuing to superintend, direct, modify, and control the operations of the agents, which he originally ordained" (*VG*, 18–19). Presumably, the reverend had forgotten the horror and devastation of the Lisbon earthquake, including its effect on Christians struggling to explain why a God responsible for secondary causes would allow such atrocity to annihilate some of his most devout followers.

But Buckland's *Vindiciæ Geologicæ* was forward-thinking on one matter. It took a risk in trying to formalize "gap theology"—the notion that a large historical interval separates the first and second verses of Genesis. Accordingly, a long stretch of time could fall between the initial creation ("In the beginning God created the heaven and the earth") and the earth's ongoing amorphousness ("And the earth was without form, and void; and darkness was upon the face of the deep").

To Buckland, then, the word "beginning" in Genesis referred to an undefined period before man, when the newly formed earth bore numerous plants and animals that had since become extinct. He was thus able to incorporate his own catastrophism theory—the notion that a global deluge had devastated all planetary life except the last remaining species that Noah had carefully rescued—into a version of Old Earth creationism. He could do so without resorting to biblical literalism or, just as critical, without offending the powerful clerics who had gathered to hear his inaugural lecture. "We argue thus," he declared, in a syllogism framed by a rhetorical question: "It is demonstrable from Geology that there was a period when no organic beings had existence: these organic beings must therefore have had a beginning subsequently to this period; and where is that beginning to be found, but in the will and *fiat* of an intelligent and all-wise Creator?" (*VG*, 21).

There was, he insisted, only "apparent nonconformity" between geological research and popular understanding of the Earth's creation—just as there was only an "apparent inconsistency" between "tangible facts" and "literal interpretation of Scripture" (*VG*, 22, 23). Accordingly, the hiatus in historical time between Genesis 1:1 and 1:2 that Buckland accepted did not, for him, represent a problematic gap between the poetry of the Bible and the increasingly rigorous prose of science. The Church of England showed its support for that argument by later appointing him dean of Westminster.

Although it took him decades to accept the full consequences of Buckland's thinking, the reverend's admiring student Charles Lyell, taking inspiration from his lectures, quickly grasped that if geology was to advance, its practitioners must "free the science from Moses."[21] To Lyell, a devout Unitarian (who views God as one rather than encompassing the Trinity), that task initially seemed easier to accomplish in theory than in practice. He could accord the planet and its species a capacity to evolve and adapt, yet understandably found that ability distasteful, even repugnant, when taken to its logical conclusion and applied also to man. The idea that we too have evolved—that man descends from such near neighbors as the "Ourang-Outang"—was a conclusion from which Lyell privately recoiled. Cognizant of his stature in the field, however, as well as the growing need to respond to proponents of species development such as Jean-Baptiste Lamarck, Lyell's many admirers tried to force him to take a stand.

The ensuing struggle, including its theological consequence and psychological price, came down to how much doubt Lyell and his argument could bear. Suffering intense anguish over faith and growing evidence of species development from fossil records, Lyell tried to maintain a convincing front. He offered such bravura declamations of Lamarck's and others' early theories of evolution that, for many Victorian intellectuals, Lyell seemed to settle the debate. Only in private did he concede that the question of evolution (then known as species "development" or "transmutation") troubled him, not least because he staked much of his career on its *not* being a possible outcome for man.

The gap that divided Lyell's public scientific statements from his private and religious doubts about them is to a large degree intensely Victorian. It encapsulated a profound, almost foundational anxiety that haunted many of his contemporaries, including Thomas Carlyle and, later, Leslie Stephen. In the process of following their journals, letters, and works, we witness a fascinating set of relays between science and literature, where fiction transforms—as it tries to make sense of—the scientific theories that detractors and supporters fiercely contested at the time. It is less often acknowledged that science itself was strongly influenced by metaphors that Victorian culture popularized, including its sublime images of time.

Lyell's evocative style helps to explain that influence. His use of literary figures conveys the impact of scientific arguments about the expansiveness and immeasurability of the universe. Indeed, his arguments and works not only drew in large numbers of general readers but also captivated the imagination of such writers as George Eliot and Alfred, Lord Tennyson, who invoked him, respectively, in *The Mill on the Floss* and *In Memoriam.*

Rather like Darwin, Lyell earnestly (if incompletely) engaged with evolutionary theories that he for a long time disbelieved. For that reason, his work cannot be dismissed as having been offered in simple bad faith, as at least one contemporary critic has charged.[22] The issues at stake are more complex, including doubt, resistance, denial, and, finally, grudging concession. At stake, after all, was nothing less than the history of the planet and of *Homo sapiens* as a species. Small wonder that Lyell painstakingly worked out hypotheses to their logical conclusions, trying earnestly to make them fit evidence that pointed in a different direction.

Lyell made no pretense of "connecting" geology with scripture, as Buckland had. He made clear that his geological statements would succeed or fail on their own merit, giving *Principles of Geology* a subtitle that sounded scientific and secular, and certainly humbler than Buckland's: "An Attempt to Explain the Former Changes of the Earth's Surface, by Reference to Causes Now in Operation." That stress on looking backward from current evidence, which Hutton's *Theory of the Earth* had popularized, made clear from the start that Lyell saw geological developments as continuous with the past, rather than as ending with Moses' account of the flood besieging Noah, or God's proclamation after the deluge: "I will not again curse the ground any more for man's sake" (Genesis 8:21).

To Lyell, the world presented an exciting array of cryptic signs and buried stories that were archived in its crust and in fossils, if the geologist could but discover and decipher them. Geology, in his hands, became a new way of seeing and reading, based on the evidence. And scientists had misinterpreted that evidence (Lyell let his readers infer) because the Bible had steered them down a different path. Another world awaited them that was older and stranger than most of them realized. As he declared, in a sentence capturing his literary style, "We may restore in imagination the appearance of the ancient continents which have passed away."[23]

Lyell's desire to foster an archaeology for the planet, based on a cyclic history of the Earth, had dizzying philosophical implications that made him "venture to doubt" various "article[s] of faith" (*PG*, 16)—the global effects of Noah's flood being one of them. Picking up where Hutton had left off, with his poetic but thoroughly disorienting assertion, "We find no ves-

Figure 4. John and Charles Watkins, *Sir Charles Lyell, 1st Bt,* albumen carte de visite, 1860s. © National Portrait Gallery, London.

tige of a beginning, no prospect of an end," Lyell produced an argument for "deep time" that underlined the immensity of the planet's history.[24]

Just as Hutton had, Lyell discovered that his cyclic view of that history raised large questions about extinction, a serious conundrum for both scientists, given their respective arguments and beliefs. Why indeed would God create species to flourish, only to render large numbers of them extinct? Was that a sign, as Hutton had wondered, of a deliberate flaw in God's model or an indication that he was letting nature take its own course? And if the latter, what were the implications, for humanity as for Christianity, of a dynamic—even hostile—model of nature, which let whole species disappear without apparent reason?

"Whereas Hutton had confined himself almost entirely to processes of inorganic change," John Greene notes, "Lyell defined geology to include the study of organic change as well. This was in keeping with the progress made in the study of the fossil record since Hutton wrote."[25] But the inclusion posed a serious intellectual and religious challenge, forcing Lyell either to accept that evolution affected all species or else to maintain, against all evidence, that humanity was exempt from such changes.

"Although we are mere sojourners on the surface of the planet, chained to a mere point in space, enduring but for a moment of time," he declared as optimistically as he could, "the human mind is not only enabled to number worlds beyond the unassisted ken of mortal eye, but *to trace the events of indefinite ages before the creation of our race,* and is not even withheld from penetrating into the dark secrets of the ocean, or the interior of the solid globe" (*PG,* 102; emphasis mine).

Instead of turning to scripture and trying to confirm its scientific bona fides, then, as Buckland and Paley had done, Lyell allowed the present to recede like a series of infinitely diminishing Chinese boxes—except that, in his poetic analogy, the boxes became earlier epochs: "Worlds . . . seen beyond worlds immeasurably distant from each other, and beyond them all innumerable other systems are faintly traced on the confines of the visible universe" (*PG,* 16). If one could somehow trace their line to a vanishing point, one probably would not alight at an end or beginning; but the act of working backward would produce a history. It would forge a connection, however tenuous, between that moment, light-years ago, and now.

The recourse to simile and metaphor was no accident. "Deep time" doesn't anchor meaning in the way that Genesis does; it leaves science with a host of questions, including over the reliability of its claims and calculations. With centuries and millennia as hopelessly inadequate measurements, the intervals of space involved become so sublime that the mind can find no reasonable scale for them. As Lyell put it lyrically, describing his reaction to reading Hutton, "The imagination was first fatigued and overpowered by endeavouring to conceive the immensity of time required for the annihilation of whole continents by so insensible a process [as minute, protracted sedimentation and erosion]. Yet when the thoughts had wandered through these interminable periods, no resting place was assigned in the remotest distance" (*PG*, 16).

One of the crises stemming from Hutton's work was, sure enough, that it seemed to distance (even, potentially, to remove) from the Earth's history the presence and reassuring intervention of a beneficent architect. The planet underwent changes without apparent rhyme or reason. If a blueprint for the universe existed, other than what was written as scripture, then it was becoming increasingly difficult to find it. Still, as Adrian Desmond asserts persuasively in *The Politics of Evolution*, the fact that Lamarck's theory of evolution put creationist explanations on the defensive was precisely a source of its appeal to atheists and socialists who in the 1820s and 1830s "supported a brand of evolution . . . far more radical than anything Darwin envisaged." "Theirs was evolution in a real 'revolutionary' context," he explains, promoted by those wanting "the dissolution of Church and aristocracy, and calling for a new economic system."[26] In later chapters, we'll see how this groundswell of support for pre-Darwinian evolution helped to make the topic more acceptable to middle-class readers concerned about being labeled "infidels" and "atheists."

The absence of an apparent blueprint for creation (beyond Genesis) provoked a different reaction in scholars such as Lyell, whose response to such doubt-filled moments (anxious misgivings followed by hesitation and, eventually, disbelief) soon developed into a pattern. "In the course of my tour" of volcanic Mount Etna on Sicily, he acknowledged, "I had been frequently led to reflect on the precept of Descartes, 'that a philosopher should once in his life doubt everything he had been taught.'" But he neither welcomed that doubt nor allowed it to permeate all that he knew: "I still retained so much faith in my early geological creed," he added, that "when visiting . . . parts of the Val di Noto . . . all idea of attaching a high antiquity to a regularly stratified limestone . . . vanished at once from my mind."[27]

Given all of the evidence that he could muster for the planet's long-

drawn-out development, including that the flood affecting Noah was almost certainly limited and not especially unique, Lyell also found his
thoughts returning increasingly to the species question. It was rapidly becoming *the* hot-button issue of the time, a heated subject for Sunday sermons and religious treatises, as we shall see. With Lyell's reluctant help,
science increasingly put the burden of proof on Christianity. For if uni-
form changes were visible everywhere, including in the extinction of
species, what—other than biblical insistence—made us exempt from the
transmutations affecting almost everything else on Earth?

The faithful argued passionately that God had singled us out, giving us
temporary dominion over the planet. And perhaps surprisingly, given his
bid to "free [geology] from Moses," Lyell held a similar belief for much of
his career.[28] A scientist who generally preferred appeasement to conflict,
he shied away from theological controversies, not least because he still had
to make a living.[29] Alienating the clergy could end one's chances of being
appointed a professor at Oxford or Cambridge (Lyell ended up at the University of London). Indeed, in ways that distinguished England from its
European counterparts, clerics tended to control university appointments.
(At Cambridge, amazingly, the professoriate also had to agree to be celibate,
though exceptions were sometimes made to those already married.)[30]

The Reverend Henry Milman, one of Lyell's closest associates, became
an unwitting victim of such parochialism. Milman's *History of the Jews*
(1830) was too cutting-edge for the time. It drew on German biblical criticism to argue that the Jews were an "eastern tribe" and on documentary evidence to downplay the existence of miracles.[31]

Ultimately, nothing in Milman's book "went beyond what could be
found in the notes to an expensive Bible edited by one of his most learned
opponents."[32] Yet it was widely denounced, by Sharon Turner, author of
the hugely popular *Sacred History of the World* (1832), as by the young John
Henry Newman, subsequent leader of the Tractarians, Oxford's Anglo-
Catholic movement. "The crime," Lyell noticed, was "to have put" such
arguments forth "in a *popular* book."[33] Milman's work appeared in John

Murray's relatively inexpensive "Family Library" and seems, incredibly, to have generated more heat because it was written largely for a lay audience.

Lyell resented such control and narrow-mindedness. He envied the United States its nondenominational universities and railed (to friends, at least) that England was "more parson ridden than any [country] in Europe except Spain."[34] As Roy Porter acknowledges, Lyell criticized not only "'theological sophists,' Catholics, Puseyites, and Scriptural geologists like Andrew Ure ('an unprincipled hypocrite and libertine' . . .), but [also] Anglican bishops, the hierarchy of the Church of England, and ecclesiastical power in general."[35]

Private denunciations of clerical power are not, however, the same as a public stand against it. Although Lyell was an ardent liberal Whig who advocated electoral reform and the disestablishment of the Anglican Church, he also had his own beliefs, which he seems to have kept quite separate from his criticisms of organized religion.[36] Those beliefs surface at the end of *Principles of Geology,* in a closing sentence that underscores—perhaps with Milman's fate in mind—that speculating on the Earth's beginning "appears to us inconsistent with a just estimate of the relations which subsist between the finite powers of man and the attributes of an Infinite and Eternal Being" (*PG*, 438). Lyell's Unitarian beliefs do not make him a conventional doubter, yet his intellectual difficulty in squaring those beliefs with scientific arguments he contested and even ridiculed makes him quintessentially Victorian and a key source of interest for this book.

Lyell ended up backloading quite a lot into *Principles.* One sentence earlier, he had added rather hurriedly, as if gliding over a long-postponed subject, that although "it appears that the species have been changed" (the passive clause carefully abstaining from any suggestion of how or why), "yet they have all been so modelled, on types analogous to those of existing plants and animals, as to indicate throughout a perfect harmony of design and unity of purpose" (*PG*, 438).

The argument could almost be a throwback to Paley's *Natural Theology.* Yet Lyell's claim, read carefully, concedes far less than it may at first seem. As James Secord observes, "In the *Principles* the rock of faith rest[s] solely on God's maintenance of the economy of nature and on the status of humans as moral, rational beings."[37] Lyell had thus chiseled away quite extensively at Paley's arguments.

But he had to keep the plank in place—in part because religious arguments about the Earth's creation still had so much meaning for him. Only in the closing pages of his three-volume study could he be "led with great reluctance into [a] digression" on Noah's flood (*PG*, 433). Tiptoeing around that delicate subject, the cause of so much rancor and so many column inches at the time, he wrote that in all likelihood it was a localized flood that had taken place near what we now call the Black and Caspian Seas. There, subsidence—perhaps even an earthquake—had made possible the sudden release of large amounts of water from much higher ground.

Lyell's distaste for using secular explanations to settle theological disputes is palpable, not least because the former had such an unsettling effect on his convictions. As Michael Bartholomew observes, he "subscribed to the specifically *natural* theological opinions of his contemporaries, even though *Principles* was seen by some of them to embody a denigration of those beliefs."[38]

Lyell was quick to intuit how much shock and dismay his words would cause other believers. (Moses' account of the Flood had called it global; to limit the Flood to even a relatively small geographical region was a major, and controversial, step.) His faith and propriety also led him to conclude that religion was a private affair between oneself and God. That conclusion —mealy-mouthed to some—gave belief a sacrosanct dimension, which, in his view, science should either abstain from encroaching on or do so only with great reluctance and respect.

When for instance the atheistic Scots physician George Hoggart Toulmin decried Christianity in *The Eternity of the World* (1785), Lyell privately compared him to English soldiers who had raided Burmese temples for war trophies: "To insult their idols was an act of Christian intolerance, and, until we can convert them, should be penal. If a philosopher commits a similar act of intolerance by insulting the idols of an European mob (the popular prejudices of the day), the vengeance of the more intolerant herd of the ignorant will overtake him."[39] Attacking beliefs that the "mob" was not willing to give up "is not courage or manliness in the cause of Truth," Lyell insisted. "Nor does it promote its progress."[40] He was doubtless right on that last count. While allusions to a European "mob" and an "intolerant herd" betray prejudices of his own, Lyell grasped that people are extraordinarily reluctant to relinquish their beliefs. In some cases, they would prefer to die for them than abandon them, and certainly not see them attacked gratuitously.

The strongest bone of contention among Lyell's critics—and the clearest sign of his difficulty in parting with certain long-held beliefs—was his long-delayed acceptance of evolutionary theory. The issue turned into a drama of exceptional significance for Lyell, not least because he devoted so much of his career to refuting it.

"It cost me a struggle to renounce my old creed," Lyell later acknowledged in 1863.[41] That was putting it mildly. It would take him almost three decades of contemplation and hedging (with numerous updated editions of *Principles* and the publication, finally, of Darwin's *On the Origin of Species*) before he would quietly end that fight and bow to what had become inevitable. He did so, justifiably, claiming some credit for bringing about the new state of affairs. Certainly, Darwin was prepared to concede that he had been unfair to Lyell—that there was much more in *Principles* than he had given his friend credit for—though he was still disappointed in Lyell's long-drawn-out resistance to evolutionary theory.[42]

Lyell first encountered arguments for species "transmutation" in 1827, when he read a borrowed copy of Lamarck's *Philosophie zoologique*. That study, which outlined a fairly basic theory of organic descent for all creatures, including man, had appeared in Paris almost two decades earlier. Lyell's reaction, at least to his friend Gideon Mantell, was dismissive, comparing the work to light fiction. The book had delighted him "more than any novel I ever read," he scoffed, "and much in the same way," because such theories "address themselves to the imagination."[43]

Certainly, such theories *do* affect the imagination—just as Lyell's account of "deep time" forces us to wrestle with the concept of infinity. Behind the scenes, however, Lyell found Lamarck's argument extremely unnerving. In *Principles* he voices surprise that it "has met with some degree of favour from many naturalists," not just in Paris but also among such London colleagues as Robert Edmond Grant, a member of the Geological Society Council who taught fossil zoology at the city's university.[44] Even in his 1827 letter to Mantell, Lyell admits, in barely concealed horror, that if Lamarck were right, his theory "would prove that man may have come from the Ourang-Outang."[45] The chaos and confusion to ensue would be too awful to imagine—a theme that recurs with almost painful repetition in Lyell's notebooks far into the 1850s. In the following statement to Mantell, for example, it is not immediately clear if he is voicing an exclamation or asking a heartfelt question: "How impossible will it be to distinguish and lay down a line, beyond which some of the so-called extinct species have never passed into recent ones."[46]

In public, Lyell regrettably decided to play to England's rearguard audience, which was only too happy to dismiss the latest intellectual fad from Paris. In 1832, London's *Monthly Review* derided "transmutation" as "the most stupid and ridiculous" idea to have been hatched by "the heated fancy of man."[47] Lyell was neither so brash nor so foolish, but he did sniff in *Principles* that Lamarck's arguments "were not generally received" before almost going out of his way to attack them as "staggering and absurd" (*PG*, 184, 189). "When Lamarck talks 'of the efforts of internal sentiment,'" he jeered, "he gives us names for things, and with a disregard to the strict rules of induction, resorts to fictions, as ideal as the 'plastic virtue,' and other phantoms of the middle ages" (188).

Criticizing Lamarck's theory as "fiction" and the effect of an overheated "imagination" was becoming almost a trademark reaction. Yet the charge of antiquated thinking closely fit Lyell here. And the theory that he publicly ridiculed preoccupied him, with implications he could neither accept nor dismiss. "The chief objection to the hypothesis of transmutation," he privately acknowledged in his journals, "was naturally the inseparable connexion which it established between Man & the lower animals."[48] "If we exclude" man from transmutation, he worried in 1856, three years before the "earth-shaking" publication of Darwin's *On the Origin of Species by Means of Natural Selection,* "the only sound argument for the popular theory of progress in the organic World is gone. If we include him, the great book which the Geologist is trying to decypher becomes at once identified with Natural Theology as well as with Natural History."[49]

Caught between this Scylla and Charybdis, Lyell settled uncomfortably on the compromise that man is "an exception" to progressive development. Like many Victorians, he saw evolution as degrading, even disgusting—a process not befitting a noble species. That reaction is understandable, given the newness of the theory and the shock of wrestling with its far-reaching implications. Evolution also brought to Lyell's mind fears about barbarousness, miscegenation, and even sexual corruption: "If Man be modern," his notebook frets, "& if the negro & white man have come from one stock, & if such distinct races, if discovered in quadrumana, would have been pronounced species, then new species have been formed since the human pair originated."[50]

Those worrisome "ifs" highlight a religious scientist struggling to accept the almost unavoidable conclusion: "new species have been formed since" Adam and Eve. If in a strict biological sense we are no longer the same as the first "human pair," then what are God's intentions for us, Lyell wondered? If we have evolved in ways similar to other species, then were Adam and Eve somehow imperfect to begin with, and do we nonetheless hold a specially appointed task, with dominion over other creatures?

After the cornerstone of Lyell's faith began to shift and he could no longer call man "the crowning link in the chain of progressive development," a slew of questions hit him almost immediately:[51] "If there are . . . intermediate steps between the sensible or rational & the insane, why claim

such dignity for Man as contrasted with the brutes. When does the suck-
ing infant attain the rank of an intelligent dog? Has the child an hour before its birth a soul? Or an hour after?"[52]

After Lyell allowed himself to entertain such questions, the dam seemed
to break. A flood of queries followed, about insanity, idiocy, and especially
race. There's no avoiding that Lyell's anxiety about evolution was coexten-
sive with his prejudices over what he called "the hundreds of millions of savage or semi-barbarous races."[53] Those questions, in turn, generated still
more unanswered enigmas. "Then comes the question whether less civilized
races deteriorated from a more highly gifted or more advanced race, or
whether the first stock was of low capacity & improved into higher."[54]

"Not only did evolution repel Lyell's highly refined aesthetic sense,"
including his image of humanity, notes James Secord astutely; "it [also]
undermined his lofty conception of science as the search for laws governing a perfectly adapted divine creation."[55] That Lyell abstained from public commentary on this issue did not end his profound unease over man's
"bestial" origins. As he put it in November 1858, "If the geologist . . . blends
[man] inseparably with the inferior animals & considers him as belonging
to the Earth solely, & as doomed to pass away like them & have no farther
any relation to the living world, he may feel dissatisfied with his labours &
doubt whether he would not have been happier had he never entered upon
them & whether he ought to impart the result to others."[56]

The full intensity of Lyell's "repugnance"—his word—at perceiving
that men "may have come from the Ourang-Outang" was enough to make
him doubt his role as a geologist. As his private notebooks confirm
throughout the 1850s, such emotions were as real and painful for a devout
scientist as they were for men of the Church who firmly believed that science and religion were not drifting apart but could in fact hold together.

As Lyell eventually acknowledged to himself, such weighty matters
"evinced . . . something more than mere philosophical doubt."[57] They hung
invisible question marks around everything that he had come to believe
about man's privileged role on earth, with the universe still a beneficent

entity designed to assist us. Science had begun to turn such assumptions into reflections of a demand for the universe to make sense, with humanity somehow still at its center as "Time's noblest offspring," to quote Bishop Berkeley's words from roughly a century earlier.[58] But as Lyell eloquently observed, the mounting contrary evidence still left "mankind in the same state of aspiration & hope, of trust in God, of yearning after something higher yet to come, of a feeling of individuality, [and] a belief that the discarding of this would not only lower the hopes but deteriorate the moral standard—that a belief in immortality betters & renders happier *& is therefore more probably true than* a philosophy which teaches that we are bubbles reflecting for a moment the wonders of the universe & then bursting & returning to annihilation."[59] One could hardly ask for a more lyrical statement of what religion is designed to achieve. Nor is one likely to read a more articulate account of what believers still ask religion to make possible. For Lyell, though, to state that belief in immorality bettered humanity and was "therefore more probably true" than a philosophy teaching otherwise makes clear where religious faith collided with his commitment to scientific evidence. Unsurprisingly, then, the more he brooded on those questions, the less they satisfied him. His notebooks are full of statements about living almost unavoidably in "a state of doubt," and doing so in great discomfort.[60]

As he continued to attend church fairly regularly, Lyell was "given to thoughtful and agonizing reflections" on the ever-widening gap between scripture and evolution. As his biographer Leonard Wilson put it, Lyell "couldn't quite accept the consequences of a chaotic and meaningless universe," even though his geological theories pointed almost unavoidably to that conclusion.[61]

"There was a real agony in his mind over religious doubt," Wilson continued. "I think he always had doubts," both intellectual and religious, and tried as hard as possible to reject them, "but the doubts were always at the back of his mind."[62]

Tennyson, future poet laureate, famously would invoke Lyell's *Princi-*

ples in his elegy *In Memoriam* (1850), by far the Victorians' most popular poem, especially the corrosive effect of Lyell's expansive notion of time, change, and periodic extinction on "our little systems" (philosophy, science, and theology). "From scarped cliff and quarried stone / [Nature] cries, 'A thousand types are gone: / I care for nothing, all shall go.'"[63] It is nature, "red in tooth and claw," whose "evil dreams" cause Tennyson's speaker to "stretch lame hands of faith, and grope." For it is nature—alien, violent, and indifferent—that has "shriek'd against [man's] creed," in particular his ardent belief that love is "Creation's final law."[64] Tennyson felt moved to voice such anguish and religious uncertainty despite his wanting to bolster faith that everything would work out well in the end:

> Oh yet we trust that somehow good
> Will be the final goal of ill,
> To pangs of nature, sins of will,
> Defects of doubt, and taints of blood;
>
> That nothing walks with aimless feet;
> That not one life shall be destroy'd,
> Or cast as rubbish to the void,
> When God hath made the pile complete.[65]

Tennyson was not, of course, the only writer influenced by Lyell. Among others, George Eliot almost openly invoked his *Principles* in *The Mill on the Floss* when her narrator asserts: "To the eyes that have dwelt on the past, there is no thorough repair."[66] However, one key Victorian intellectual, Thomas Carlyle, dismissed Lyell, calling him, in his own inimitable way, "a twaddling circumfused *ill*-writing man."[67]

The invective seems intense even for Carlyle, until one recognizes the two men's shared struggle with evolution. Just as Lyell had, Carlyle wrestled with the principle, calling it a "most melancholy doctrine" that helped shear his religious beliefs.[68] Also like Lyell, he added, "Faith is properly the one thing needful." Hence "the loss of . . . religious belief was the loss of

Figure 5. Julia Margaret Cameron, *Thomas Carlyle "Like a Block of Michael Angelo's Sculpture,"* albumen print, 1867. © National Media Museum/Science and Society Picture Library, London.

every thing [*sic*]."[69] Although that last part may carry more autobiographical weight than Carlyle intended, he found living without faith extremely difficult and sensed, correctly, that others were suffering similarly.

A fellow Scot also brought up in a strict religious environment (Calvinist rather than Unitarian), Carlyle began writing *Sartor Resartus,* one of the era's most powerful statements on doubt, two months after the first volume of Lyell's *Principles of Geology* appeared.[70] By November 1833, only weeks after Lyell released his third volume, Carlyle's study had begun to be serialized. So completely do the two works overlap, indeed, that Carlyle opens *Sartor* with allusions to Lyell's geology and complaints about its philosophical implications. "Of Geology and Geognosy we know enough," he quipped in his proto-Joycean style; "what with the labours of our Werners and Huttons, what with the ardent genius of their disciples, it has come about that now, to many a Royal Society, the Creation of a World is little more mysterious than the cooking of a Dumpling" (*SR*, 3).

The dig was clearly intended as a punch. An ever more querulous social critic, Carlyle was angry that the "Torch of Science" had been so "brandished and borne about" that the mystery of life had begun to leech (*SR*, 3). "Man's whole life and environment have been laid open and elucidated," his fictional editor opines; "scarcely a fragment or fibre of his Soul, Body, and Possessions, but has been probed, dissected, distilled, desiccated, and scientifically decomposed" (4).[71]

Intended as a new kind of book that "glances," in Carlyle's words, "from Heaven to Earth & back again in a strange satirical frenzy," *Sartor Resartus*, Carlyle's most scriptural text, is scarcely read or taught today.[72] "A strange Book all men will admit it to be," its author predicted.[73] In an almost self-fulfilling prophecy, it has come to be known as the *Finnegans Wake* of the Victorian era: amazing—even astonishing—in scope and originality. Yet so baroque in style and meaning that we scarcely try to fathom why it influenced large numbers of writers from Dickens, Ralph Waldo Emerson, and George Eliot to Thomas Hardy, James Joyce, and Virginia Woolf.

Carlyle did himself no favors with his quirky style and the book's uninviting title (literally, "The Tailor Retailored"). Yet his experiment is not half as difficult to read as its reputation suggests; and its quasi-religious speculations generate such extraordinary meditations on doubt that its hapless protagonist, an imaginary German professor, is pushed to the limits of his belief and identity. Carlyle, in short, has important things to say about faith.

"The role that Calvinism plays in *Sartor Resartus*," his editors allow, is "difficult to overstate." That is partly because Carlyle was immersed in the religion from a young age. With his parents austere Calvinists, proud of their work ethic and fiercely held beliefs, the "daunting presence of God and Kirk was an everyday reality . . . [and Carlyle] revered the belief while holding the institution suspect."[74]

He had studied theology at the University of Edinburgh, with every intention of becoming a minister of his church. His father strongly encouraged him, and Carlyle seemed to comply. But doubt about his faith and direction intensified as he read. He ended up rejecting theology and with it the prospect of a future in the church.

Still, long after he had ceased to believe in Christianity as an organized religion, Carlyle (like many others) found that he couldn't give up the church completely. "The religious faith in which he had been brought up disintegrated," one of his biographers notes, "before the challenge of the newer and, it seemed, more sophisticated creed" began to irk him: the rationalism of the Scottish Enlightenment, with its skeptical debunking of religion.[75] So even though Carlyle's semiautobiographical *Sartor Resartus* was "a classic expression of crisis in faith," its author remained both inspired and tormented by what he could not quite renounce.

"To accept the tenets of Calvinism was impossible," his editors explain, "yet to reject them was equally impossible. Just before the composition of *Sartor Resartus,* he considered testing his notions of theology by writing a biography of Luther."[76] Indeed, even in its profound expressions of doubt and religious confusion, *Sartor* is permeated by various kinds of religiosity —transcendentalist philosophy, belief in the power of symbols, and even ardent devotion to work. Carlyle talks about that as part of the "after-shine" of Christianity: the religion affects one long after one has stopped believing and worshipping (*SR*, 124).

Carlyle's protagonist balances similar tensions. His name, the peculiar-sounding "Diogenes Teufelsdröckh" (literally, God-Born Devil's Dung), implies an almost Manichean split between his Hellenistic first name and his Hebraic last name. With his erudition and profession, moreover, Carlyle's hero is "a distillation of the intellectual traditions of the German professor and the rhetorical traditions of the rabbi."[77] Indeed, there are several hints in the text that Herr Teufelsdröckh, educated in the Midrash at the University of Weissnichtwo (Don't Know Where) is Jewish, albeit in ways we would now call secular.

The text's religious complexities don't end there. As the editors point out: "To the Old Testament mind (Sartor), the answer is "Yes" to [Teufelsdröckh's many] questions of faith. However, to the New Testament mind (Resartus), the answers are not so clear."[78] There is, in short, no neat balancing of Old and New Testament perspectives. On the contrary, everything biblical in *Sartor*, though respected, ends up slightly jumbled. Remnants of faith remain, but the book ends on a question mark, suggesting that it "does not pretend to contain any ultimate truth," religious or otherwise.[79]

Teufelsdröckh is a bit like a wayward, grumbling version of Christian in John Bunyan's Calvinist classic, *Pilgrim's Progress.* He must survive a series of tests (just as Christian managed to flee Doubting Castle), ideally to leave his faith stronger and more resilient.[80] But part of the comfort of Bunyan's allegory lies in its suggestion that doubt is an enemy of the self, a separate antagonist that makes doubt easier to quantify, vanquish, and elude. By contrast, Teufelsdröckh's tests, having no simple answers, are more personal and existential. The hapless professor shambles from doubt to self-doubt, then on to doubt of others.

Teufelsdröckh tries to tune his faith and perspective to acceptance that "the whole world is . . . sold to Unbelief" (*SR*, 122). But although that prospect greatly saddens him, eventually he accepts that the passage between belief and unbelief is as inevitable as the pumping of the heart (his metaphor) "as in longdrawn Systole and longdrawn Diastole" (87). The metaphor is close to invoking Hutton's and Lyell's "longdrawn" arguments about the deposition and erosion of sand and shale over infinite time. There is reassurance, too, in likening the waxing and waning of faith to something far more comforting, such as the regularity of breathing. But Carlyle's universe is largely secular; it is also troubled by a sense that God has abandoned it, leaving humanity very much to its own devices.

Teufelsdröckh takes a long time to accept that belief passes and returns, just as the seasons do. He fights the idea for years, his intellectual labor full of "long details on his 'fever-paroxysms of Doubt.'" He also describes how, "in the silent night-watches, still darker in his heart than over sky and earth, he . . . cast himself before the All-seeing, and with audible prayers, cried vehemently for Light, for deliverance from Death and the Grave" (*SR*, 88).

Doubt isn't the only object at which the professor is angry. If God turns out to exist after all, the professor fumes, how could he sit by, idle, while earthquakes and other natural disasters occur? The anger turns to bargaining, before it yields to something closer to secular acceptance. The plaintive question "Is there no God . . . ?" leads Carlyle's professor to ask what meaning "Duty" might have in a nonreligious context and whether belief in general is merely a "false earthly Fantasm" (*SR*, 121).

In Carlyle's hands, doubt and belief are remarkably close to fear, an emotion we have traced in Lyell's scientific notebooks. It is as if doubt prompts the poor, pitiable "Devil's Dung" to wonder whether fear was really the element that held everything together in the first place. "Strangely enough," he writes, "I lived in a continual, indefinite, pining Fear; tremulous, pusillanimous, apprehensive of I knew not what: it seemed as if all things in the Heavens above and the Earth beneath would hurt me; as if the Heavens and the Earth were but boundless jaws of a devouring monster, wherein I, palpitating, waited to be devoured" (*SR*, 125).

It is an extraordinary passage, full of revelation about the meaning of belief and the fear of giving it up. Indeed, it is only when the professor almost angrily confronts himself over the meaning of his fear that he is able to put it in some perspective: "What *art* thou afraid of? Wherefore, like a coward, dost thou forever pip and whimper, and go cowering and trembling? Despicable biped! what is the sum-total of the worst that lies before thee? Death? Well, Death; and say the pangs of Tophet too, and all that the Devil and Man may, will, or can do against thee!" (*SR*, 125).

"What *art* thou afraid of?" It is an excellent, and surely quite necessary question to ask in light of Lyell's and Carlyle's tangled intellectual and religious doubts. If the fear that Carlyle's professor describes is merely imaginary, then nothing confronted head-on will look as ominous. The specter-mongering terror will collapse into a heap on the floor. But it didn't quite do so for Carlyle himself, even years after his "tailor" had been "retailored." And for others as well, such as John Henry Newman and Anne Brontë, the fears that sprang from doubting the existence of God remained real enough to be palpable.

THREE

Feeling Doubt, Then Drinking It

A few months before Carlyle's doubt-drenched *Sartor Resartus* began circulating in England, John Henry Newman was wandering the streets of Leonforte, a small town in Sicily, berating himself for his "utter hollowness."[1] Carlyle's eccentric narrator had given a resounding "yea" to the universe, in hopes of combating his own relentless doubt. Newman—then a tutor at Oriel College, Oxford—had returned to Sicily alone to clarify exactly what he believed.

For both Victorians, doubt turned out to be more than a serious preoccupation; it brought to a head concerns about the Anglican Church that Newman would pursue literally and figuratively to Rome. At the same time, Carlyle, and Anne and Branwell Brontë, the focus of this chapter, would develop full-blown meditations on the nature of faith and unbelief. All harboring doubt, they found different ways to represent and work through it. Their spiritual crises and solutions are—like the story of Victorian doubt itself—inseparable from the broader cultural and religious crises that roiled Britain in the first decades of the nineteenth century.

By June 1833, somewhat tired of his own company and deliriously imagining that he'd been "given over" to the devil as a test, Newman was "aching to get home" from his travels around southern Italy.[2] Already weak from typhoid fever, an illness he viewed as punishment for his earlier wavering, he harangued himself for his want of faith and lack of "self denial."[3] Not surprisingly, with all that pressure added to the debilitating effects of illness, Newman's inability to find transportation home proved too much. "I sat down on my bed," he wrote, "and began to sob violently."[4] "I kept asking almost impatiently why God so fought against me."[5]

The Oxford tutor who played a major role in trying to reorient England's church toward Rome—indeed, the man the Vatican is now considering for sainthood[6]—had sailed from Falmouth the previous December with Hurrell Froude, his closest friend, and Froude's father.[7] (Froude senior will appear again in the next chapter, when he disinherits his youngest son, James Anthony, for writing *The Nemesis of Faith*.) Once in Italy, Newman wrote a letter home calling Rome "the most wonderful place in the world," though he viewed its church as "polytheistic, degrading, idolatrous."[8] Twelve years later, having changed his mind, he set off a firestorm in England by converting to Roman Catholicism.

Eventually, in Sicily, the right ship turned up, and Newman boarded "an orange boat, bound for Marseilles."[9] But when the wind died in the Straits of Bonifacio (the small patch of sea between Corsica and Sardinia), a thick fog fell, giving Newman the impression that the boat was lost, even stranded. In his faith or impatience, thinking he was sent another test, he sat down to compose "Lead, Kindly Light," an allegory about overcoming doubt that would soon become the Victorians' favorite hymn. He signed it, appropriately, "at sea."

"Lead, kindly Light," the first stanza exhorts,

> amid the encircling gloom,
> Lead Thou me on!
> The night is dark, and I am far from home—
> Lead Thou me on!

Keep Thou my feet; I do not ask to see
The distant scene—one step enough for me.[10]

By turning doubt into a metaphor, Newman transformed the orange boat into a beacon of hope. In other respects, "Lead, Kindly Light" makes doubt manageable by allowing it to seem predictable. Like those before him, including Bunyan, Newman helped to turn doubt into an ordeal designed to test the believer, to make him or her try harder, and even to relish doing so. In Newman's case, the result was stronger faith following conversion to Catholicism. For Anne Brontë, by contrast, the effect was a persistent "tinge of religious melancholy."[11] That's partly because the Evangelical tradition in which she worshipped viewed faith as "God-given" and thus as something that God could and did take away. The very presence of doubt was to such Christians a sign that God had rejected the worshipper and thus a calamitous judgment that the mortal wasn't sufficiently worthy to enter heaven.

Newman's path to Rome was of course very much his own, and fashioned at a time when many were leaving the Anglican Church in large numbers, either troubled by its internal rifts or unable to continue believing in its Articles of Religion (on which more soon). Even so, the central role that he played in England's Oxford Movement—combined with his later conversion to Catholicism (1845)—meant that he worked through some of the thorniest theological problems of the age: baptismal regeneration, unconditional election, reprobation, vicarious atonement, and final perseverance.

Here, too, dissent became entangled with doubt, indicating the latter's complex shading among skeptics and denominations. In his strong objections to "the school of Calvin," for example, Newman voiced skeptical positions to which unbelievers and freethinkers were similarly prone.[12] As he explained, using hyperbole to convey his thoughts on the crisis into which Calvinism had helped to throw the Established Church, "There are but two alternatives, the way to Rome, and the way to Atheism."[13]

Put this way, Newman's intense suffering by the Mediterranean starts to bear an uncanny resemblance to that of doubters such as Arthur Hugh Clough, poet and friend to Thomas and Matthew Arnold, who after much soul-searching decided to give up his tutorship at Oriel College because it required him to teach the Thirty-Nine Articles.[14] In hindsight, the dovetailing of religiously motivated doubt with that of skeptics and freethinkers is not only apt, as Newman made clear, but also helpful in underscoring why and how agnosticism arose from within a religious context.[15]

"I have a very large amount of objection or rather repugnance to sign" them from the heart, Clough wrote to friend J. P. Gell about the articles. The necessary oath was to him "a bondage, and a very heavy one, and one that may cramp and cripple one for life."[16] The author of "The Latest Decalogue" and other doubt-filled poems wrote further to Gell one year later, "If I begin to think about God, there [arise] a thousand questions, and whether the 39 Articles answer them at all or whether I should not answer them in the most diametrically opposite purport is a matter of great doubt."[17]

The Anglican Church's Thirty-Nine Articles had been established in 1563 as the cornerstone of its doctrine—indeed, as a means of cementing the Reformation and break with the Roman Church. They range from the opening article, whose second clause had become increasingly contentious ("There is but one living and true God . . . the Maker, and Preserver of all things both visible and invisible") to number 20, on ecclesiastical authority ("The Church hath power to decree Rites or Ceremonies, and authority in Controversies of Faith"). Article 33 concerns the policy of how to "excommunicate Persons, how they are to be avoided": "That person which by open denunciation of the Church is rightly cut off from the unity of the Church, and excommunicated, ought to be taken of the whole multitude of the faithful, as an Heathen and Publican, until he be openly reconciled by penance."[18] One gets a sense, at least, of how difficult it was for many scholars to swear to uphold such articles as a matter of belief and English law.

That the crisis affected Clough and Newman differently is beyond dispute, yet each of them—and many others of their generation—felt that they had come to a fork: beliefs had to be tested, to see if faith would endure. Both, accordingly, leaned heavily though differently on doubt. Newman's decision thereafter was to embrace doctrine more fervently through another branch of Christianity. But many others, finding that path impossible or undesirable, instead discovered that their beliefs faltered because of weakened attraction to the Church. After following their consciences to doubt, many then transitioned to various forms of secularism. Susan Budd notes that "the conversion to atheism usually followed two distinct phases: the conversion from Christianity to unbelief or uncertainty, . . . and the move from unbelief to positive commitment to secularism."[19] Experiencing chiefly the first phase, Clough and Carlyle put their impressive minds and energies to the advancement of nonreligious ideas. In doing so, they helped to transform the nation's culture.

The number of Victorian treatises and novels that they and other writers composed on religious doubt alone easily reaches one hundred.[20] Some of them treat doubt elliptically, as a subject too difficult to voice directly, but implying a feared loss of social order.[21] When one considers the sheer number of works and articles on the subject, including only the period's major poetic statements on doubt—from Alfred, Lord Tennyson's *In Memoriam* (1850) to Gerard Manley Hopkins' *Wreck of the Deutschland* (1875) and Thomas Hardy's "God's Funeral" (c. 1908)—one starts to glimpse the haunting, often agonizing importance of the subject for the culture at large. Even in Hardy's supposed elegy for the deity, a "man-projected Figure," the speaker cannot stop imagining what men and women will create instead to worship.[22]

Although Newman parted theological company with many of his contemporaries, his importance to them remained. As his beliefs inched ever closer to Rome, he made it easier for Victorian skeptics to join him in examining what was least attractive about Anglicanism.

Despite the obvious provocations of early Victorian geology and biology, the theological wrangles that unfolded in 1830s Oxford began as separate phenomena. The more immediate threats to the Established Church were rifts over doctrine, driven in part by religiously inflected doubt, as well as by the religious enthusiasm and zealotry that Methodism and Evangelicalism had been encouraging for more than a century.

Throughout the 1730s and beyond, Methodists were perceived in Britain as a growing threat. They were persecuted accordingly, partly because, in refusing to abide by Anglicanism's Thirty-Nine Articles, Methodist preachers gave unlicensed sermons to lay audiences, often in nonreligious settings such as fields and schoolrooms. In England, early Methodism (initially a pejorative term) helped to stoke what was later called the First Great Awakening of religious enthusiasm that swept the American colonies in the 1730s and 1740s, leaving the country's religious landscape permanently altered.

One reason emerged for the fervor in both countries: Methodism, like Calvinism, appealed directly to a strong sense of personal guilt over the death of Christ, which both denominations saw as the path to salvation. Where Anglicanism stressed ritual and ceremony, with an array of theological teachings about the Trinity, Methodism in particular pared away that structure. It stressed the fundamental importance—and simplicity—of a personal rapport with Christ, though it dwelled on other emphases, too, such as the importance of conversion and of practical piety, meaning social activism at home and missionary zeal abroad.

"In their war against the flesh," one scholar writes about Methodists, "every aspect of corruption served to heighten the end they had in view: to disgust their followers with this life and speed them into the next."[23] That's putting it strongly, but both Methodism and Calvinism aimed at inducing constant reminders of humanity's propensity to sin, in accusations that could easily border on fanaticism. As Mr. Brocklehurst, the headmaster of Lowood School, explains in *Jane Eyre*, Charlotte Brontë's 1847 classic, "I have a Master to serve whose kingdom is not of this world: my mission is to mortify in these girls the lusts of the flesh, to teach them to clothe themselves with shamefacedness and sobriety, not with braided hair and costly apparel; and each of the young persons before us [with naturally curly hair] has a string of hair twisted in plaits which vanity itself might have woven: these, I repeat, must be cut off; think of the time wasted."[24] Recoiling from such Calvinism, Brontë turns Brocklehurst—a "black marble clergyman" whose "grim face" resembles "a carved mask"—into a hypocrite who parades his daughters before his impoverished, orphaned students.[25] He does so, amazingly, with his daughters clothed in silk dresses, enjoying long flowing locks, without any awkwardness about the double standard. Toward the end of the novel, moreover, St. John Rivers, an aspiring Calvinist missionary whose "marble-seeming features . . . [are] expressive of a repressed fervour," proposes marriage to Jane Eyre on condition that they both move to India to evangelize. "God and nature intended you for a missionary's wife," he tells her. When Jane agrees to the work but not the marriage, Rivers is almost instantly scornful: "Tremble lest in that case you should be numbered with those who have denied the faith, and are worse than infidels!"[26]

Brontë's portrayal of Calvinism is clearly extreme, but its rhetoric of mortifying the flesh appealed to those who wanted stark distinctions between virtue and sin, as well as clear mandates on what to reject and despise. Its fire-and-brimstone edicts left worshippers in no doubt about who would be saved and who apparently would not. It wasn't a joyous outlook, nor was it kind to congregations. In general, Evangelicalism gave worshippers a constant terror of judgment, which took hold rapidly in remoter Anglican parishes, especially those without priests. Thereafter, sermons were designed less to communicate love and acceptance than to stir trepidation about burning pits of fire. The demand for repentance, atonement, and regeneration was harsh, but it gave followers black-and-white rules that could be reassuring in the certainty they described.

One of the best passages detailing Newman's despair over such theology is the moment in his autobiography when he sums up what pulled him in the "opposite" direction, toward Hurrell Froude and Roman Catholicism. Newman had flirted briefly with Calvinism in his teens, following an even earlier diet of freethinkers such as Hume, Voltaire, and Thomas Paine. In his admiration for Froude, however, one detects the rationale for a larger intellectual movement, like the one that he and other Tractarians would soon cultivate:

> He professed openly his admiration of the Church of Rome, and his hatred of the Reformers. He delighted in the notion of an hierarchical system, of sacerdotal power, and of full ecclesiastical liberty. He felt scorn of the maxim, "The Bible and the Bible only is the religion of Protestants"; and he gloried in accepting Tradition as a main instrument of religious teaching. He had a high severe idea of the intrinsic excellence of Virginity; and he considered the Blessed Virgin its great Pattern. He delighted in thinking of the Saints; he had a vivid appreciation of the idea of sanctity, its possibility and its heights; and he was more than inclined to believe a large amount of miraculous interference as occurring in the early and middle ages. He embraced the principle of penance and mortification. He had a deep devotion to the Real Presence, in which he had a firm faith. He was powerfully drawn to the Medieval Church, but not to the Primitive.[27]

All those factors, however, as readily propelled people from the Church as toward it. To Newman's assertions about the miraculous, for instance, one could as easily echo William Nicholson's question, quoted in chapter 1: Why would so much "miraculous interference" occur predominantly "in the early and middle ages," leaving "so few" signs of it "in *latter times?*"[28]

Indeed, that Newman's younger brother, Francis, transitioned fairly quickly from Calvinism to deism to religious doubt—more or less as Hurrell's brother Anthony would—makes clear that the very elements of faith that John Henry upheld as attractive were, for many others, sources of controversy, even deep consternation.[29] Widespread anger over Newman's final tract, about the terms and limits of the Thirty-Nine Articles of Faith, was, after all, a key reason he decided to leave the Oxford Movement, and with it the Anglican Church.[30]

In each of the above clauses about Hurrell Froude, however, Newman lists an equal-and-opposite reaction to Calvinism, which rejected hierarchies, iconography, miracles, and just about everything else that it saw as detracting from Christ, conversion, and scripture. Newman had not yet joined the Roman Church, over which he still had serious doctrinal concerns, but the Oxford Movement, he makes clear, sprang from a deep desire to restore to Anglicanism aspects of the English church that the Reformation had rejected as "Popery." What he advocated, quite bluntly, was "a second Reformation:—a better reformation, for it would be a return not to the sixteenth century, but to the seventeenth."[31]

The Reverend John Keble, then chair of poetry at Oxford, had helped to form the Oxford Movement when he preached his famous Assize sermon, "National Apostasy," in July 1833. Contesting the idea that interest in the pre-Reformation church meant that one was seeing "omens and tokens of an Apostate Mind in a nation," Keble urged his congregation to embrace that interest and the momentum it was gathering.[32]

As Newman would, Keble argued that Britain was right to revive its "Apostolical Church." He called on followers to "uphold [and] restore" that pre-Reformation tradition by asking them to weigh two startling questions: "What are the symptoms, by which one may judge most fairly, whether or no a nation, as such, is becoming alienated from God and Christ? And what are the particular duties of sincere Christians, whose lot is cast by Divine Providence in a time of such dire calamity?"[33] Confident that the "good Christian" and "true Churchman" would find "*the winning side*" and that victory would be "complete, universal, eternal," Keble went on to become a leading light of the Tractarians. He did not, however, follow Newman into the Roman Catholic Church.[34]

Rather less sanguine, by contrast, the devout Anglican John Constable painted Salisbury Cathedral—founded in 1220 and representative to him of the plight of the Church as a whole—as racked by storms but still yet weathering them.

Constable had already painted Salisbury Cathedral before, in a work commissioned by John Fisher, then bishop of Salisbury. That earlier painting, from 1825, presents the cathedral as flooded by sunlight and surrounded by blue sky. But in his even more symbolic 1831 rendition (see illustration), the swollen river mires the progress of a horse and cart, while a grave marker joltingly reminds of death. The painting seems bogged down with challenges, impediments, and endings. Nevertheless, Constable's ash tree is meant to symbolize life, and the cathedral spire—mirroring its insistent vertical line—points urgently, resiliently, to a gap in the skies promising reprieve. Constable completes the scene with a rainbow almost encircling the cathedral, as if he wanted to shield it from the lowering skies. These, his symbolism makes unavoidable, are the same threatening clouds that menace Oxford just a few dozen miles northeast.[35]

Painting a rainbow above Salisbury Cathedral epitomized Constable's anxiety at the time, including about the movement that Keble, Newman, and their colleague Edward Pusey were promoting, but putting an end to all the wrangling in 1830s Oxford proved to be far more difficult. While Thomas Arnold (Matthew's father and headmaster of the elite Rugby School) publicly rebuked the Tractarians, as they had become known, as "Oxford Malignants," privately he went further, castigating them as "idolaters." In words that soon reached Newman, he wrote to Arthur Penrhyn Stanley, a former pupil, "I do not call them bad men, nor would I deny their many good qualities; . . . but fanaticism is idolatry, and it has the

Figure 6. John Constable, *Salisbury Cathedral from the Meadows,* oil on canvas, 1831. © National Gallery, London.

moral evil of idolatry in it; that is, a fanatic worships something which is the creature of his own devices."[36]

As the number of doctrinal issues facing the Church grew, however, the idea that fanaticism and factionalism were problems stemming largely from the Tractarians became harder to maintain. Two decades later, pamphlets would circulate in London with such titles as *Reasons for Feeling Secure in the Church of England.* That pamphlet was written by the Reverend Edward Monro, vicar of Harrow in Middlesex. Though couched as a defense of the Established Church, it is noticeably anti-Catholic in its none-

too-subtle attempts at stopping more worshippers from leaving the Anglican Church. The article is subtitled, "A Letter to a Friend, in Answer to
Doubts Expressed in Reference to the Claims of the Church of Rome," and
it insists on its opening page: "A clear line must be drawn with regard to the
claims of the Roman Communion upon us. We can no longer go on playing with Romanism, or live on the borders of her encampments, while we
are members of the Communion of the Church of England."[37]

With the Church of England increasingly embattled and distracted by
the surrounding "encampments" of doubters, Catholics, and nonconformists, the scientific debates sketched in the previous chapter gained momentum. Not only did they encounter less resistance, but they also helped
to make a strong case for liberalism, reason, and free thought. Yet as Mill
conceded in his treatise *On Liberty* (1859), "the marvels of modern science,
literature, and philosophy" weren't sufficient to end "the *odium theolog-
icum*"—or "theological hatred"—that in his view was driving and dividing
the devout. On the contrary, "a battlefield" had erupted over Christian doctrines, whereby enthusiasts found it "serviceable to pelt adversaries with"
them. "It is understood," Mill added bitingly, that such doctrines "are to be
put forward (when possible) as the reasons for whatever people do that
they think laudable."[38]

Geology and natural history were not, then, the sole or even the initial
reason why scholars left the Church. As David DeLaura explains, extending Mill's point about doctrinal disputes, "The dominant factor" in that
departure "was a growing repugnance toward the *ethical* implications of
what [many] had been taught to view as essential Christianity—especially
a set of interrelated doctrines: Original Sin, Reprobation, Baptismal Regeneration, Vicarious Atonement, Eternal Punishment."[39] "Only after this
alienation was fixed," he concludes, did public doubters such as Francis
Newman, James Anthony Froude, and George Eliot "show serious interest
in the Higher Criticism (as support for attacking offensive orthodox teach-

ings) and evolution (as indicating a way of life more in harmony with the meliorist ethic of the age)."[40]

Further evidence of recoil from Calvinism came from four writers living some distance from the controversies swirling in Oxford. As renowned for their Romantic literature as they are for wandering the moors of their father's parish in Yorkshire, Anne, Emily, Charlotte, and Branwell Brontë had much to say about religious faith and doubt.

"What shall I do . . . if there be no God above, / To hear and bless me when I pray?"[41] One of Anne Brontë's best poems, "The Doubter's Prayer," raises but cannot answer this startling question. That Brontë asked it at all—and published it for others to see—was not only meaningful but bold and courageous. She was just twenty-three at the time, the daughter of an Irish-Anglican curate. Six years later, still attending church but torn by doubt about religious doctrine, she died of advanced incurable tuberculosis.

Brontë's doubt surfaced largely in response to Calvinist principles, which haunt her poems and novels as sources of real contention. Yet the pressing question in "The Doubter's Prayer" (1843)—what to do if God does not exist—goes to the heart of an even greater dilemma over faith and proof that preoccupied her throughout her short life.

Anne Brontë is less well known than her sisters, Emily and Charlotte, but she has been called "the bravest of the Brontës"—not without reason. Not only did she daringly portray "vice with a frankness from which even a Thackeray shrank," writes biographer Winifred Gérin, "and claim . . . for women equal legal rights totally denied them at the time, but she penetrated into the very mysteries of religious dogma and proclaimed beliefs which even ten years later were to shock Victorian society."[42]

An asthmatic child, Anne "remain[ed] a prey all her life to the dread doctrines of 'Election' and 'Reprobation,'" Gérin reports. These probably came to her filtered through her strictly Methodist aunt, who co-parented

Figure 7. Patrick Branwell Brontë, portrait of Anne Brontë, poet and novelist (detail of fig. 8). © National Portrait Gallery, London.

after their mother died of cancer in her late thirties. It was her aunt who burdened Anne with a "crushing sense of sin from which it took her all her life to extricate herself."[43] "She lived . . . under a sense of the daily imminence of death and, something that her aunt made more dreadful still than death, the imminence of Judgment." So while Anne "revolted against the doctrine of damnation as applied to others, . . . of her own salvation she remained sadly long in doubt."[44]

Brontë's poem conveys deep understanding of that uncertainty; it also draws attention to each associated emotion. The poem describes the almost visceral agony of failing to *feel* the presence of God. Whereas in earlier chapters we saw doubt represented chiefly as an idea or argument, in Brontë's lyric we are shown the panic of vanishing belief. "To the Protestant," Marianne Thormählen explains, "especially one who grew up in an Evangelical home, faith is God-given."[45] One can pray for it, but God must also hear—and be willing to bestow—such faith to those asking to receive it.

Anne's difficulty, Gérin adds, "was beyond conventional remedy. It was the truth she wanted; help, not a palliative. The future creator of Helen Huntingdon could not be put off with ready-made replies. She would inquire for herself."[46] In doing so, however, Anne's theological questions seem to have unleashed a nagging fear that belief in God may be a "vain delusion."[47]

One point cannot be overstated. "The Doubter's Prayer" is not a cold, dispassionate exercise; it is full of torment. "If e'er thine ear in mercy bent ... / To save lost sinners such as me," Anne's speaker cries, "Then hear me now, ... *O give me—give me Faith!*"[48] As her voice rises in despair, appealing to God to "drive these cruel doubts away," she seems almost beside herself at the thought of losing her beliefs. Yet the one element that seems as if it could anchor faith—proof of God's existence—remains elusive, requiring still more of what she lacks: religious trust. The thought that God might *not* exist is terrifying to her. Yet the more the poem tries to stanch that doubt, the more it accents an almost insoluble predicament: its very prayer is aimed at a being who, the speaker allows, may not really be there.

Although some critics view "The Doubter's Prayer" as an expression of Anne's religious despair, others claim as plausibly that she may have ventriloquized the published doubts of her brother, Branwell, or blended them with her own.[49] Either way, her poem posits a hypothesis that, for many at the time, would have bordered on heresy:

> If I believe that Jesus died,
> And, waking, rose to reign above;
> Then surely sorrow, sin and pride,
> Must yield to peace and hope and love. (lines 41–44)

Ordinarily, the "then" in this stanza would answer the "if" that precedes it. But the "if" clause is so unsettling in what it suggests, that "peace and hope and love" cannot stay its designated conclusion. The argument slips; and peace, hope, and love are unable to do their intended work. The poem ends with the fear of unbelief still ringing, like the hum of a struck bell. The conditional clause, "*If* I believe that Jesus . . . rose," still resonates at the final line, leaving the poet and her audience uncertain as to what comes next.

That Brontë's father was an Anglican curate adds a layer of intrigue to her "Doubter's Prayer." Educated at Cambridge and well versed in theological debates, the Reverend Patrick Brontë made the Church his life. As his daughters and son would, he rejected what he called the "appalling doctrines of personal Election and Reprobation" that oriented Calvinism.[50] He opted instead for a blend of Wesleyan Methodism and Evangelicalism that made education a priority, for his daughters as well as for his son. He also formed ties to the Clapham Sect, a group of progressive reformers (including William Wilberforce) that fought for the abolition of slavery, Catholic emancipation, and penal reform.

Like her father, Anne "was a very sincere and practical Christian," Charlotte explained a year after her younger sister died of pulmonary tuberculosis, but "hers was naturally a sensitive, reserved, and dejected nature." According to Charlotte, still writing under her male pseudonym "Currer," the dejection stemmed from "a tinge of religious melancholy" that "communicated a sad shade to her brief, blameless life."[51] Although much else in Charlotte's biographical essay on Anne and Emily has struck critics as exaggerated (partly because Charlotte cultivated a myth that her sisters were guileless and naive), the phrase "religious melancholy" captures Anne's wrestle with not only Calvinism, but also the Evangelical Christianity that she practiced until her final, illness-ridden days.[52] In her 1912 biography of Anne and her sisters, May Sinclair was blunter still: "What her soul suffered from was religious doubt."[53]

Among her siblings, Anne was not alone in her concerns about theological doctrines and practices. Her sisters, too, wrote often about them. In novels like *Jane Eyre* and *Villette* (1853), Charlotte presented complex, sometimes jarring perspectives on different forms of Christianity—Presbyterian, Lutheran, Episcopalian, and Catholic—largely to offset a personalized form of faith from its generally unappealing Church representatives. As a result, at least one review denounced *Jane Eyre* as "pre-eminently an anti-Christian composition." In its "murmuring against the comforts of the rich," the *Quarterly Review* warned, the novelist was "murmuring against God's appointment." Nor was the novel's "proud and perpetual assertion of the rights of man" to be appreciated, for of these apparently "we find no authority either in God's word or in God's providence."[54]

"Conventionality is not morality," Brontë firmly responded in the novel's second edition, and "self-righteousness is not religion. To attack the first is not to assail the last. To pluck the mask from the face of the Pharisee, is not to lift an impious hand to the Crown of Thorns."[55] Nevertheless, or perhaps because of such reviews, her historical novel *Shirley* (1849) went on to air (before overruling) the atheism of its male protagonist, Robert Moore. During a heightened row with her meddling uncle over future husbands and their faiths (or lack thereof), the title character, Shirley Keeldar, also boldly tells her uncle:

> Your thoughts are not my thoughts, your aims are not my aims, your gods are not my gods. We do not view things in the same light. . . . As to your small maxims, your narrow rules, your little prejudices, aversions, dogmas, bundle them off: Mr. Sympson— go, offer them a sacrifice to the deity you worship; I'll none of them: I wash my hands of the lot. I walk by another creed, light, faith, and hope, than you.[56]

The argument reads like a long-deferred row that has gathered steam for want of airing. When Mr. Sympson responds incredulously, "Another creed! I believe she is an infidel," Shirley tries to clarify: "An infidel to *your* religion, an atheist to *your* god." But the word *"atheist"* makes him apoplectic; Brontë gave his italicized repetition of it three exclamation points.

In, moreover, Brontë's last complete novel, *Villette*, the protagonist Lucy Snowe calls her complex musings on life and belief a "heretic narrative" from "an unworthy heretic." She uses the term as a noun or adjective on four other occasions, in part for ironizing elements of the Catholic Church before falling in love, as an avowed Protestant, with an ardent Catholic.[57]

Emily, meanwhile, set her own pantheistic faith against "the thousand creeds / That move men's hearts." These she went on to dismiss, in one poem, as

> Vain . . .
> unutterably vain,
> Worthless as withered weeds
> Or idlest froth amid the boundless main
>
> To waken doubt in one
> Holding so fast by thy infinity.[58]

The alliteration in "worthless . . . withered weeds" almost chokes the life out of such creeds. To Emily, moreover, the creeds actually "waken doubt" in those already predisposed to believe and thus seem almost hostile to Christianity rather than, as intended, a means of defining and nurturing it.

With Branwell Brontë creating unbelieving and doubting characters such as Alexander Percy, who voice much the same philosophy as his own, the Brontë siblings didn't shy away from religious controversy. They embraced and even courted it, writing powerful indictments of ecclesiastical practice that joined the ranks of criticism from dissenters and skeptics concerned about the future of England's Established Church.

A startling paradox seems to surround Anne Brontë's fiction and her life: her quiet, almost withdrawn personality clashes with her writing, which can be bold, even unflinching in its depiction of rage and violence. Critics condemned her second novel in particular for being "extravagant," "unnecessarily coarse," and conveying "a morbid love of . . . the brutal."[59] Like her sisters, she adopted a male pseudonym, Acton Bell, but that doesn't begin to explain the energies unleashed in her second novel.

The very qualities that make *The Tenant of Wildfell Hall* (1848) so bracing to analyze today were at the time a "stumbling-block [for] most readers," making the work "utterly unfit to be put into the hands of girls."[60] These, ironically, were the very readers Anne wanted to forewarn about the risks of an ill-considered marriage. "I would rather whisper a few wholesome truths," she explained in a follow-up preface, "than much soft nonsense." Obviously trying to hide her annoyance at hostile critics, she demurred: "When we have to do with vice and vicious characters, I maintain that it is better to depict them as they really are than as they would wish to appear."[61]

Most reviewers, unfortunately, were impervious to her appeals. An anonymous critic in *Fraser's Magazine* chastised the work's "foul and accursed under-currents," including the novel's perspective on religious doubt, which is more complex and incisive than such blanket condemnation implies. For one thing, the village vicar, the Reverend Michael Millward, is shown as judging his parishioners too quickly and harshly. One observer calls him "a man of fixed principles [and] strong prejudices . . . , intolerant of dissent in any shape, acting under a firm conviction that his opinions were always right, and whoever differed from them must be either most deplorably ignorant, or wilfully blind" (*WH*, 19). The judgment is technically by Brontë's first narrator, Gilbert Markham, who with a male friend shares a quasi-humorous perspective on religious zeal; but it doesn't differ greatly from concerns about pious rigidity that Brontë described elsewhere, especially in her letters and in such poems as "A Word to the 'Elect.'"

What may have irked the *Fraser's* reviewer most is that the *style* of Christianity that Brontë admired—a joyous, nonjudgmental kind—finds few adherents in her novels. In *Agnes Grey* (1847), the first novel, what makes a preacher effective is a recurring concern. Does attractiveness mix poorly with piety, the novel asks, and so blend religious and marital adoration? In *Wildfell Hall*, by contrast, religious guides are unreliable, and the drama of physical attraction is limited mostly to the heroine's future husband, Arthur Huntingdon. The novel details his sordid, largely unrepentant collapse as a hedonist and serial adulterer who treats his wife and child atrociously. Indeed, when the novel opens, and Markham struggles to make sense of Helen Huntingdon to his friend, she is trying to pass herself off as a widow—one, we later learn, who has escaped the clutches of an abusive husband.

Biographical details play a complicated role here. Anne appears to have drawn on scenes she witnessed at Thorp Green Hall, Yorkshire, where she and Branwell worked as tutors. Yet much of the depiction of Arthur seems also to have been shaped by Branwell, especially in his final, profligate years, when—addicted to alcohol and laudanum—he ran up big debts, created havoc in the vicarage at Haworth, and led his sisters, father, and then himself to the brink of despair. And though "the precise circumstances of Branwell's disgrace have [long] been a matter of controversy among Brontë scholars," as biographer Edward Chitham puts it, it is still "legitimate to ask where Anne found her material for *Wildfell Hall*."[62]

Whatever the sources of her inspiration, Anne seems to have wanted to rewrite—even to de-Romanticize—the forms of violence that saturate her sister's *Wuthering Heights*, a novel she echoes in both her title, *Wildfell Hall*, and the names of her characters.[63] Yet just as Heathcliff's godless charisma seems almost designed to prevent readers from simply dismissing him in Emily's novel, in an odd twist Arthur Huntingdon is given some of the best lines of *Wildfell Hall*, including about belief and doubt. "What *is* God—I cannot see him or hear Him?" he asks and observes, moments before dying. "God is only an idea," he states "contemptuously"; "it's all a fable" (*WH*, 446, 441).

Arthur's confident atheism quickly turns to panic, however, about the risk of premature unbelief. To his insistence that "it's all a fable," Helen immediately responds: "Are you sure, Arthur? Are you *quite* sure? Because if there is any doubt, and if you *should* find yourself mistaken after all, when it is too late to turn—" (*WH*, 441). She, at least, seems certain what awaits him, in contrast to the speakers of many of Brontë's poems, who don't always know. "The sufferer was fast approaching dissolution," Helen observes dispassionately, almost impersonally about her husband, "dragged almost to the verge of that awful chasm he trembled to contemplate, from which no agony or tears could save him" (444). Helen isn't necessarily right. She is revealing both her concerns and her beliefs, which sometimes come across as starchly pious, even prim. Indeed, her language about Arthur's demise—in Calvinist rhetoric—is language Brontë elsewhere rejected as judgmental, uninviting, and borderline cruel.

In "A Word to the Calvinists," which she published in *Poems* and later retitled "A Word to the 'Elect,'" Anne Brontë added ironic quotation marks to "Elect" and sardonic emphasis to a set of accusations that already seem fierce: "You may rejoice to think *yourselves* secure," her speaker almost sneers in the opening line,

> But is it sweet to look around and view
> Thousands excluded from that happiness,
> Which they deserve at least as much as you,
> Their faults not greater nor their virtues less?
>
> And wherefore should you love your God the more
> Because to you alone his smiles are given,
> Because He chose to pass the *many* o'er,
> And only bring the favoured *few* to Heaven?[64]

The poem tackles the Calvinist doctrine of "unconditional election," whereby a small minority—predestined—is guaranteed a place in heaven.[65] One reason for the doctrine's controversy: it upended the Protestant argument that entrance to heaven is based on a life of faith and good works. Instead, Calvinism created something of an advanced quota for heaven.

An elect were guaranteed salvation *almost* no matter what they did on earth.

In *Wildfell Hall*, concern about "election" is beside the point. Arthur is so intransigent, he is hoist with his own petard. His reasonable skepticism —"What *is* God . . . ? God is only an idea"—tips into churlishness about even suggestions of last-minute atonement: "Where's the use of a probationary existence," he opines, "if a man may spend it as he pleases, just contrary to God's decrees, and then go to Heaven with the best—if the vilest sinner may win the reward of the holiest saint, by merely saying, 'I repent'?" (*WH*, 445).

A reasonable point, to be sure, but since it is difficult to imagine a person voicing the quibble moments before death, Brontë's second novel in effect turns her protagonists into puppets just when their religious doubt becomes most interesting. The emotion of doubt reverts to something like a line from Hume's *Dialogues Concerning Natural Religion*. As the reviewer for *Fraser's* observed, justly, "One is inclined sometimes to suspect that they are caricatures."[66]

In looking to stage a debate about the *merits* of religious doubt, albeit through the novel's back door, Brontë in effect backs off too quickly— sooner than in her poetry—and opts for stilted words befitting neither character nor context. The dying man, a reviled hedonist who previously had called God an idea, is given half a page to modify his earliest expression of doubt before his wife explains, with more revelation than she perhaps knows: "I do not wish to be set down as an infidel" (*WH*, 395).

In a novel about marital injustice, it is only fitting that Arthur review his past behavior. But he is allowed neither insight nor maturity; he simply reverts to his former monstrousness, begging—apparently in earnest—for his wife to join him in perdition, to make his case for redemption at the gates of hell: "Helen, you *must* save me! . . . I wish to God I could take you with me now! . . . you should plead for me" (*WH*, 441, 446).[67]

Given the heat that Brontë had already taken for her novel's "foul and accursed under-currents," it is clear why she would want to avoid any hint that she is on the side of an "infidel."[68] In effect, though, she kills two birds with one stone, allowing atheism and agnosticism—already made inseparable from Arthur's hedonism and amorality—to be all but eliminated by his death. Paradoxically, doubt in the novel is not so easily suppressed. Even before Arthur falls sick, Helen asks herself: "Have I no faith in God?" (*WH*, 368). The novel implicitly answers that with her later caveat, to her diary: "if I could only have faith and fortitude to compose my thoughts" (395).

Although religious doubt haunts Brontë's second novel, her poems tend to take it more seriously, in part by painstakingly capturing, in the first person, the emotion tied to vanishing faith. In "A Prayer," for example, despite the speaker's claim to have a "trembling soul that would fain be Thine," she chides her "feeble faith" with existential anxiety about what could happen to her without it: "O, do not leave me desolate!"[69] Similar concern agitates "Despondency." Indeed, the speaker's acknowledgment that "Faith itself is wavering now" slips between a question and an exclamation: "O how shall I arise!"[70]

The poet also found the conditional tense and subjunctive voice conducive to her expressions of doubt. In "To Cowper," for instance, her eulogy to the Romantic poet and writer of hymns alights rapidly on his "dark despair" and "wilder woe," as if the religious doubt that "crushed and tortured" him might almost eclipse her own. Despite insisting that such uncertainties "are gone" from her, the poem undercuts that message with a striking conditional: "if God is love / And answers fervent prayer."[71] Other poems by her are strewn with subjunctives, including these halting qualifiers: "If thy hand conducts me," "If but thy strength be mine," and "if I hold thee fast."[72]

In a self-divided, almost self-accusative way, Brontë's use of the subjunctive weakened her attempts at ringing assertions of faith. A voice of doubt insisted on being heard, no matter what the occasion. The subjunctive adds ambivalence in her hymnal confessionals, often precisely when they're trying to settle theological conundrums. But while her sensitive hymns record the emotion of lost faith and the heartbreaking difficulty of doubt, they pale in drama beside her brother's franker atheism, which he seems to have reached at an even younger age.

The habit of ignoring or dismissing Branwell is now so firmly rooted in Brontë scholarship that it has become self-perpetuating. That May Sinclair could in 1912 publish a study entitled simply *The Three Brontës* is a telling sign of occlusion that probably dates to Charlotte's efforts to scrub her difficult brother from the literary and artistic record. Her letters about him are angry and reproachful, attesting to "the emptiness of his whole existence."[73] It didn't help that Branwell literally painted himself out of his best portrait, a now-famous rendition of his sisters.

In 1912, when six autographed fragments of the children's early work came up for auction, Esther Alice Chadwick (a collector of oral history from Haworth) sniffed about the peculiarity of two of Branwell's works commanding a high price. He "has been discarded," she wrote, "and considered unfit to be associated with his sisters, either as an author or a brother."[74] Biographies of him also capture a flavor of this judgment, from Daphne du Maurier's *Infernal World of Branwell Brontë* (1961) to Joan Rees' *Profligate Son* (1986) and to Mary Butterfield and R. J. Duckett's *Brother in the Shadow* (1988).[75] Du Maurier presents Branwell as almost schizophrenic in belief and behavior:

> The two sides of Branwell's nature stood in balance. The one affectionate, ardent, devoted to his family and above all his father, hoping—for their sake as well as for his own—that either by writing or by painting he would prove so successful that not only they but the whole world would come to recognize his talent; the other diffident, mocking, skeptical, doubting as much in his own powers as in a Power above, and sometimes so fearful of the black abyss of Eternity that the only way to quieten apprehension would seem to be a plunge into vice and folly.[76]

Figure 8. Patrick Branwell Brontë, *The Brontë Sisters (Anne Brontë; Emily Brontë; Charlotte Brontë [Mrs. A. B. Nicholls])*, oil on canvas, c. 1834. © National Portrait Gallery, London.

Two substantial editions of his poetry attest to a prodigious output, quite a lot of it focused on unbelief and religious doubt. Indeed, Branwell was not only fiercely precocious but also a man who peaked very early, perhaps even burning out before his twenties. By the age of eleven or twelve, he had written several prose pieces, including a six-page *History of the Rebellion of My Fellows,* and named himself editor and publisher of *Branwell's*

Figure 9. Self-portrait of Patrick
Branwell Brontë, poet, painter, and
tutor, 1840. © The Brontë Parsonage
Museum, Haworth, West Yorkshire.

Blackwoods Magazine. He brought out at least four issues of the magazine, and perhaps as many as seven. Additionally, he wrote a "two-volume travel book, at least thirty-four poems or verse fragments (including an attempt at Latin verse), a verse drama" approximately thirteen hundred lines long, and fourteen poems in collaboration with Charlotte.

Editor Victor Neufeldt describes Branwell's output during these years as "a kind of volcanic eruption with all the sense of undisciplined exuberance the image suggests."[77] The description is especially apt in light of the quandary it raised a few years later, when serious decisions about what path and profession Branwell should pursue bore down on him with intense pressure. Despite his having tried poetry, painting, tutoring, and bookkeeping, Branwell somehow couldn't stick to any of them.

From this historical distance, with often scant evidence to go on, it is impossible to know whether Branwell's abuse of laudanum and alcohol caused his depression and downfall or was an effect of it. We can say that it put an end to his literary and artistic talent, which "withered and died like a sprig of bright shamrock perishing among the heather."[78] Less poetically, biographer Winifred Gérin describes his temperament as "histrionic," which captures the drama with which he lived out his last declining moments.[79]

In "The Doubter's Hymn" (1835), drafted eight years before his sister wrote her "Doubter's Prayer," one of Branwell's characters, a rogue philosopher called Alexander Percy, meditates on life, belief, and mortality. He imitates Lord Byron and surely Hamlet in thinking through several outsized metaphysical questions:

> What is Eternity?
> Is Death the sleep?—Is Heaven the Dream?
> Life the reality?[80]

The penultimate question is a significant one, obviously difficult to answer but still needing to be asked, especially with the ambiguity surrounding that capital "D" in "Dream." "The Doubter's Hymn" begins with more declarative authority:

> Life is a passing sleep,
> Its deeds a troubled dream,
> And death the dread awakening
> To daylight's dawning beam.[81]

Branwell was eighteen when he wrote that (he died of tuberculosis, exacerbated by alcohol and opium abuse, at age thirty-one). Yet even though his style and philosophy were clearly derivative, it is worth asking why he titled the poem a "hymn"—indeed, to *what* or to *whom* it aspired to be hymnlike, given its stated doubts. The poem does not appeal for their removal, as Anne Brontë's would. Nor does it ask for—or seem particularly to want—stronger faith. In that sense it lacks the wrenching anguish of his sister's prayer, though it is bolder about intellectual doubt. The poem sounds a note of serious skepticism toward its end, as interest rather than despair:

> . . . When we arise,
> With 'wildered gaze to see
> The aspect of those morning skies,
> Where will that waking be?[82]

Notably, Branwell's question takes no comfort in classical or Christian models of the hereafter. The speaker seems genuinely undecided and, it must be said, willing to let that uncertainty stand as a question mark over everything presumed known about the afterlife, including whether indeed there is one.

When Percy's second wife, Mary, dies from consumption in the poem, Branwell is careful to make Percy's former doubts harden into atheism. "He felt certain," we are told, in a manuscript du Maurier recovered decades later, "that under any circumstances they must part forever."[83] Later alone, after Mary has died, the sentiment becomes even more emphatic: "While . . . the past is sliding into nothing, [I] know . . . that I shall Never, Never See Thee More."[84]

In the summer of 1834, Branwell traveled to Leeds to see an exhibition sponsored by the Northern Society for the Encouragement of Fine Arts. It was there that he found a prototype for Alexander Percy. The sculpture that transfixed him was a large bust of Satan, modeled after the scene in Milton's *Paradise Lost* known as Satan's Address to the Sun. At that point, in book 4 of the poem, Milton oscillates between condemnation and sympathy for Satan, to ensure that we feel a strong tug of interest in the fallen angel's intelligence and earlier partnership with God.

The bust had been sculpted by Joseph Leyland, a talented twenty-three-year-old from Halifax, just fifteen miles from Haworth, whom Branwell later befriended and tried to emulate.[85] Leyland had certainly caught the tension in Milton's depiction of Satan. A reviewer for the *Morning Chronicle* noted that "the characteristic marks" of the sculpture were "a scornful lip, distended nostrils, and a forehead more remarkable for breadth than

prominence, indicative of great mental capacity, bereft of moral principle."
The reviewer added, "Mr. Leyland has made his Satan a being, not fearful
merely, but of that Satanic beauty which is so true to the conception of Milton."[86] Branwell's adoption of Leyland's sculpture as his model for Alexander Percy suggests that he, too, wanted to portray doubt and atheism on a
grand scale. (Leyland's sculpture does not appear to have survived. Unfortunately, many of his works were either lost or destroyed.)

Four years later, still powerfully indebted to Byron and his now-cele-
brated Romantic atheism, Branwell returned—less melodramatically this
time—to the subject of unbelief in "Harriet II" (1838).[87] The poem is named
after Harriet O'Connor, a character in the Angrian tales who leaves her
husband for Percy. He in turn abandons her, an act that not only dashes her
romantic hopes but also shatters her religious beliefs:

> I have lost—long lost—my trust in Thee!
> I cannot hope that Thou wilt hear
> The unrepentant sinner's prayer!
> So, whither must my spirit flee
> For succour through Eternity?[88]

Belief in God as contingent on love on earth is a strongly Romantic
tenet, differing considerably from Anne Brontë's and John Henry Newman's more tightly scripted doubts about Calvinist doctrine. Although both
found themselves leaning heavily on doubt, their different uses of it highlight a growing diversity of perspectives on it. Religious doubt would soon
be characterized as an opportunity, a psychology, and even a creative en-
deavor. Nonetheless, Anne Brontë reminded readers of doubt's more
volatile emotions. In doing so, she gave voice to a fearful anguish that God
had abandoned the world, leaving the Victorians at the mercy of an uncertain destiny.

FOUR

Natural History Sparks
Honest Doubt

F ew books are sufficiently influential to have a lasting impact on a nation's culture. But in mid-Victorian Britain, two came close to achieving that effect, and both were written at least fifteen years before Darwin's *On the Origin of Species* appeared. In different ways, each concerned religious doubt and evolution. Neither book is a household name today, in part because one of them appeared anonymously and generated such heat that the identity of its author remained concealed until years after he had died. The other book, also the cause of serious controversy, was burned at Oxford University before its author, a deacon, was asked to renounce his fellowship.

Tensions over creationism and science had simmered through the 1830s, as Charles Lyell's notebooks and John Henry Newman's tracts confirm, but they didn't ignite until a decade and a half later, when a powerful salvo appeared in 1844 bearing the title *Vestiges of the Natural History of Creation*. It is no exaggeration to say that the book became a widespread topic of conversation across the country, putting doubt at the forefront of countless public, household, and church-based discussions. The book set out to establish what its author called "*the mode* in which the Divine Author proceeded in the organic creation."[1] Simply thinking about that *mode*, and calling it one, turned out to be incendiary.

In *Victorian Sensation,* his vivid account of Britain's intense reaction to the book, James Secord notes: "It was effectively impossible, only a few weeks after *Vestiges* [had] appeared, to comment on it without being aware of sharing an experience with a wider national and even international community of readers. . . . *Vestiges* was [as Darwin explained] the one book that all readers of the *Origin of Species* were assumed to have read."[2]

Written by the Scots author, editor, and publisher Robert Chambers, *Vestiges* caused more than a public "sensation"; it sparked one of the most significant cultural discussions of the century, and not just in Britain. It was widely read on both sides of the Atlantic and throughout Europe. In Britain, perhaps a bit surprisingly, readers took to the book enthusiastically, in part because it was well written, but also because it ostensibly rejected atheism. The first newspaper reviews were admiring, calling it, in the words of the *Lancet,* "a very remarkable book, calculated to make men think." Others praised not only the "ingenuity" of its argument (*Spectator*), but also the author's "extraordinary ability," "clearness of reasoning," and "the grandeur of the subjects . . . he treats" (*Atlas*).[3]

Within a few weeks, *Vestiges* was a major topic of discussion from dinner parties to newspaper columns. Not wanting to miss out on the conversation (and greatly intrigued, it must be said, by the mystery of its authorship), large sections of the reading public felt that it was imperative to peruse it. Even the queen and members of the royal family clamored to get hold of copies. It is not difficult to see why. In bringing together a large number of fields and disciplines, including geology, natural history, phrenology, and chemistry, Chambers offered the latest synthesis. He put before the public what he called "the first attempt . . . as far as I am aware . . . to connect the natural sciences into a history of creation" (*V,* 388).

He was, as it happens, wrong on that and several other important counts: Erasmus Darwin (Charles' grandfather) had begun to write about evolution as early as the 1780s, in a popular poem called *The Loves of the Plants* (1789);[4] and some of Chambers' science was eyebrow-raising, to say the least, in remodeling classification groups and suggesting that insects could be created by electricity. Still, as Secord reminds us, the "extraordinary publication, reception, and secret authorship" of *Vestiges* meant that "evolution moved off the streets and into the home."[5]

In doing so, the book generated fierce clerical and scientific reactions. As one reviewer thundered, "To style this book infidel would be pronouncing upon it too mild a condemnation."[6] This was but a foretaste of the hostility that Evangelicals managed to foment around the book. As they turned *Vestiges* into a symptom of their concerns, including premillennialist fears of the Apocalypse, they implicitly conceded that the book was enormously effective in making people think about a subject that they had largely accepted as biblical. Florence Nightingale wittily observed, "We had got up so high into *Vestiges* that I could not get down again, and was obliged to go off as an angel."[7] Everyone was either fascinated by the experience or terrified by what it suggested.

With a culture as complex as nineteenth-century Britain's, it would be rash to try to pin down the moment when scientific and secular works gained enough momentum to affect how the country saw and understood itself. That process took at least three decades, following the influence of debates and discoveries from well over a century before. Still, to focus on the upheaval in mid-Victorian England, when the issue achieved critical mass, major debates in the early 1860s turned out to be turning points for cultural arguments that had flared in the 1830s and begun to attract wide audiences in the 1840s. The primary instigators of those cultural arguments were *Vestiges* and J. Anthony Froude's *Nemesis of Faith*, the second of the two books alluded to earlier.

In the course of those decades, theological explanations for scientific phenomena lost significant ground in Britain, and secular arguments once limited to a relatively small group of freethinkers began to draw greater interest. In her landmark study *Varieties of Unbelief,* Susan Budd conveys the scale of that interest and widening skepticism by tracking the growing numbers of secularist obituaries in freethinking journals such as the *Reasoner* (1852–61), *National Reformer* (1860–93), *Secularist and Secular Review* (1876–84), and *Freethinker* (1881–1968). The first of these had five thousand subscribers in 1853, and with the other journals above it recorded in detail "the conversion experiences of one hundred and fifty secularists . . . , with supporting evidence from nearly two hundred briefer biographies." The journals did so, she points out, to refute the popular notion that free thought and unbelief might be fashionable stances in life, but deathbed repentances would ultimately favor Christianity.[8]

As intellectual, theological, and lay readers struggled to absorb dramatic scientific discoveries, one sign of the ensuing turmoil and transition on both sides of the Atlantic was a growing number of articles on and about religious doubt.[9] Their titles shift significantly from pleas for "Deliverance from Doubt" (1857) to more balanced analyses of "Faith, Doubt, and Reason" (1863), as scholars began to weigh doubt's function, value, and even its ethical necessity.[10] One called it "the very mother of a perfect faith."[11] Christianity, in turn, became a major object of inquiry. Scholars wanted to give its practices and history as much close examination as the Church could bear. Mill's *On Liberty* (1859) made its history a frequent touchstone for concerns about "the evils of religious or philosophical sectarianism." "It is," he wrote, "the opinions men entertain, and the feelings they cherish, respecting those who disown the beliefs they deem important which makes this country not a place of mental freedom."[12]

Enlightenment arguments about rationalism, rights, and scientific method had circulated decades earlier, especially in continental Europe. In Britain, moreover, Jeremy Bentham's Utilitarian approach to religion had gained some traction, identifying followers with criticism of the Church. His approach included estimating the use-value of religious systems and gauging whether "utility" justified their existence.[13] Still, such arguments generally circulated among a limited audience of professional and gentlemen scholars largely oriented to biblical and creationist perspectives. A significant lag occurred before German and French Enlightenment texts reached Britain, partly because of publication and translation delays, but also, more fundamentally, because of resistance to their arguments.

The intellectual gap between the Continent and Britain began to narrow in the late 1840s and early 1850s, with progressive journals (the free-thinking *Westminster Review,* for instance) introducing readers to such philosophers as Arthur Schopenhauer; Auguste Comte, untiring advocate for a secular "religion of humanity," an attractive concept for religious skeptics; and Ludwig Feuerbach, author of *The Essence of Christianity* (1841), whose opening section carries the title "The True or Anthropological Essence of Religion." A growing number of Victorian scientists, drawn to empirical emphasis on method and evidence, also challenged the clergy's scientific and cultural authority.

It is easy to see why these and related arguments were threatening to British theologians and why they and other scholars tried desperately to keep them at arm's length. While Comte believed that humanity would progress in three doubt-filled stages, from theocracy to metaphysics before finally reaching a positive phase governed by science and sociology, Feuerbach styled God as "feeling released from limits," which strongly implied that believers are drawn to doctrinal positions that befit their temperaments. If "God is the highest feeling of self," in Feuerbach's terms, then "in God man is his own object," confronting needs and desires that are very much earthly in origin.[14]

In her novel *Jane Eyre,* published six years later in 1847, Charlotte Brontë advanced a similar idea by describing how St. John Rivers' extreme Calvinism is an extension of his austere temperament, rather than, as many Victorians would have thought, its logical cause. As Rivers "scarcely impressed one with the idea of a gentle, a yielding, an impressible, or even of a placid nature," he ends up betraying that psychology when asking Jane, while proposing marriage, "Do you think God will be satisfied with half an oblation? Will He accept a mutilated sacrifice? It is the cause of God I advocate: it is under His standard I enlist you."[15] The idea that religious doubt and religious extremism were psychologically inflected was steadily gaining momentum.

Much eighteenth- and nineteenth-century Continental philosophy (by Immanuel Kant, Johann Gottlieb Fichte, and G. W. F. Hegel, for example) had made doubt and self-questioning integral to how we form judgments. As Robert Flint observed in his 1903 study *Agnosticism,* "the great revolutions of speculative thought . . . all originated in extensions of the operations of doubt."[16] Complicating a standard line about the ensuing spread of rationalism, Ayaan Hirsi Ali explains: "Enlightenment thinkers, preoccupied with both individual freedom and secular and limited government, argued that human reason is fallible. They understood that reason is more than just rational thought; it is also a process of trial and error, the ability to learn from past mistakes. The Enlightenment cannot be fully appreciated without a strong awareness of just how frail human reason is. That is why concepts like doubt and reflection are central to any form of decision-making based on reason."[17]

A further reason why secular arguments gained while those of theology slipped is the expansion of literacy in the culture. In addition to enlarging the number of people interested in books and ideas, higher literacy rates helped to strengthen long-standing ties in England between working-class radicalism and free thought. That tie had been formed because freethinkers tended to break with aristocratic assumptions about the order of things, including God's role in orienting the Established Church. As we saw in chapter 2, the secular embrace of evolution by political and religious radicals in the 1820s and 1830s helped pave the way for its later debate among middle-class readers, who could discuss *Vestiges'* support for evolution without automatically being thought irreligious. As the demand for books increased and the cost of producing them fell dramatically, the skepticism once limited to David Hume and others gained enough momentum in the culture to become unstoppable.

A third key factor, as we saw in the previous chapter, is that in the 1830s the Church was increasingly splintered and distracted by disputes with Evangelical Methodism and Calvinism. Demands to emancipate Catholicism were at an all-time high. Not surprisingly, Anglicanism was less able to defend itself against the arguments that assailed it—including that religion was part of human discourse, not exempt from its rules and practices.

Finally, Victorian secularism differed greatly from its eighteenth-century precursors. Dramatic gains in scientific understanding had refined methods and standards of proof, making opposition to scientific inquiry look increasingly flat-footed. Chambers' *Vestiges of the Natural History of Creation* is a prime example, which helped to make "scriptural geology" sound more outdated than as a neutral description.[18] The Church and the scientific establishment took a wait-and-see line with Chambers' radical claims, clearly hoping that his book would disappear. When the first wave of reviews was overwhelmingly positive and the book became a sensation, a full-on assault took place. The author was publicly denounced as an "infidel" and charged, by furious reviewers, with promoting atheism. A backlash had begun that would take at least two decades to dissipate.

Vestiges was Chambers' twenty-sixth book, and certainly his best-selling, surpassing even Darwin's *Origin of Species* and reaching a twelfth edition by 1884. Most of his other books and pamphlets were histories of Scotland, covering its traditions, ballads, and royalty. But though *Vestiges* was mostly a departure from Chambers' usual subject matter, as a publisher and editor he was well informed about evolutionary theory and able to represent its arguments incisively.

The son of a cotton manufacturer, Chambers set up a printing press with his elder brother, William, printing cheap pamphlets and books, as well as *Chambers's Edinburgh Journal,* which soon became influential. Secord notes that it "had a religious target, the evangelical wing of the Scottish Presbyterians. Within the charged world of Scottish theology," he adds, "the *Journal's* 'neutral' position on religious questions sparked intense controversy."[19]

Figure 10. Robert Chambers, a line and stipple engraving by
D. J. Pound after Jabez Edwin Mayall, 1860. © National Portrait
Gallery, London.

The Chambers family worshipped at a Presbyterian church, but to say
that their minister was unhappy with the journal would be putting it mildly.
When he held up a copy of it to excoriate, the family and supportive friends
walked out en masse. The minister had sermonized that omitting discussion of Christian salvation from a "so-called family periodical" was "tan-
tamount to atheism."[20] According to Secord, "Robert rarely went to services after [that] (how often he had gone before his marriage is not clear),
while Anne took the children to the Episcopalian church."[21]

Although Chambers' private correspondence is "fiercely anticlerical," in *Vestiges* he was firm, even adamant, that God anchors evolutionary arguments. How we interpret that gap, or whether we detect one, depends heavily on our starting point. Critics of Chambers would see it as bad faith; others, perhaps with Charlotte Brontë in mind, would hold that criticizing the Church as an organization can stem from the strongest piety.

If we view Chambers as ingenuous—as wanting to encourage theological debate from the perspective of a critical believer—we would point to the deism of his argument, a philosophy arguing that God created the world, then left it alone for nature to take its course. Any transmutation among species would thus be written into a blueprint. As Chambers put it, such arguments had to take into account "the original Divine conception of all the forms of being which . . . natural laws [are] only instruments in working out and realizing" (*V*, 231).

One can, however, overstate the religiosity of his argument and person. Secord claims that the former was "largely strategic," to encourage resistant readers to consider an argument they would otherwise rule out of hand. Even more shrewdly, perhaps, Chambers was able to prod the clerisy into debate from the vantage of a religious position.[22]

Despite his deist position, Chambers supported Lamarck's theory of species transmutation, an early form of evolutionary theory. He thus incensed critics by accepting what his more cautious fellow Scot Lyell had publicly refuted (and privately agonized over). In his deism, however, Chambers tried to pivot by criticizing Lamarck for inadequately describing a process that Chambers called God given, or at least God orchestrated.

Choosing his words carefully, he sought to clarify precisely "*the mode in which the Divine Author proceeded in the organic creation*" (*V*, 153). Not exactly mechanistic, his approach came across as coolly impersonal, conjuring a God more interested in systems than in souls. At the same time, detachment gave Chambers enough flexibility to discuss evolutionary and geological change while appearing to satisfy conservatives demanding that the argument have a religious foundation. "We have seen powerful evidence," he wrote, Hutton and Lyell very much in mind, that "the earth's formation . . . was the result, not of any immediate or personal exertion on the part of the Deity, but of natural laws which are expressions of his will" (153–54). "What is to hinder our supposing," he added almost mischievously, taking the argument further than either Scotsman before him, "that the organic creation is also a result of natural laws, which are in like manner an expression of his will?"

The echo that Chambers set up with "expression of his will" may have dampened the shock caused by such astonishing sentences, especially as both threaten to end before their reassuring subclauses can modify things heavenward. Without the final clause, for instance, one would read: "The earth's formation . . . was the result, not of any immediate or personal exertion on the part of the Deity."

Perhaps owing to this provocation, the backlash came not from the general public—which was, for the most part, intrigued, almost seduced. It came from religious leaders and the scientific establishment, with scientists attacking Chambers' claims about evolution and clergy chastising him for promoting a "rank materialism . . . [that] may end in downright atheism."[23] The review in which this last charge appeared was vitriolic; the *Edinburgh Review* also felt it necessary to give the anonymous author (the Reverend Adam Sedgwick, Woodwardian Professor of Geology at Cambridge) eighty-five more pages to explain why Chambers' argument about evolution was "mischievous, and sometimes antisocial, nonsense."[24] In the same review, Sedgwick also memorably called Lamarck's theory of species transmutation "as baseless as the fabric of a crazy dream."[25] Not only was Sedgwick equating support for evolution with delusion, even delirium; in doing so, he was entangling science in a new round of metaphors and similes.

To the charge of atheism, Chambers insisted, politely and quite reasonably: "I had remarked in no irreverent spirit, but on the contrary, that the supposition of frequent special exertion anthropomorphises the Deity" (*Explanations,* 134). He was trading piety with a version of Hume's warning in *Dialogues Concerning Natural Religion* that God must be kept austere, to avoid suppositions that he is always at hand, to intervene in even the most mundane details. As Chambers asked in *Vestiges,*

> How can we suppose that the august Being who brought all these countless worlds into form by the simple establishment of a natural principle flowing from his mind, was to interfere personally and specially on every occasion when a new shell-fish or reptile was to be ushered into existence on *one* of these worlds? Surely this idea is too ridiculous to be for a moment entertained. . . . Are we to suppose the Deity adopting plans which harmonize only with the modes of procedure of the less enlightened of our race? (*V*, 154, 157; emphasis in original)

Variants of that assumption of course still exist today, from U.S. football teams that pray for victory before each game to those who insist that God is their group's or nation's ally, with truth exclusive to the faithful and damnation likely for almost everyone else.

The *Edinburgh Review* was merciless in listing Chambers' errors, a large number of them compounded by his quirky enthusiasms; but Chambers was quick to capitalize on the higher ground he had seized, insisting that he merely wished to restore dignity to a theological position that would otherwise degrade God. Even when attacking theologians on theology, that is, he managed to sound both pious and, for the most part, humble: "To a reasonable mind the Divine attributes must appear, not diminished or reduced in any way, by supposing a creation by law, but infinitely exalted" (*V*, 156).

"To a reasonable mind" was one of Chambers' many ingenious phrases, since it positioned his angriest critics as unreasonable, and thus wrong. Chambers was in fact wrong himself about several speculative matters, including whether plants could grow like frost crystals, dogs could play dominoes, and several other odd notions. Even so, his rhetorical authority makes it seem wise, not blasphemous, to point out that the Book of Genesis is "not only not in harmony with the ordinary ideas of mankind respecting cosmical and organic creation, but is opposed to them" (*V*, 155).

"When we carefully peruse [Genesis] with awakened minds," he continued, half-flattering some readers and outmaneuvering others,

> we find that all the procedure is represented primarily and pre-eminently as flowing *from commands and expressions of will, not from direct acts.* Let there be light—let there be a firmament—let the dry land appear—let the earth bring forth grass, the herb, the tree—let the waters bring forth the moving creature that hath life —let the earth bring forth the living creature after his kind—these are the terms in which the principal acts are described. The additional expressions,—God made the firmament—God made the beast of the earth, &c., occur subordinately, and only in a few instances; they do not necessarily convey a different idea of the mode of creation, and indeed only appear as alternative phrases, in the usual duplicative manner of Eastern narrative. (155; emphasis in original)

According to Chambers, "reasonable mind[s]" will quickly perceive that "the prevalent ideas about the organic creation" were simply "a mistaken inference from the text," meaning the first verses of the Bible (156).

A quick counterpunch came from Samuel Richard Bosanquet, a wealthy lawyer who in 1845 published two editions of a pamphlet called *"Vestiges of the Natural History of Creation": Its Argument Examined and Exposed.* This tract, Secord notes, was advertised prominently across London by placards announcing "that an atheist agitator with a prison record for blasphemy would be speaking on *Vestiges.*" The agitator in question wasn't identified, but it obviously was not Chambers, given his continued wish for anonymity as the book's author. "A year later," Secord adds, referring to a time when the authorship of *Vestiges* was still well concealed (though a matter of fierce speculation), "announcements promised an entire series of lectures on the book by the country's most notorious woman atheist. The audience for such talks rarely exceeded one hundred, but street advertising was, without question, vital to cementing the association of *Vestiges* with religious disbelief."[26]

Among reviewers, too, *Vestiges* was soon cast as forcing readers to choose between piety and unbelief.[27] While the *North British Review* implied, in Secord's words, that *Vestiges* was "parading atheism under a Christian banner," others were outraged, even to the point of inciting violence.[28] The *Nonconformist* condemned the "infidel" book as a "most erroneous and pernicious work." Even the moderate and Anglican *Christian Observer*, decrying the book's "infidel[,] and even atheistic . . . tendencies," declared that it ought to be greeted with "a few sentences of vigourous invective" and a clenched fist.[29]

To these and many other charges, Chambers fought back diligently and calmly. While catching a number of awkward factual mistakes when revising the book for less expensive editions, he also in 1845 published *Explanations: A Sequel,* which took on his detractors, offered a robust defense of natural law, and argued that science needed to embrace rather than quell discussion about human destiny and its place in nature.

Many of the more outrageous and ill-informed charges against *Vestiges* began to take, however. One was that it was written by an amateur merely "paving the way" for Darwin, Alfred Russel Wallace, Thomas Huxley, and later, more elaborate theories of evolution based on natural selection. It didn't help that Darwin himself, with some self-interest and some justification, took the same line, arguing that Chambers did "excellent service in this country in calling attention to the subject [of evolution], in removing prejudice, and in thus preparing the ground for the reception of analogous views."[30] However, that relegates *Vestiges* to a shadow role before *On the Origin of Species,* when its impact on the general public was immeasurably greater, as Secord proves so emphatically. Even among scientists in the 1840s and 1850s, one senses that their overreaction to sensitive subjects, like species transmutation, was because Chambers had in fact hit his target most successfully.

Alfred Tennyson was fortunate to order his copy of *Vestiges* just after the first reviews appeared (the first edition sold out quickly). Diary entries by the future laureate show that he was "quite excited" to get his copy; much later, he insisted that he had found "nothing degrading in the theory."[31]

Tennyson saw Chambers as advancing "speculations with which I have been familiar for years, and on which I have written more than one poem." But *Vestiges* broke with Lyell's *Principles of Geology* (the earlier work that Tennyson alludes to here) over species transmutation. Put another way, it is Chambers, not Lyell, who orients the devastating question in Tennyson's *In Memoriam,* "Are God and Nature then at strife?"[32] Lyell had struggled mightily to argue that they were not.

Tennyson's lengthy elegy for friend and fellow poet Arthur Hallam shared with Chambers' *Vestiges* the distinction of being one of the most read and most talked about works of the century. And though as we've seen Tennyson also went on to characterize nature as "red in tooth and claw," in a bloodied, proto-Darwinian understanding of natural cruelty, the effect of *Vestiges* on the Victorian poet was to spark a profound crisis over *why* such cruelty should occur, in such quantity. Tennyson called the crisis and its apparent solution "honest doubt." As he declared, ventriloquizing the "perplext . . . faith" of his once-closest friend and possible lover: "There lives more faith in honest doubt, / Believe me, than in half the creeds." The elegy presents these lines as Hallam's response to another's assumption that "doubt is Devil-born," a Calvinist premise that Tennyson wanted the Victorians to contest.[33] To his own bleakly post-Romantic understanding of nature, however, "honest doubt" was the most—perhaps the only—intelligent way of grappling with his talented friend's death at the age of just twenty-two.

In rescuing doubt from Calvinist accusations of spiritual weakness and the even sterner rebuke that unbelief was a sin, Tennyson helped to imbue the trait with integrity. In his work, as in several others, the result was greater willingness to ask whether religion had enough answers to explain strong evidence of brutality in nature, including against humanity.

Another budding intellectual strongly influenced by Chambers was James Anthony Froude, younger brother to Hurrell (Newman's closest friend) and the son of an archdeacon, who read *Vestiges* as a young fellow at Exeter College, Oxford. Like many other Oxford students swinging, as Secord puts it, "toward liberal divinity or outright unbelief," Froude found that the book "led him to reject miracles in nature . . . and [the] divine inspiration of Scripture."[34]

Although Froude and Tennyson later became friends, it is unlikely that the younger Froude would have known the poet's exact thoughts on "honest doubt," published the year after his own *Nemesis of Faith* appeared. So it is all the more striking that both writers reacted to *Vestiges* by calling for, and themselves enacting, candid expressions of religious skepticism. These were bolder, more direct, and far-more personal expressions of religious uncertainty than the culture had yet seen. Tennyson also saw such doubts as having "*more* faith than . . . half the creeds," an obvious provocation in itself. But Froude went further, tackling what he called the "savage fanaticism" of various kinds of "rigid Protestantism."[35]

His objections were destined for angry rebuke, though few could have anticipated quite the form it would take. For his candor, Froude suffered the shock and insult of seeing his book burned at his own university. He also entered a legal tug-of-war with the university over the possibility of being charged with perjury. Taking orders to be a deacon was not just a theological commitment; it was a binding legal contract.

Like all deacons in training, Froude had pledged to uphold the Anglican Church's Thirty-Nine Articles, the source of so much contention throughout the 1830s. Froude had followed those debates closely, given his brother's close ties to Newman. While he studied at Oxford, however, his own relation to the articles soured. As Froude told fellow novelist and friend Charles Kingsley—and made quite clear in *The Nemesis of Faith*, his

Figure 11. Sir George Reid, portrait of James Anthony Froude, novelist and historian, oil on canvas, 1881. © National Portrait Gallery, London.

second novel—"I hate the Articles."[36] When he seemed to break them by publishing that work of autobiographical fiction, lawyers seriously discussed whether he could be charged with a crime. In the end, they opted for other forms of punishment, more or less demanding that he resign his fellowship.[37] Still, Froude was faced with a dilemma and a significant backlash. "I must live somehow," he explained in the same letter to Kingsley, "and England is not hospitable."[38]

Although occasionally histrionic, the first half of the novel describes how Markham Sutherland, a doubting clergyman, is exiled from the small British community he tries to serve. The trigger is when a village Bible group denounces him for not referring to the book enough times in his sermons.

Some weeks earlier, Sutherland had in fact begun to harbor doubts about the Church and his faith, but he had tried to follow his friend's sober advice: self-repression. His tongue-tied syntax says it all: "I think I can do what you say is the least I ought to do—subdue my doubts" (*NF*, 45). For several months, the practice works. After a "religious tea-party" leads to frank, almost confessional talk of the Bible, however, a few villagers use the opportunity to go on the offensive, declaring of their spiritual counselor "in a tone of satiric melancholy: 'he never preaches the Bible'" (57, 61). Although he disagrees, insisting, "I believe I read it to you twice every day," the parishioners are upset and declare, quite seriously, "The enemy is among us" (61, 64).

The village boycotts his services. Tensions rise, and the local bishop asks Sutherland to explain himself. He gives Sutherland a careful hearing as well as a paradoxical answer, common at the time: "Only He who is pleased to send such temptation [in doubt] can give you strength to bear it" (*NF*, 74).

That premise differs greatly from Sutherland's more secular and psychological insistence that he is simply one who feels "compelled to doubt" (*NF*, 81). The gap between these perspectives is telling, even predictive of later trends in the country. Indeed, Sutherland eventually views his doubts as merited, as a healthy predisposition. By his lights, then, to threaten punishment and damnation for such a trait is dangerously extreme, an alarming overreaction to natural questioning.

Sutherland and Froude turn doubt into an ethical rather than a theological category. "Acting upon a doubt" becomes not a sin, Froude says, but a "responsibility," though one that people often "shrink from" (*NF*, 85). To his protagonist, that is, doubt requires that one *engage* with faith and belief, rather than pretend that on both counts all questions are answered and nothing is wrong. In this way, the novel strengthened a growing belief in England that doubt was not a source of evil but an integral component of moral and ethical systems.

In Froude's case, at least initially, the approach backfired—partly because it was indeed viewed theologically, as a sinful failing. Although he tried repeatedly to explain himself, insisting that with *Nemesis*, "I cut a hole in my heart and wrote with the blood," those in positions of authority turned a deaf ear, silently justifying his initial complaint.[39] He was not given the kind of hearing at Oxford that Sutherland had received from his bishop. Instead, he encountered a larger audience, both hostile and supportive, when newspapers began reporting on the scandal and reviewing the book that had caused it.

"Why is it thought so very wicked to be an unbeliever?" That is one of the key questions troubling Markham Sutherland (*NF*, 84). His answer, harnessed to psychology, likens dogma to a group reflex: "Because an anathema upon unbelief has been appended as a guardian of the creed," he states angrily and inelegantly. "It is one way, and doubtless a very politic way, of maintaining the creed, this . . . anathema." Such an outcome is also, he can't help adding, "vulgar" (84).

Similar charges were leveled at Froude—not only for blanket criticisms of the devout but also for his scattershot dismissal of serious, history-drenched concepts such as "sin," which at one point Sutherland calls "a chimera" (*NF*, 92). "*The Nemesis* is certainly an unpleasant book," insisted Kingsbury Badger in his 1952 essay "The Ordeal of Anthony Froude." One of his complaints: the book "exposes a mind perplexed by a jumble of biblical criticism."[40]

Froude had in fact absorbed large amounts of scholarship documenting the Bible's inconsistencies. That is one reason his protagonist doubts that the Bible is infallible, asking pointedly of the faith that the devout place in miracles, "But why do they believe it at all? They must say because it is in the Bible" (*NF*, 20). Such lines help explain why the novel's publication was a serious blow to his father, given his position as archdeacon. With Froude's also visualizing a "religious tea-party" so effectively (57), it is not difficult to imagine the scenes between austere father and wayward son that ensued following publication. Not least was the awkwardness, in the 1840s, of one's youngest publicly dissecting the weaknesses of the Church while pondering the merits of unbelief.

It was hardly the first time that Froude had disappointed his father, though the man was, by all accounts, notoriously hard to please. Partly as a result, the son's books are shot through with strongly pronounced father complexes. Sometimes, too, that complex turns father-son relations into a religious allegory, with Froude styling himself almost as an angry Job addressing God the Father alongside his own father in God. But other factors motivated Froude to write, including intellectual doubt about the possibility of miracles, growing concern about the articles that he had sworn to uphold, and the problems that he faced trying to reconcile Genesis with the dozens of historical tracts he was studying.

Chambers' *Vestiges* had one impact on writers such as Froude and Tennyson but quite another on popular preachers like the Reverend John Cumming, the firebrand Evangelical from Aberdeenshire, who would have been the first to criticize Froude's Sutherland for not quoting the Bible enough. In *The Church before the Flood* (1853), in a passage the future George Eliot would call an "exuberance of mendacity," Cumming declared, "The idea of the author of the *Vestiges* is, . . . that if you keep a baboon long enough, it will develop itself into a man."[41]

The author of roughly 180 other books, including *Apocalyptic Sketches* (1849), *The Romish Church, a Dumb Church* (1853), and *The Destiny of Nations as Indicated in Prophecy* (1864), the reverend was a highly influential Calvinist preacher. He found evidence for the End Times, two scholars

Figure 12. Elliott and Fry, portrait of the Reverend John Cumming, minister of the Presbyterian Church of England, albumen print, 1860s. © National Portrait Gallery, London.

write, in "everything from the French Revolution to the Irish potato famine to the invention of the telegraph and steamship." He also thought that the "Christian dispensation would come to a glorious end" circa 1867.[42] Although Cumming was something of a crank whose ferocious anti-Catholicism was strongly criticized, he preached each Sunday to a congregation numbering between five and six hundred and was a powerful presence in the National Scottish Church in Covent Garden, central London.

Evolution and unbelief were among the reverend's biggest obsessions. One of his many books, *Is Christianity from God? or, A Manual of Christian*

Evidence (1847)—written, his subtitle asserts, for "scripture readers, city missionaries, Sunday school teachers, &c."—lambasted what he called the "Creed of the Infidel." Couched as a satire of the Nicene Creed so often used in Christian liturgy, it states:

> I believe that there is no God, but that matter is God, and God is matter; and that it is no matter whether there is any God or not. I believe also that the world was not made, but that the world made itself, or that it had no beginning, and that it will last for ever. I believe that man is a beast; that the soul is the body, and that the body is the soul. . . . I believe not in the evangelists; . . . I believe not in revelation; *I believe in tradition: I believe in the Talmud: I believe in the Koran;* I believe not in the Bible. I believe in Socrates; I believe in Confucius; I believe in Mahomet; I believe not in Christ. And lastly, I *believe* in all unbelief.[43]

It would be easy to dismiss this fascinating, self-revealing "web of contradictions," as George Eliot would later call them; unbelief logically rules out belief in the Talmud and the Koran, as well as the Bible. It is also ludicrous to put failure to "believe . . . in the evangelists" on a par with interest in the teachings and philosophical traditions of Socrates and Confucius (to do so, even implicitly, highlights the reverend's grandiosity). But refusal to believe in the Bible was his primary concern. Accordingly, Cumming's caricature of doubters and atheists renders both, in Eliot's summation of his words, a type of "intellectual and moral monster . . . who unites much simplicity and imbecility with . . . Satanic hardihood."[44]

Why bother to engage with Cumming, then? Because the claims and fears that he expressed so often and so vehemently resonated with a large cross-section of the Victorian public. He was, "as every one knows, a preacher of immense popularity," Eliot explained, who found a way to tap deep-seated fears of change, perhaps especially the idea that science could invalidate belief, rendering it null and void.[45] That is one reason Cumming denounced Lord Byron, without irony calling one of his poems "*an infidel's brightest thoughts.*" Byron had insisted that "*the heart* is lonely still," but death will be a return to "the *Nothing* that I was / Ere born to life and living woe!"[46] To Cumming, that was heresy, plain and simple.

In 1855, several years before she adopted the pen name George Eliot, Marian Evans decided to take on the firebrand preacher in the *Westminster Review*. She didn't mince her words. In "Evangelical Teaching: Dr Cumming," a blistering review of his many books, the future novelist condemned his "tawdry" assertions, "vulgar fables," and "astounding ignorance" ("ET," 42, 53, 47). The review article was one of Eliot's first publications, though she would write several more high-profile reviews on agnosticism and free thought for the *Review*. She was in an excellent position to do so, having translated the work of such key German philosophers and historians of religion as Ludwig Feuerbach and David Friedrich Strauss.

Though she bore the title of assistant editor, Eliot was editor of the *Review* in all but name, as John Chapman's chaotic personal and professional life forced her to assume his responsibilities, too. During her two years at the helm of this progressive intellectual journal, she befriended such regular contributors as the sociologist Herbert Spencer, the scholar-writer Francis William Newman (younger brother to John Henry), and the liberal George Henry Lewes, the man with whom she would soon share a home, though he was married and unable to procure a divorce.[47]

Founded in 1824 by Jeremy Bentham and James Mill (John Stuart Mill's father), the *Westminster Review* was not only a leading proponent of liberalism; it also introduced British readers to major Continental thinkers, and gave important backing to evolutionary theory at a time when it had few public defenders. With the biologist Thomas Huxley comanaging its science section and later reviewing Darwin's *On the Origin of Species,* the journal was the first to use the term "Darwinism." The *Review* was, in short, one of the periodicals that Carlyle's Teufelsdröckh had in mind when he called journalists "the true Kings and Clergy" governing Britain. Like several other organs, the *Review* contributed to a fundamental shift in think-

Figure 13. Samuel Laurence, portrait of George Eliot [Marian Evans], 1857. © The Mistress and Fellows, Girton College, Cambridge.

ing, including by encouraging greater public acceptance of religious doubt and uncertainty.[48]

In a joint statement with Chapman about the *Westminster Review*'s editorial position on religion, Eliot wrote that it would "unite a spirit of reverential sympathy for the cherished associations of pure and elevated minds with an uncompromising pursuit of truth. The elements of ecclesiastical authority and of dogma will be fearlessly examined and the results of the most advanced biblical criticism will be discussed without reservation."[49]

Her review article on Cumming was similarly "fearless," though she published it anonymously, as was customary at the time. A portion of her rebuke was probably personal. As biographer Gordon Haight puts it, the reverend "offered Marian ample ammunition for an annihilating account of the beliefs she had held so earnestly in girlhood."[50] Nor did the ironies end there. To Eliot, the reverend's aggressive certainty looked suspiciously like a way to silence the religious doubts that had in fact beset *him* at university.

Eliot began her review article by asking, wittily and bitingly, how one might thrive as a "mediocrity," so that "a smattering of science and learning will pass for profound instruction, . . . platitudes will be accepted as wisdom, bigoted narrowness as holy zeal, [and] unctuous egoism as God-given piety" ("ET," 38). "Let such a man become an evangelical preacher," she urged impishly, especially if his interpretation of scripture is "hard and literal," his "insisting on the Eternity of punishment . . . unflinching," and his "preach[ing] less of Christ than of Antichrist" (38). In that last phrase, one hears an echo of Jane Eyre's equal irritation, in Brontë's celebrated novel of eight years earlier, that the Calvinist preacher St. John Rivers aimed more to scold and terrify his congregations than to minister to their emotional needs.

Eliot's criticism far-surpassed the Reverend Cumming's spiritual and emotional dryness. She chided his religious assertions as "slippery and lax" ("ET," 51). Although he viewed focusing on "evidence" as a "symptom of sinful scepticism," countless others, she insisted, find "doubt . . . the stamp of a truth-loving mind" (45, 51). Eliot wasn't alluding to Tennyson only when she echoed his refrain about honest doubt. She followed with a Latin aphorism of her own that translates: "There are some for whom it is an honour not to have believed, and their unbelief is a guarantee of future faith."[51]

Eliot was insistent about the need for doubt because she recognized that Cumming's brand of certainty was designed to mute serious questions of his own. "I was tainted while at the University by the spirit of scepticism," he states bluntly in *Apocalyptic Sketches:* "I thought Christianity might not be true."[52] By calling his doubts a "taint" and speaking about them in the past tense, Cumming obviously hoped to show resilience to readers perhaps plagued by questions of their own. But his phrasing was probably more revealing than he intended. His doubts were so intense that apparently they gave him "no peace till [he] had settled" whether the Bible was authentic. "I . . . read from that day, for fourteen or fifteen years, till this, and *now* I am convinced," he explained, a decade later still, "upon the clearest of evidence, that this book is the book of God as that [from which] I now address you."[53]

An "ingenuous mind," Eliot argued, would engage the arguments of Newton, Linnaeus, Werner, Hutton, and others with "a humble, candid, sympathetic attempt to meet the[ir] difficulties" ("ET," 52, 42, 52). But because Cumming couldn't permit that, he opted for a "mode of warfare" that distorts and ridicules the position of these and other skeptics (43): "Everywhere he supposes that the doubter is hardened, conceited, *consciously shutting his eyes to the light*—a fool who is to be answered according to his folly—that is, with ready replies made up of reckless assertions, of apocryphal anecdotes, and, where other resources fail, of vituperative imputations" ("ET," 52; emphasis mine).

Reading such lines, one cannot help wishing that Anne Brontë had lived long enough to see them. Certainly, they resonate strongly with her own concerns about Calvinism, in "A Word to the 'Elect.'"[54] In her trenchant criticism, Eliot overturns the oft-stated claim by believers that agnosticism implies a refusal to see the light and accept the Word. Instead, she renders doubt a sign of integrity and honest difference. Either impervious to such criticism or steeled by it, the reverend continued regardless. He published dozens more books, most of them featuring his own version of the apocalypse.

In Hutton and especially Lyell we have traced the personal and intellectual doubts of several key scientists, but Eliot exemplifies midcentury humanistic concerns about the nature of belief, religious and otherwise. Among the nineteenth century's most talented and respected novelists, she was quite forthcoming about her agnosticism, almost two decades before Huxley coined the term in 1869.[55] At the same time, she was widely celebrated for cultivating in her novels an ethic of fellow feeling so ardent that, for some readers, it borders on a "religion of humanity."[56] Certainly, no one could accuse Eliot of letting agnosticism relax her moral strictures. Her life story and philosophy upends the commonplace—still heard today—that religion keeps us in check, to stave off amorality.

Devout in her youth, Eliot was raised by an orthodox Anglican who strongly supported the Tory ideals of church and state. By her early teens, she had filled a notebook with religious verses and added a few of her own, including one called "On Being Called a Saint." It begins: "A Saint! Oh would that I could claim / The privileg'd, the honor'd name." The poem hints at a form of self-denial that has pleasures of its own. It also claims to envy the saints their role in "judg[ing] the world . . . / When hell shall ope its jaws of flame / And sinners to their doom be hurl'd."[57]

It would be inaccurate and grossly unfair to view the author of *Middlemarch* and *Daniel Deronda* through the lens of such juvenilia, but that early writing does capture a strain of zeal in Eliot's personality that she was among the first to recognize. The same "stern, ascetic views," she called them, also motivate a few of her characters, including the young Maggie Tulliver in *The Mill on the Floss,* who for a while is drawn to acute self-denial even as she reads Keble's *Christian Year* (1827), a popular book of poems that celebrated the Christian calendar and "the Church's middle sky, / Half way 'twixt joy and woe."[58] Yet while Keble's collection feels too much like a "hymn-book" to move Maggie, Thomas à Kempis, the medieval mystic, is said to give her a "strange thrill of awe" in proclaiming: "Love of thyself doth hurt thee more than anything in the world. . . . Thou must set out courageously, and lay the axe to the root, that thou mayest pluck up and destroy that hidden inordinate inclination to thyself, and unto all private and earthly good."[59]

By the time she could include such passages in her novel, and in part from the sentiment that they convey, Eliot had lost her faith. It left her quickly and decisively. We can almost name the day—January 2, 1842—just after she purchased Charles Hennell's *Inquiry Concerning the Origin of Christianity* (1838). Hennell had set out to write a positive book about the role of miracles in the gospels. But after two years' careful research, he concluded that although Jesus was "a noble-minded reformer and sage, martyred by crafty priests and brutal soldiers," there was insufficient evidence to support such fundamental matters as his supernatural birth, miraculous works, and resurrection.[60] Hume had published similar claims decades earlier, but Hennell was forthright in saying to a larger audience that if Christianity were assessed on strictly empirical grounds, one could explain its formations quite easily through natural law.[61]

That is where faith takes over, many countered, as belief in something that cannot finally be proven. That Christianity and other religions should be held to standards of material proof was also beside the point, and even part of the problem, because faith transcends rationalism.[62] For many Christians at the time, however, including Eliot, it mattered greatly that Christianity have strong historical validity. Otherwise, as in her case, belief in its assertions might come to an end.

Biographer Rosemary Ashton notes of Hennell's book that Eliot's copy "has her name inscribed on the flyleaf with the date 'Jany 1st 1842,'—a most suggestive date," Ashton continues, "since it was the very next day which she chose for her rebellion against church-going."[63] The decision sparked what Eliot called a "Holy War" with her father,[64] during which he "with-dr[e]w into a cold and sullen rage."[65] And though she may have begun reading another copy of Hennell's book slightly earlier, it is striking that thereafter she not only formed a strong friendship with him and his wife, Rufa (as well as his freethinking sister, Cara Bray, and her husband, Charles), but also decided to translate a biography of Jesus by the German biblical critic David Friedrich Strauss, which advanced an argument quite similar to Hennell's. That biography, *The Life of Jesus, Critically Examined,* had been published in Germany in 1835, three years before Hennell's book came out, though it was unknown to him when he began his own study.

That two books with similarly stated doubts about Jesus appeared within a few years of each other is perhaps less surprising when one considers the growth of interest at the time in historical approaches to the Bible, a form of scholarship known as higher criticism.[66] The approach had taken off in Germany at the turn of the nineteenth century, largely because of such powerful early practitioners as Johann Gottfried Eichhorn and Wilhelm Martin Leberecht de Wette. It quickly became a branch of theology with considerable clout in Germany, especially in the university town of Tübingen, near Bavaria.

Higher criticism took several decades to reach Britain. But when it did so, as we shall see, it set off a crisis deeper than even Darwin's *Origin of Species* in 1859. Eliot, therefore, was forward-thinking, when she referred, in her first published review article four years earlier, to such scholars and their peers as "a large body of eminently instructed and earnest men who regard the Hebrew and Christian Scriptures as a series of historical documents, to be dealt with according to the rules of historical criticism" ("ET," 49). Without her reviews and translations of such philosophers as Feuerbach and Spinoza, it is also fair to add, the impact of higher criticism on Britain would surely have been slower and weaker.

Conversions of any kind can be abrupt and intoxicating, offering black-and-white distinctions on matters that strike others as containing many shades of gray. Eliot reacted to her loss of faith with a zeal that could be described as either making up for lost time or as an equal and opposite reaction to what she previously had held as true. In a review of Robert William Mackay's *Progress of the Intellect,* she protested: "Our civilization, and, yet more, our religion, are an anomalous blending of lifeless barbarisms, which have descended to us like so many petrifications from distant ages."[67] For Eliot, religion had become an anachronism that was holding the Victorians back. It was vital to consider what could replace it.

By the time she began writing fiction full-time, in her late thirties, Eliot had refined her intellectual arguments. By 1854, having translated Spinoza's *Tractatus Theologico-Politicus*, a critique of religious intolerance that the Dutch philosopher published anonymously in 1670, she had also finished translating Feuerbach's *Essence of Christianity* (1841), the powerful philosophical treatise which argues that God is a projection of humanity's need for recognition, forgiveness, and love. "Religion is human nature reflected, mirrored in itself," Feuerbach maintained, and thus "God is the mirror of man."[68] In short, religion is man-made.

Although that sounded blasphemous to many ears, Feuerbach noted quite reasonably of all forms of monotheism that "*what faith denies on earth it affirms in heaven; what it renounces here it recovers a hundred-fold there.*"[69] He also insisted that if Church doctrine were returned to its original human scale, the idea that God Is Love would revert to its foundational premise: Love Is God. Eliot's 1854 translation of Feuerbach's fascinating treatise is not only still in print but to this day is considered definitive.

It is through Feuerbach, moreover, that we best make sense of Eliot's intriguing statement in her review of Cumming, one year later: "There are some for whom it is an honour not to have believed, and *their unbelief is a guarantee of future faith*" ("ET," 51; emphasis added). In so writing, Eliot did more than join Tennyson and Froude in restoring integrity ("honour") to doubt and unbelief; she also extended Froude's interest in the ethical "responsibility" that follows. And though Eliot's fiction adds a twist to that move by underscoring the challenges of binding doubt to ethics, rather than to morality, it is only through fellow feeling, her novels show, that the ethic has any chance of succeeding.[70]

In *Silas Marner*, to give just one example of the fragility of that compromise, the title character is a simple weaver who lives in a small Calvinist community in rural England called Lantern Yard. He suffers periodically from catalepsy, however, and falls into trances during which he becomes oblivious to what is happening around him.

Taking advantage of his friend's ailment, William Dane decides to steal the church money while Silas is in a trance. He then blames the theft on his friend by planting Silas' knife at the scene of the crime. Adding insult to injury, Dane snags Silas' fiancée, Sarah, before his former friend is excommunicated from the group and faith he once cherished.

For Silas, the false charges are unbearable: the narrator says that he is "stunned by despair."[71] "God will clear me" is his rallying cry, but when he is banished by "those who to him represented God's people," his trust in celestial justice is shattered (*SM*, 12). After hearing his verdict, he tells his accusers: "There is no just God that governs the earth righteously, but a God of lies, that bears witness against the innocent" (14). Ever quick to seize the opportunity, his erstwhile friend uses the statement to confirm Silas' guilt: "William said meekly, 'I leave our brethren to judge whether this is the voice of Satan or not'" (14).

Already suffering from acute self-doubt, the weaver tries to take "refuge from benumbing unbelief" by working his way through the crisis (*SM*, 14). He eventually recovers—even thrives financially—in a nearby village. That is, until one of the squire's sons decides to steal his savings. Deprived again of what he needs and values, his faith in humanity tested to the limit, Silas is forced to reengage with his neighbors by asking them to help him find the culprit. But although the gold eventually turns up, years later, Silas never achieves redress from Lantern Yard. When he decides to return there, thirty years later, still on the off-chance that something may have surfaced to convince his accusers that he was innocent, he finds a grimy factory where the chapel and house once stood.

Confrontation, clarification, apology: Eliot's novel makes none of these actions entirely feasible. The "hole" created by the Calvinists' accusation remains unanswered and unanswerable. The novel finds other ways to console Silas, including through friendship and love for his adopted daughter, Eppie, but the impression left by the false judgment of the Evangelical community is lasting and severe.

Eliot doubtless drew on some personal experience in representing Silas' traumatic encounter with his community: When she decided to live un-married with George Henry Lewes, her brother Isaac infamously cut ties with her for the next twenty-five years (and urged their younger sisters to do the same). He restored their bonds only in old age, after Lewes had died and Eliot had remarried. The scandal that swirled around her and Lewes was all the more intense, ironically, because her first published novel, *Adam Bede* (1859), printed anonymously, generated intense public interest. When her authorship was finally revealed (after a clergyman, no less, had allowed credit for the work to be attributed to him), the novel quickly turned her into a reluctant celebrity.

Eliot's "religion of humanity," we might say, was as tested in life as in her fiction, where a gap opens between religious and secular models that is not easily resolved. Properly established after her loss of religious faith, her ensuing attack on Evangelical zeal, and her deep familiarity with philoso-phies of religion, Eliot's secular path was quite similar to Froude's. She con-gratulated him for writing *The Nemesis of Faith* and reviewed his book fa-vorably. To both writers, doubt made free thought a possibility. Indeed, it was by wrestling over what could replace religion that Eliot, Froude, and their close associates found it possible to put their faith and abundant in-telligence in a culture that might finally try to do without God.

FIVE

Uncertainty Becomes
a Way of Life

I n the summer of 1860, England was awash with rain. The season was
so wet and sunless that almost a century and a half would pass before
another June would produce heavier rain.[1] In Oxford, however, amid
the gloomy spires and sodden quadrangles, one bright spot stood out.

On June 30, the British Association for the Advancement of Science
gathered to meet. The papers presented that final morning of the assembly
were given over to discussing Charles Darwin's controversial best-seller,
*On the Origin of Species by Means of Natural Selection, or the Preservation of
Favoured Races in the Struggle for Life.* The book, like Robert Chambers'
Vestiges, had already begun to send shock waves through the nation. The
Reverend Baden Powell, Oxford's Savilian Professor of Geometry (and father to the founder of the Scout Movement), had praised its ideas on evolution, arguing that Darwin's "masterly volume" detailed "the grand principle of the self-evolving powers of nature."[2] The stakes at the June meeting
were thus felt to be high. Both the scientists and men of the cloth who
wanted to discuss the book's argument found themselves on either side of
a fairly sharp divide.

Today the Oxford University Museum is partitioned into administrative offices, with only a plaque inside to mark the occasion, but on that morning the hall hummed with a crowd of more than seven hundred. The presentations on Darwin's book had not been widely publicized, but the tension was considerable. The crowd grew restive as John William Draper, an English-born scholar visiting from the United States, meandered through an hour-long talk on "The Intellectual Development of Europe, Considered with Reference to the Views of Mr. Darwin and Others." Several in the audience heckled him; one even tried to cut in. The clergy, who had turned out in large numbers, ended up shouting him down.

Draper's paper, the first of its kind on social Darwinism and a forerunner to his subsequent books on the conflict between science and religion, succeeded in stirring a debate that erupted shortly after he stepped down.[3] The chair of the session, John Stevens Henslow (Darwin's former mentor from Cambridge), called on several more speakers before the floor was given to Samuel Wilberforce, bishop of Oxford. And when Wilberforce began ridiculing evolutionary theory, it looked as if the assembled traditionalists and clergy would win the debate by a landslide. The agile, practiced speaker—whom many called "Soapy Sam" because of his habit of rubbing his hands as he spoke—had been coached by one of Darwin's rivals. He also hit home with personal jokes that insulted his opponents. "Was it through his grandfather or his grand*mother*," he is alleged to have sneered to Thomas H. Huxley, Darwin's defender, "that he claimed his descent from a monkey?"[4]

Huxley had been pressed into speaking for Darwin, who was sick at the time, and doubtless knew what opposition awaited him. But like the clergy around him, the feisty biologist was in no mood to back down. He thought Darwin was right, and he had come to the meeting to say so. As the crowd began chanting for him to speak, Huxley slapped his knee and, in a recollection that clearly might err in his favor, murmured to a nearby scientist in biblical prose, "The Lord hath delivered him into mine hands."[5]

According to most accounts, the hall quieted to a hush as Huxley spoke

Figure 14. Carlo Pellegrini, portrait of Samuel Wilberforce,
bishop of Oxford, watercolor, *Vanity Fair* (London), July 24,
1869. © National Portrait Gallery, London.

Figure 15. Thomas H. Huxley, biologist, chromolithograph, *Vanity Fair* (London), January 28, 1871. © National Portrait Gallery, London.

with forceful self-control. He had listened carefully to the lord bishop's speech, he told the now-silent crowd, "but had been unable to discern either a new fact or a new argument in it—except indeed the question raised as to my personal predilection in the matter of ancestry."[6] It was a sharp reply, but Huxley apparently did not leave it there. To astonished gasps, he recalled adding that he would "rather have a miserable ape for a grandfather" than a man who was willing to distort the truth.

One woman apparently screamed, then fainted, at hearing a bishop insulted so publicly—just as Huxley had been, of course. She was Lady Brewster, wife of the renowned Scottish physicist and philosopher Sir David Brewster. But as the clergy shouted in anger, demanding that Huxley retract his accusation, most of the rest of the audience broke out in hearty applause. To those clapping for him, Huxley had at last given Darwin a proper hearing. The Church also left the meeting claiming victory. Because it had been backed into a corner by traditionalists, however, Christianity in Britain came to seem as if it was fighting a rearguard battle against science itself. Increasingly dissatisfied with that stance, large numbers of Britons would soon join Huxley in viewing religious doubt as a robust alternative that made agnosticism integral to cultural debate and scientific inquiry.

Huxley's debate with Wilberforce has since become apocryphal, doubtless at the risk of some coloring and the eclipsing of other, less dramatic events in the century.[7] But to participants on both sides, the debate felt historic, and it was quickly described as such. The *Press*, a London weekly, wrote excitedly: "The theory of Dr Darwin . . . , on the origin of species by natural selection, gave rise to the hottest of all debates."[8] In hindsight, too, it marks a watershed in the nineteenth century's battle over reason and faith. As John Hedley Brooke notes, the Oxford debate "has come to symbolize not merely the conflict between Darwinism and the Bible but the victory of science over religion."[9] The reasons are bound up with the remarkable book that scholars and members of the clergy would continue vociferously to debate.

Darwin had already caused quite a stir, as the Church was painfully aware. *On the Origin of Species through Natural Selection* had sold its initial print run of 1,250 copies almost the day it appeared. With warm initial reviews and vigorous word of mouth, it quickly flew through several more printings. The papers that galvanized the debate on Darwin's treatise were themselves a sign that his treatise on random variation in species, borne from a "struggle for existence and adaptive 'selection' by the environment," was too important to ignore.[10] The debate gave Darwin credibility and meant that his arguments were more likely to be aired than dismissed out of hand.

There is, however, more to the issue than we often hear. Darwin was extremely torn over what he had unearthed; indeed, the discovery fairly appalled him. As Christopher Hitchens notes astutely, Darwin "was very reluctant to accept its . . . implications and referred throughout [the book] to 'creation' without mentioning 'evolution.' (The naturalist himself feared that these very implications, if followed, would be like 'confessing a murder.')"[11] That last phrase accents Darwin's guilt, even self-blame, in identifying an issue that would change the way humanity thought about itself, its past, and its role in the world.

Not all of that torment was tied to religion, to be sure, but some of it was. Darwin had once considered training for the priesthood and had described in letters his pride in occupying the same rooms at Cambridge as William Paley, author of *Natural Theology,* so it is easy to see why he recoiled from the practical implications of his discovery. His wife, Emma, was also strongly religious.[12] Darwin's "spiritual odyssey from orthodox Christianity to agnosticism [therefore] seems of immense significance in light of his discovery of the theory of natural selection."[13] His reactions to uncovering that principle are best described in his *Autobiography,* published in 1887, five years after his death, at a time when Britain's leading journals were already publishing major statements and debates on agnosticism.[14] The pages conveying his religious doubts are a powerful combination of candor, humility, and eloquence.

"It is not possible," Darwin recalled explaining in his journal, after "standing in the midst of the grandeur of the Brazilian forest, . . . to give an adequate idea of the higher feelings of wonder, admiration, and devotion, which fill and elevate the mind" on such occasions.[15] Even as an older man, looking over "the endless beautiful adaptations which we everywhere meet with," he wrote, "it may be asked how can the generally beneficent arrangement of the world be accounted for?" (*A*, 73).

Despite much of what one hears about the godlessness of the *Origin of Species,* Darwin's 1859 theory of natural selection implicitly assumes that a higher being preordained species adaptation to help creatures adapt to changing conditions—hence Darwin's noting that his argument "deserve[d] to be called . . . Theist" (*A*, 77). Not until *The Descent of Man,* twelve years later, did he become more forthright in viewing adaptation as a purely material response to shifting circumstances on earth, without the necessary intervention of a higher being.

The shift in emphasis came partly from Darwin's concession that while "the morality of the New Testament . . . is . . . beautiful, . . . its perfection depends in part on the interpretation which we now put on metaphors and allegories" (*A*, 72). The literary figures that Hutton, Lyell, and Adam Sedgwick had invoked to make sense of scientific discovery ended up redounding, in Darwin's eyes, on religious doctrine too. At the same time, Darwin recoiled from the argument that large amounts of "suffering in the world" can be explained "by imagining that it serves for [man's] moral improvement" (75). However attractive that precept is for some, he wrote, "it revolts our understanding to suppose" that the benevolence of God "is not unbounded, for what advantage can there be in the sufferings of millions of the lower animals throughout almost endless time?" (75).

Though Darwin found religious arguments about suffering increasingly implausible, he left some speculative room for them: "I cannot pretend to throw the least light on such abstruse problems" as the "First Cause," he wrote late in life, and whether the evolution of humanity was "the result of blind chance or necessity. . . . The mystery of the beginnings of all things is insoluble by us; and I for one must be content to remain an Agnostic" (*A*, 78, 77, 78).[16]

You could call this hedging or fence-sitting (as some have), but Darwin was not avoiding the hard questions. He was confronting them head-on and discovering that science and religion parted company on several fundamentals, leaving the "mystery of the beginnings" a riddle that science neither had solved nor, in his eyes, likely would.

In one of his most candid moments, Darwin acknowledged the comfort that religion confers—especially in welcoming a faith that surpasses scientific understanding. "To those who fully admit the immortality of the human soul," he wrote, describing the slow extinction of some species and moments when nature is decidedly unlovely, the gradual "destruction of our world" through loss of species "will not appear so dreadful" (*A*, 77). There is comfort, too, he noted, in representing death not as an end but as a continuation, even as a prelude to something better.

But those arguments increasingly failed to move him personally. Nor did he consider them plausible intellectual grounds for presuming "the existence of God" (76). Over time, he wrote, "the state of mind which grand scenes formerly excited in me, and which was intimately connected with a belief in God, did not essentially differ from that which is often called the sense of sublimity; and however difficult it may be to explain the genesis of this sense, it can hardly be advanced as an argument for the existence of God, any more than the powerful though vague and similar feelings excited by music" (76).

It is easier to proclaim that Darwin was right or wrong about religious faith than it is to keep both options as workable hypotheses. Certainly Darwin's private willingness to consider each side put him in a fairly unusual position that supporters and detractors today easily overlook, perhaps in a desire to make him a standard-bearer in the ongoing battles over evolution and intelligent design.

Standard-bearer he may have become, but the label gives an inaccurate picture of a man both revered and reviled for identifying how the strongest species adapt over eons to their natural environments. Such openness came at personal cost to Darwin. "I gradually came to disbelieve in Christianity as a divine revelation," he recalls, "but I was very unwilling to give up my belief" (*A, 72*).

As the Oxford debate attests, Darwin would succeed where Chambers largely had not, in forcing the Church publicly to contend with scientific perspectives on natural history rather than to reject them out of hand as outlandish or blasphemous. Perhaps oddly, however, the February 1860 publication of seven Broad Church essays on Christianity, in a volume simply called *Essays and Reviews,* helped to stoke the meeting at Oxford and kindle interest in Darwin's treatise. The volume did so from the seemingly modest aim of describing and analyzing historical approaches to the Bible —work that had been thriving in Germany for more than three decades but was just starting to take off in England.[17]

Partly because of its growing popularity, that scholarship was held up to eloquent critique by the High Church Anglican Henry Longueville Mansel, soon to be Waynflete Professor of Moral and Metaphysical Philosophy at Magdalen College, Oxford. In 1858, Mansel gave the Bampton Lectures at the university, which he titled *The Limits of Religious Thought Examined.*[18] Extending Kant's interest in the concept of God, in *Religion within the Limits of Reason Alone* (1793), Mansel aimed to "defend . . . the doctrine of biblical infallibility" by arguing that "God and the transcendental world are beyond" the limits of man's knowledge, and thus "unknowable."[19] His lectures caused a stir and attracted a large audience, but did little to protect Christianity from historical scholarship. On the contrary, two years later, Huxley used Mansel's argument about God's unknowability to assert that agnosticism, or persistent doubt, was the only tenable position for freethinkers to adopt.

Essays and Reviews featured an impressive lineup of scholars to address Mansel's and others' claims of biblical infallibility, including the Reverend Baden Powell; Benjamin Jowett, one of the country's leading classicists;

and Mark Pattison, priest, author, and rector of Lincoln College, Oxford. The controversy this volume caused was remarkable, arguably dealing a more severe blow to the Established Church than even Darwin's theory. The suggestion that some aspects of the Bible might best be interpreted historically, even figuratively, was devastating for congregations brought up to believe that the Bible was literally *the* Word of God.

The scholars were respectful, but firm, in suggesting otherwise; their work was also rigorous and readable. Flying rapidly through nine editions in its first year, *Essays and Reviews* sold more than twenty thousand copies in its first two years and at least the same number again over the 1860s as a whole.[20] It soon became known among scholars for melting what one contributor called the "unmeaning frostwork of dogma."[21] It also generated a book-length response, *Aids to Faith,* promoted heavily by Samuel Wilberforce, which tried to revive interest in miracles and the Mosaic record in "those whose faith may have been shaken by recent assaults."[22]

Rich in detail and historical discovery, *Essays and Reviews* almost inevitably made the Bible resemble a loose collection of papers rather than a coherent vision from eyewitness accounts. The best lines were probably Jowett's, who wrote unsparingly: "The unchangeable word of God, in the name of which we repose, is [actually] changed by each age and each generation in accordance with its passing fancy." He continued, "The book in which we believe all religious truth to be contained, is the most uncertain of all books," because it is inconsistent and "interpreted by arbitrary and uncertain methods."[23]

Those who deny such variability, Jowett cautioned, and prefer a "minute and rigid enforcement of the words of Scripture," put expectations on the Bible that it cannot hope to satisfy. It is not the Word, he declared, if by Word we mean something so absolute and unchanging that it lacks any historical sense of how it came to mean in the first place. Insisting otherwise would have unfortunate effects, he told readers, such as encouraging blind faith and closing down inquiry altogether: "Doubt comes in at the window, when Inquiry is denied at the door."[24]

To avoid such close-mindedness, Jowett argued that interpreters of the Bible should try to "recover the original . . . meaning" of the book. They should do so, moreover, by basing their interpretations on "a knowledge of the text itself." But it was the third of Jowett's recommendations, to "read Scripture like any other book," that sparked most outrage and anxiety.[25] As the Reverend Charles W. Rishell of Boston University's School of Theology later warned, "The very assumption [of the higher critics] is dangerous to the influence of the Bible." A reason for serious "fear of the[m]," he wrote, is that "their first assumptions . . . undermine its authority."[26]

Jowett's suggestion that one "read Scripture like any other book" scandalized colleagues like Rishell, who insisted that "a book whose author or co-author is God must be treated with a reverence not due to a purely human production."[27] Of course, trusting the veracity of Rishell's point about the Bible's "author or co-author," though critical to his perspective, was a sticking point for Jowett. Still, it would be wrong to view Jowett, Pattison, and other contributors as radicals or as wanting to replace all forms of faith with secular alternatives. The unintended "assault" from *Essays and Reviews* came from trading rote learning with interest in the Bible's historical variability and rigid literalism with shades of metaphor. As the scholar Jude Nixon notes, the authors wanted not to denigrate scripture but to "make [it] speak again, to make the rocks cry out."[28] To do so, they felt obliged to acknowledge that the Bible, as a series of writings, was not a settled or complete text but an "incomplete, fragmented figure." No wonder many were aghast at hearing that such miracles as the parting of the Red Sea or Jonah's living for three days inside a large fish might best be thought extended metaphors modified by each generation that reported them.

If one adopted the higher criticism approach to the gospels and the Old Testament, Hebrew professor Rowland Williams conceded, one would almost necessarily "naturalize the great deluge, read . . . Genesis as an incomplete history of origins, find . . . the biblical chronology unreliable, and interpret . . . the narrative of the Red Sea crossing" with "the latitude of poetry."[29] Yet as many had been brought up to believe that the Bible's miracles were not in the least metaphorical, the stakes concerning how one read the Bible escalated rapidly. The issue was more critical, for many, than whether science was right to argue that species evolved.

That not all of the Bible could be taken literally was hardly, for every contributor to *Essays and Reviews,* a reason to give up Christianity. Even so, scholarly perspective on the Bible inevitably altered understanding of the religion, including its historical origins. Like the German scholar Baron von Bunsen for instance, who had translated the Bible, then published a fascinating study of it and Christianity—*God in History*—that tracked humankind's evolving conceptions of the deity, some of the scholars in *Essays and Reviews* hinted that much of the Mosaic record might best be viewed as partial and figurative.[30]

Although the historical scholars eventually won the debate, and literalist approaches to the Bible receded in England, they returned with a vengeance in the United States. So much so, we'll see, that the battle of the 1925 Scopes trial over the teaching of evolution failed to settle the issue.

While many British Victorians grasped that literalist accounts of Genesis placed an extraordinary burden on the historical record, they also made clear that doubt was not a trait one would always necessarily welcome. It could be threatening, a source of intense fear and anguish; it could also make the world seem rudderless and leave believers with the sense, as J. Hillis Miller puts it, that God had "disappeared," perhaps never to return. Even the devout poet Gerard Manley Hopkins, one of Miller's subjects, suffered acutely from that anxiety.[31] *The Wreck of the Deutschland* (1875–76), voicing his complex theodicy, is an elegy Hopkins composed after seventy-eight people (including five Franciscan nuns fleeing harsh anti-Catholic laws in Germany) perished at sea following a naval disaster.[32] Later sonnets of his such as "No worst, there is none," "Carrion Comfort," and "I wake and feel the fell of dark, not day," also published posthumously in 1918 but composed in the mid-1880s, accent an even stronger sense of despair. They represent doubt as a parasitical element that feeds on the poet, turning his religious self-accusation into a visceral form of anguish. "I am gall, I am heartburn," his speaker declares in the last of these sonnets, voicing despair and confusion over what in fact is wanted of him. "God's most deep decree / Bitter would have me taste: my taste was me."[33]

A few years earlier, in 1878, the author W. H. Mallock tried to describe how the "disappearance of God" affected his generation by declaring, our "hearts are aching for the God that [we] no longer can believe in." He continued: "One may almost say that with us one can hear faith decaying. . . . This decay [has] been maturing for three hundred years, and [its] effects prophesied for fifty."[34]

Mallock's "aching for the God that [we] no longer can believe in," paired with the comparable despair of Hopkins and many others, voiced a powerful, understandable conundrum about nature and governance that had sprung up everywhere. In one of Sir Edwin Landseer's bleakest paintings, for example, the English artist and sculptor used the failure of a polar expedition several years earlier to accent—rather than try to conceal or explain—nature's indifference to the suffering of humanity. *Man Proposes, God Disposes* (1864), Landseer's unusually maudlin narrative painting, is based on Sir John Franklin's failed attempt to discover the Northwest Passage two decades earlier, in 1845.

In its title and content, the painting bitterly records a gap between human aspirations and the outcomes that heaven apparently has authorized, for reasons unclear and unknown to man. In one sense that gap turns into a question mark that hovers over the painting. At the same time, the painting almost sadistically requires that viewers reimagine the grisly end of Franklin and his relatively large (one-hundred-plus) team of explorers from evidence that had only recently come to light. As one of the polar bears rips the tattered remnants of a royal ensign still clinging to the mast, human ribcages in full view, a broken telescope near the left bear symbolizes the explorers' tragic ambitions. At the same time, for Landseer, as for

Figure 16. Sir John Landseer, *Man Proposes, God Disposes,* oil on canvas, 1864.
© The Royal Holloway Collection, London.

the viewer, it isn't easy to explain why God would decide to "dispose" of explorers and scientists in such a gruesome way.

Rather than finding grim reassurance in the belief that God had somehow authorized such cruelty, other writers and painters found such tormenting dilemmas led to bafflement, shock, and unbelief. In 1882, criticizing the way that Christians worship God, a "madman" in one of Friedrich Nietzsche's books famously declares, "God is dead! . . . We are all his murderers." A generation of writers—stunned by that assertion—then tried to grapple with its terrifying implications. As the madman asks with piercing eyes and haunting diction, "How were we able to drink up the sea? Who gave us the sponge to wipe away the entire horizon?"[35]

One could view such remarkable questions, mad or sane, as a way of releasing humanity from a constraining, outdated mythology and thus as paving the way for atheistic existentialism. Or such pronouncements could seem, as Carlyle had written of materialism half a century earlier, a gratuitous form of "Downpulling," where the desire to demythologize the gods leaves a bare, denuded universe "void of Life, of Purpose, of Volition, even of Hostility."[36] To still others, the death or disappearance of God left humanity without an agent capable of releasing it from guilt. Full and absolute atonement therefore felt impossible.

To Nietzsche, certainly, monotheistic premises were no longer viable. Still, as the infamous passage in his *Gay Science* makes clear, even in its various translations, he did not view the results naively. Quite the contrary. To him—as to his "mad" character—the violent act returned Christians to the same existential dilemmas that their religion had seemed to eclipse: "God is dead! God remains dead! And we have killed him! How can we console ourselves, the murderers of all murderers? The holiest and the mightiest thing the world has ever possessed has bled to death under our knives: who will wipe this blood from us? With what water could we clean ourselves? What festivals of atonement, what holy games will we have to invent for ourselves?"[37] The death of God puts humanity in a desperate bind, Nietzsche's madman cries, leaving it without even the illusion of a beneficent presence to forgive it its crimes and failings. In what, thereafter, could humanity put its trust, its longing for comfort, and its need for redemption? As Nietzsche's Zarathustra stressed but one year later, *"All Gods are dead: now we want the Superman to live."*[38]

While Hopkins was far from drawing such conclusions, he was not alone among British poets in asking similar agonized questions about solace and redemption. In Matthew Arnold's famous lyric "Dover Beach," published in 1867 but drafted perhaps as early as 1851, the "Sea of Faith" is presented as sounding a "long, withdrawing roar."[39] It is no longer "full," the speaker laments, "like the folds of a bright girdle furl'd" around the world, apparently protecting it from harm. With the fabric removed and the tide far out, there's neither "certitude, nor peace, nor help for pain." Just the "turbid ebb and flow / Of human misery."

It is a bleak prospect carrying shades of melodrama, one of Arnold's poetic weaknesses. Indeed, in his earlier poem *Empedocles on Etna,* composed in 1852, Arnold had tackled that religious uncertainty head-on, with results so morose that he decided not to publish them. His lengthy elegy describes the pre-Socratic philosopher's distress as he circles Mount Etna, Sicily's volcano, uncertain whether God exists. Eventually he leaps to his death, finally convinced that there is no God. Although over the top, the poem looks intelligently at the way classical humanity used the gods to help explain uncertainty and calamity:

> Loath to suffer mute,
> We, peopling the void air,
> Make Gods to whom to impute
> The ills we ought to bear;
> With God and Fate to rail at, suffering easily.[40]

With a flavor of Feuerbach's even earlier argument that humanity fashions God into an extension of its demand for recognition and love, Arnold's Empedocles tries to adopt the stoical position that one should endure such ills rather than try to impute them to a metaphysical force. In his view, though, that is more an ideal than a realistic goal. For he anticipates how bereft humanity will feel without a force to guide and forgive it:

> We shall be the strangers of the world,
> And they [mind and thought] will be our lords, as they are now;
> And keep us prisoners of our consciousness,
> And never let us clasp and feel the All
> But through their forms, and modes, and stifling veils.
> And we shall be unsatisfied as now,
> And we shall feel the agony of thirst,
> The ineffable longing for the life of life
> Baffled for ever[.]

All those "we shalls" might begin to sound almost biblically prophetic, yet the passage and poem end in confusion and torment. With the promise of revelation dismissed as mythology, humanity must look to itself for meaning and direction or risk floundering with its failing gods.

Some of the articles on doubt that appeared in the 1860s on both sides of the Atlantic expressed similar fears, including, as one might expect, the risk and spread of godlessness. In his 1864–65 lectures to the Young Men's Christian Association, R. W. Dale argued that Christians could transition "from doubt to faith," in ways that would only strengthen belief.[41] W. S. Balch went further, lamenting the widespread "Doubt and Unbelief, the opposition and indifference that prevail in Christendom at the present time." He fumed: "That men will doubt where they do not understand, is not surprising, . . . But that they will oppose and condemn what is actually and only good is past comprehension."[42]

Articles advising "how to talk with doubters" soon jostled with others explaining "how to deal with doubt and doubters," and a third group even listing remedies for "the treatment of [religious] doubts." These included: "1. *Enter into sympathy with the experience produced by doubt; . . . 3. Show him the source of his doubt, and lovingly point out its folly; . . . and 6. Persist with the doubter as long as your presence is entirely welcome.*"[43] The order of advice wasn't quite on a par with the insights of Arnold, Nietzsche, and Hopkins.

The article "How to Deal with Doubt and Doubters" was more judgmental than sympathetic. It called doubt "the mildew of all spiritual blight and failure," even as it recognized, in italics, that "*some doubt is incurable,*" even "*inevitable.*" Only the "Holy Spirit" and "*faithful teaching*" can "conquer [the] perversity," the writer admonished; "the radical cause of doubt is spiritual blindness and deadness and perverseness."[44]

Although these and many other Christians fought a rearguard action, other commentators (some still devout) tried to draw out the value of "intellectual doubt," so rejoining religious uncertainty to the previous century's philosophical skepticism. They argued that doubt was now a "discipline in religion," and not merely a "common mind-trouble" but a widespread sign of "mental uncertainty."[45] Others, seeking common ground between religion and science, argued for the inherent "value of doubt." As an editorial in the *Outlook* explained, doubt "promotes inquiry, condemns credulity, forbids unquestioning faith, [and] builds on individual investigation and rational judgment." Where "the scientific spirit commends doubt . . . ," the editors hastened to add, "so does the Christian spirit." It was "the ecclesiastical spirit," in their view, that "condemns doubt, forbids inquiry, commends credulity, demands unquestioning faith, [and] builds on the authority of tradition."[46]

As a result of such distinctions, the gulf that had arisen between Christianity and evolution did not strike everyone as inevitable. In 1889, the Oxford chaplain, canon, and tutor Aubrey Lackington Moore published a volume called *Science and the Faith* that tried to reconcile Christianity to Darwinism by arguing that they were not actually in conflict. Natural selection was one of the ways that God worked, the Christian Darwinist asserted. "Panic fear of new theories" was therefore "as unreasonable as the attempt to base the eternal truth of religion on what may eventually prove to be a transient phase of scientific belief."[47] Moore's claims for religion's "eternal truth" obviously sidestepped Christianity's complex history, including its many sectarian splits, which hardly pointed to "eternal" truths. Nevertheless, a 2009 exhibit at the Yale Divinity School Library on transatlantic Christian Responses to Darwin called Moore "the clergyman who more than any other man was responsible for breaking down the antagonisms toward evolution then widely felt in the English Church."[48] *Science and the Faith* kindled enough interest for Moore the following year to bring out a companion volume, *Essays Scientific and Philosophical,* which included a follow-up essay on Darwinism.[49]

With other devout intellectuals such as the Harvard botanist Asa Gray, an Evangelical Calvinist, trying to reconcile evolution and Christianity; the Scottish evangelist Henry Drummond pursuing the same outcome; and the English Conservative philosopher A. J. Balfour, later prime minister of Britain (1902–5), defending Christianity from the empiricist theories of science that Darwinism had strengthened, a noticeable split had formed between Christians drawn to progressive, scientific debate and those who felt that religion must at all costs oppose science (and evolutionary theory, in particular).[50] While for instance Josiah Keep voiced grave "doubts concerning evolution" (among them, that the theory "seems to conflict with our ordinary ideas of nature, and to be contrary to what is going on in the world at the present time"),[51] commentators drawn to doubt's "value," "balance," and inevitability tried to recast the question, to let it encompass broader interest in the nature and function of religious belief.[52] Why, they wondered, do we so badly need to believe? And what does religious faith answer to? Is it a prompt from God or something ardent within us that wants, above all, to have answers to why we are here and what our lives are for?

With the stakes so high for Christianity and secularism, there is little wonder that this surge in interest took place, over not only religious doubt and philosophical skepticism but also from a general sense of uncertainty and apprehension about the future. As the American author and clergyman Henry van Dyke explained in his *Gospel for an Age of Doubt* (1896), "In calling the present 'an age of doubt,' I do not mean that it is the only age in which doubt has been prevalent, nor that doubt is the only characteristic of the age. I mean simply that it is one of those periods of human history in which the sudden expansion of knowledge and the breaking-up of ancient moulds of thought have produced a profound and widespread feeling of uncertainty in regard to the subject of religion."[53]

Among the first of the century's essays on uncertainty, as a phenomenon in itself, was Laman Blanchard's brief sketch in the *New Monthly Magazine*, where he called "the present time" one in which "it is absolutely impossible to make sure of anything."[54] Because we live in such a "state of incertitude and want of fixed principle," he fretted, sounding eerily contemporary, "the only things we can make sure of are doubts."[55] Blanchard's article is a list of grievances and peeves, including bad theater and poor manners. Yet in his almost morbid preoccupation with railroad accidents and steamboat collisions, he managed to draw attention to forms of randomness and chaos that couldn't easily be folded into the idea that "God moves in a mysterious way," a biblical claim to which the Romantic poet William Cowper, despite his own pervasive religious doubt, had penned a well-known hymn.[56]

Long before Albert Einstein became a household name for his more narrowly defined "relativity principle" from 1905 and Werner Heisenberg in 1927 devised his celebrated uncertainty principle in Niels Bohr's institute at Copenhagen,[57] arguments about life's chaos and randomness received a full philosophical airing in the second half of the nineteenth century.[58] They did so, Christopher Herbert stresses in *Victorian Relativity*, largely as ethical assessments of what uncertainty, religious and otherwise, could mean for humankind.[59]

Rather than being nihilistic in pairing relativity with agnosticism, for instance, Herbert Spencer argued positively that religion, science, and many other disciplines should grapple with "the Unknowable," a blind spot in human understanding that faith had once seemed to fill.[60] One couldn't dismiss the category, he advised, as just an outgrowth of religious mythology. To do so was to fall into a new trap (a different kind of absolutism), which saw everything as driven or explained by material factors. The Unknowable remained, for science as for religion, a quandary and thus a reminder of what Spencer said is "utterly inscrutable" to us (*FP*, 84). In their different ways, he thought, religion and science implicitly concede that human understanding is built on "relative" knowledge. They also imply quite strongly that such gaps in understanding will remain.

Spencer was not naive in imagining a simple truce between religion and science on these terms. He recognized that Christianity (like other religions) chafed against the idea that uncertainty extended beyond man, to encompass also the existence of God. That is where hope of reconciliation with science tended to break down. As he put it, doubtless overstating the point, "Religion secretly fears that all things may some day be explained; and thus itself betrays a lurking doubt whether that Incomprehensible Cause of which it is conscious, is really incomprehensible" (*FP*, 87). In short, what Spencer called the Unknowable might not, he asserted, be *permanently* so. He thought that was worth acknowledging at the outset, to avoid building faith on false certainties.

Spencer was a powerful presence in British academia in the 1860s and 1870s, far more so than today, because he managed to turn evolution into a progressive theory of development in fields as diverse as biology, politics, and sociology. His model of agnosticism as a type of "negative Absolute" also led to a wealth of articles on the topic, in such journals as the *Fortnightly Review, Westminster Review,* and *Spectator,* as well as in a number of newer journals devoted entirely to the topic: the monthly *Agnostic,* for instance, the *Agnostic Annual,* and the *Secular Review: A Journal of Agnosticism.*[61] Soon forums and debates on agnosticism were springing up everywhere, with participants including physicist John Tyndall and mathematician-philosopher William Clifford, as well as school teacher Frederick James Gould, author of the pamphlet *Stepping-Stones to Agnosticism* (1890) and the mediocre novel *The Agnostic Island* (1891), concerning a settlement of doubters in New Guinea and the missionaries who visit them.[62] Dissident secularists also found agnosticism a good way to promote their ideas and respectability. As one might predict, much ink was also shed on the parsing of intricate differences, such as "temporal" and "permanent" agnosticism, and where the line should fall between "pragmatic" agnosticism and the contradictory sounding "agnostic theism."[63] After all, the term *agnosticism* contains many shades of gray; it includes subtleties that religious doubt made it seem necessary to air, not smother.

But even as Spencer's form of agnosticism set the terms of debate, the silence of his friend Thomas Huxley—the multitalented skeptic, champion of Darwinism, and advocate for intensifying scientific criticism of religion—grew louder and more pregnant with meaning. In his rigorous debunking of Gnosticism—diverse ancient belief systems that, according to Huxley, represented themselves as "more or less successfully solving the problem of existence"—Huxley had coined the adjective "agnostic" in 1869.[64] Yet he did surprisingly little over the next two decades to promote the term. Stranger still, he resisted claiming even modest proprietorship over it.

For the last decade of his life, it transpires, Huxley was quietly fuming that his friend had taken most of the glory for promoting the term *agnostic.* The issue was not simply one of professional jealousy. Originally, Huxley had inflected the term to mean "*against* Gnosticism" rather than, say, "without Gnosticism" or "awaiting Gnosticism." In Huxley's eyes, then, Spencer had pushed the concept onto terrain that he—the term's originator—had never intended. Their intellectual differences turned out to be quite significant.

Huxley explicitly opposed the idea that agnosticism could serve as even a placeholder creed or religious philosophy. Rather than finding common ground with religion, he explained, "in my judgment agnosticism can be said to be a stage in its evolution, only as death may be said to be the final stage in the evolution of life."[65]

Huxley was also emphatic that Christianity and other forms of Gnosticism had not solved the problem of existence and were not likely to do so. As he told the clergyman-novelist Charles Kingsley in September 1860, "I neither deny nor affirm the immortality of man. I see no reason for believing in it, but, on the other hand, I have no means of disproving it."[66] Later statements reveal that Huxley had what he called "a pretty strong conviction that the problem [of existence] was insoluble."[67]

To Huxley, then, Spencer's agnosticism was not only fuzzy, it was also a form of latent religiosity. As he eventually explained, the so-called Unknowable was, as a concept, "merely the Absolute [revived], a sort of ghost of an extinct philosophy, the name of a negation hocus-pocused into a sham thing."[68] Spencer had succumbed to reverse idolatry, his erstwhile friend lamented, in worshipping a negative abstraction, whereas the "one object of the Agnostic (in the true sense)," Huxley insisted (by which he meant in his sense), "is to knock this tendency on the head whenever or wherever it shows itself."[69] "In violating the very essence of agnosticism, Huxley implied, Spencer was not really a true agnostic."[70]

It may seem paradoxical to be firm, even dogmatic, about agnosticism, but Huxley did have a point about Spencer's interest in the Absolute. From Huxley's point of view, Spencer was failing to give doubt enough importance to influence his thinking and philosophy. He was also being weak on religion, when Huxley wanted to address some of its worst social effects: "People who talk about the comforts of belief appear to forget its discomforts," he declared, including "the harm done to the citizen by the . . . uncharitableness of sectarian bigotry; . . . by the spirit of exclusiveness and domination of those that count themselves pillars of orthodoxy; . . . by the restraints on the freedom of learning and teaching which the Church exercises, when it is strong enough; . . . [and] by the introspective hunting after sins," to say nothing of "the fear of theological error, and the overpowering terror of damnation, which have accompanied the Churches like their shadow."[71]

Considering his differences with Spencer, why did Huxley not do more to intervene in use of the term *agnostic?* Why, too, was his strategy for promoting the concept so lackluster, given its growing importance to scientific, philosophical, and theological debate? "Perhaps I have done wrongly in letting the thing slide so long," he later acknowledged weakly in 1889, "but I was anxious to avoid a breach with an old friend."[72] He had "wanted to present a united front," Bernard Lightman argues, "until 1889 when he was in the middle of an acrimonious quarrel with Spencer."[73]

Huxley's reticence was probably strategic, too, in taking a wait-and-see approach to how the term fared. "In effect, Huxley dropped his emphasis on agnosticism until he was attacked by Balfour in *The Foundations of Belief* and [was] forced to defend his neologism."[74] That sounds uncharacteristically reserved for "Darwin's bulldog," the man who, almost thirty years earlier, had come close to accusing the bishop of Oxford of prostituting the truth. But fighting many other battles, including with science and religion, Huxley seems to have thought it best to conserve his energy and hold his tongue for as long as he could.

Leslie Stephen was a lot more forthcoming than Huxley. The year after he legally renounced holy orders as a priest and deacon in 1875, he published in the *Fortnightly Review* an essay called "An Agnostic's Apology," with "apology" meaning "justification" or "formal defense," rather than expression of regret. By turns accusatory, even sarcastic, the essay was the first on agnosticism to appear by someone who not only applied the term to himself but also upheld its value against what he saw as the bankruptcy of Church doctrine. Despite some awkward phrasing, the essay remains a bracing, controversial read.

Today Stephen is perhaps best known for fathering Virginia Woolf and the Bloomsbury painter Vanessa Bell. But he was also the first editor of the *Dictionary of National Biography*, with twenty-one volumes to his credit, and author of *The History of English Thought in the Eighteenth Century* (1876) and *The Science of Ethics* (1882), only the second book to establish an ethical system modified to fit Darwin's theory of evolution.[75] As editor of the *Cornhill Magazine* from 1871 on, moreover, Stephen played a key role in advancing the careers of undiscovered talents such as Thomas Hardy, Robert Louis Stevenson, and Henry James.

Stephen was the son of Sir James Stephen, a leading Evangelical and a distinguished undersecretary of state in London's Colonial Office. Like the Reverend Patrick Brontë, father of the famous sisters and less famous brother, Sir James belonged to the Clapham Sect, a group of mostly Wesleyan social reformers. Partly because of this devout background, but also because of his own faith and the necessity of university dons taking orders, Leslie Stephen became an Anglican clergyman at Cambridge. He took a step further than James Anthony Froude, that is, in progressing from deacon to priest in 1859.

Within three years Stephen had stopped conducting services. Having read widely in philosophy and taken the words of Hume, Bentham, and

Mill very much to heart, he was beset by nagging doubt and losing his faith. A picture that he later gave of like-minded colleagues reveals differing opinions on how to cope with such doubt but also growing recognition of its seriousness and impact:

> The average Cambridge don of my day was (as I thought and think) a sensible and honest man who wished to be both rational and Christian. He was rational enough to see that the old orthodox position was untenable. He did not believe in Hell, or in "verbal inspiration" or the "real presence." He thought that the controversies on such matters were silly and antiquated, and spoke of them with indifference, if not with contempt. But he also thought that religious belief of some kind was necessary or valuable, and considered himself to be a genuine believer. He assumed that somehow the old dogmas could be explained away or "rationalized" or "spiritualised." . . . He shut his eyes to the great difficulties and took the answer for granted.[76]

Stephen, however, could neither "shut his eyes" to such problems nor take rote answers for granted. After leaving the university and traveling to America, where he befriended Oliver Wendell Holmes and James Russell Lowell, he returned to London to work as a journalist and editor.

He waited another decade before solemnly renouncing his holy orders in the spring of 1875. Even so, the occasion was tinged with drama and despair. Virginia Woolf recalled testimony from friends who feared that her wretched father would take his own life: his "state of mind was such that [Henry] Fawcett [his close friend] entertained serious fears that he might cut his throat during the night."[77]

Earlier on that evening of renunciation, Stephen had asked Thomas Hardy to call on him, no matter how late the hour. After climbing the stairs to his friend's study, Hardy found Stephen pacing back and forth, highly agitated. His biographer writes, "The dressing-gown which Stephen was wearing over his clothes accentuated his height so that he looked like a seer in robes as he passed in and out of the shadows, the lamp illuminating his prophetic face each time he passed the table. On it there lay a document."[78]

It was Stephen's intent to renounce his holy orders: he had called Hardy to be his witness. As A. N. Wilson notes, "This was years before Hardy wrote *Jude the Obscure* or 'God's Funeral,'" two major late-Victorian statements on religious doubt and religious power, "yet, of all Stephen's acquaintance, which must have included many of the more eminent agnostics of the day, Hardy was chosen, surely aptly, to be the witness for the final severing of his links with the Church."[79]

"An Agnostic's Apology" appeared the following summer (June 1876), shortly after Stephen's first wife, Harriet Marian, had died, and the essay may capture some of his anger at no longer feeling consolation in traditional Christian belief. However, "Apology" was also a powerful indictment of the limits of faith and doctrine. "Man knows nothing of the Infinite and Absolute," Stephen insisted, silently adopting Huxley's position. "Knowing nothing," then, man "had better not be dogmatic about his ignorance."[80] It was, in hindsight, a reasonable line to take. But Stephen did not stop there; he ended with a parting shot that betrayed his anger at those likely to attack his position: "Whilst you trumpet forth officially your contempt for our scepticism," he asserted, "we will at least try to believe that you are imposed upon by your own bluster" ("AA," 860).

The main body of Stephen's analysis is calmer and more persuasive. "There is no certainty" is one of his key premises ("AA," 847). And rather than accept that difficult truth, humanity, he said, has either wrestled with doubts or tried to cast them away: "Every doubt which we entertained about the universe is transferred to the God upon whom the universe is moulded" (848). According to Stephen, then, religion does not resolve our questions about the meaning and purpose of life; it tries instead to make doctrine bring an end to inquiry. Unanswered questions persist, however, and redound punitively on those presumptuous enough to ask them: "One insoluble doubt has haunted men's minds since thought began in the world. . . . One school of philosophers hands it to the next. It is denied in one form only to reappear in another. The question is not which system excludes the doubt, but how it expresses the doubt" (859).

To Stephen, now veering more toward Spencer's line, religious agnosticism captures a hunger for answers that the Church either will not or cannot satisfy: "We wish for spiritual food, and are to be put off with these ancient mummeries of forgotten dogma. If Agnosticism is the frame of mind which summarily rejects these imbecilities, and would restrain the human intellect from wasting its powers on the attempt to galvanise into sham activity this [corpse] of old theology, nobody need be afraid of the name" ("AA," 842–43). The agnostic's doubt should not be "condemned," he concluded, when he or she merely "asserts—what no one denies—that there are limits to the sphere of human intelligence" (841, 840).

Stephen used his anguish over renouncing holy orders to develop almost a manifesto for religious doubt. Like many other late Victorians undergoing a similar crisis, he applied varieties of philosophical skepticism to test whether religious faith and belief were sound. The debates that played out in the popular press and scholarly journals grew intricate and wide-ranging. They focused not simply on Spencer's *First Principles* and Darwin's *Autobiography*, which appeared in 1887, but also on Balfour's *Defence of Philosophic Doubt* (1879), which used doubt to attack science and unbelief, and, later, such works as William James' more nuanced psychological focus in *The Will to Believe* (1897).[81]

No simple consensus emerged from these works and papers, and it would be misleading to suggest otherwise. The varieties of doubt that circulated then soon rivaled in number and complexity the beliefs to which they responded. But interest began to center strongly on "the duty to doubt," "the ethics of doubt," and "the idealistic remedy for religious doubt."[82] Skepticism was no longer heresy; it was the sign increasingly of an open, questioning mind. And doubt was no longer anathema; to many, it was not just a personal lifeline but a means of clearing space for responsible unbelief.

In a further sign of the cultural shift, voters in Northampton in 1880 elected Charles Bradlaugh, an avowed atheist, to be their member of Parliament. His election presented the country with a serious constitutional crisis because British politicians were still obliged to "take an oath upon the faith of a Christian."[83] In refusing to compromise, Bradlaugh was prevented from taking his seat in the House of Commons. Yet voters in his district continued to return him, partly because he was an excellent champion of working men.[84] Six years' debate on the topic ensued, during which Bradlaugh's atheism was widely discussed. In 1886, the House of Commons finally relented and allowed him to take his seat. By that point, responsible unbelief had become part of a national conversation, and atheism had come to seem almost naturally aligned with liberty and ethics.

The phrase "idealistic remedy for religious doubt" was, for instance, applied in 1892 to the work of Oxford philosopher Thomas Hill Green, better known to his readers as T. H. Green, who "stressed the ethical meaning of Christianity and pleaded for a more liberal interpretation of Scripture."[85] In doing so he positioned himself with the contributors to *Essays and Reviews.* Like many of them, he believed that Christianity could "constitute . . . a new intellectual consciousness" that would help humanity forge a new moral life.[86]

Green was a significant influence on the novelist Mrs. Humphry Ward, Matthew Arnold's niece and the author of the runaway best-seller about a clergyman whose loss of faith generates a personal crisis comparable in scale and intensity to Leslie Stephen's. The novel, *Robert Elsmere* (1888), took off almost overnight, becoming a sensation on both sides of the Atlantic, with readers such as Walter Pater calling it a masterpiece.[87] For readers today it might seem ponderous and overly schematic, partly because its characters tend to speechify about faith and obsess about the gains and losses of various philosophical schools—positivism, aestheticism, agnosticism, and idealism. Still, the novel is firm in giving greatest credence to idealism. As Elsmere finally urges, in the spirit of Green, "*To reconceive the Christ! It is the special task of our age!*"[88]

Robert Elsmere was one of dozens of novels to appear in the second half of the century, many of them following near-identical plots: A clergyman loses his faith, to the consternation of parishioners, wife, and himself, before finding comfort in a secular alternative better fitting his temperament and beliefs. The secular alternative marks a shift in emphasis from Froude's *Nemesis of Faith*, signaling a growing number of options for disillusioned clergymen and a more charitable response to their plight. And the sheer number of such novels helps to convey that "reconceiv[ing] the Christ" and similar statements had become a cultural mantra. To Arnold it was a process of redefinition: "The thing is, to recast religion."[89] To John Morley, in his book *On Compromise*, published one year later, the task awaiting intellectuals was the need to establish almost a new religion, devoid of dogma but very much reliant on revived models of faith: "Both dogma and church must be slowly replaced by higher forms of faith."[90]

In his study of Victorian doubt, Lance St. John Butler observes that the poets, novelists, and intellectuals of the period were busy creating "a discourse that simultaneously relied on religion, and undermined it."[91] The paradox was everywhere apparent, as writers, harnessing skepticism about Christian dogma, tried to mold it to fit principles that were more appealing to them. Morley put it this way: "Whatever form may be ultimately imposed on our vague religious aspirations by some prophet to come, who shall unite sublime depth of feeling and lofty purity of life with strong intellectual grasp and the gift of a noble eloquence, we may at least be sure of this: that it will stand as closely related to Christianity as Christianity stood closely related to the old Judaic dispensation."[92] The idea that doubt was inherently godless and heretical was rapidly being supplanted by assurances that it was actually full of hope, insight, and (mostly secular) faith, and just awaiting a plausible place to house all three. For that reason, Morley's analogy focused on the "minor differences" among faiths: "The modern denier, if he . . . entertains hopes of a creed to come," is similar "to the position of the Christianising Jew," in the sense of being between faiths, without quite belonging to any.[93]

The arguments about secularism by Morley, Arnold, and others were often necessarily vague. They come across today as full of ardor for the hope that culture will save us from ourselves and thus be the element in which we will find lasting redemption. It is a hope that is easy to belittle, though faith in culture would seem to increase in importance when religion plays a diminished social role. Not surprisingly, the arguments were sprinkled with Christian terms and rhetoric: "The myth of height (alternative version of the myth of depth)" was, Butler writes, "hard at work: 'aspirations,' 'sublime,' 'lofty,' 'higher forms' (even 'evolution') are all Christian notions with a penumbra of connotations acceptable to non-Christians."[94] The nation still needed prophets, secular or otherwise.

George Frederic Watts' painting *Hope* (1885) is but one symbolist rendition of that anxious awaiting. In this striking allegorical work—one of several (such as *Life and Love*) that Watts intended to form part of an epic symbolic cycle called the "House of Life"—a blindfolded figure sits astride a globe, plucking a harp and listening attentively to the sound.

In Watts' painting, there is only one string left to pull; all the others have frayed or disappeared. He also chose to alter convention by giving Hope (not Justice) a blindfold, perhaps less to indicate impartiality than ignorance of the future. The painting conveys some of Watts' religiosity, for his "Hope" echoes earlier depictions of women and globes. (The most obvious and controversial of these, Ludovico Cigoli's *Assumption of the Virgin* [1586–87], had painted the Virgin Mary standing on a cratered moon.)[95] Yet Watts' depiction of "Hope" is ultimately secular. Though his work is clearly informed by a long tradition of religious art, his painting opts for symbolism, replacing Mary with a vulnerable, solitary figure whose understanding and knowledge seem altogether mortal.

As the title of Watts' painting conveys, however, Hope does not give up. Absorbed in her music-making, she waits, ardently, for something better. (For Christianity, after all, she represents one of the three theological virtues, with Faith and Love.) The questions relative to the painting are whether the globe that she sits astride should be viewed as Earth (Watts'

Figure 17. George Frederic Watts with associates, *Hope,* oil on canvas, 1885. © The Tate Gallery, London.

globe is lacking in geographical detail) and how long that final string will last before her music becomes impossible to make or hear.

As the years wore on, the horror and suggestion of sin that religious doubt once posed in Britain largely receded. It was mostly eclipsed by discussion of whether secular culture could take the place of religion (and if so, how). That discussion neither ruled out nor ignored a brief religious revival in the 1890s that was partly due to symbolist and aestheticist interest in religion as a system of signs and symbols. However, as Bernard Lightman observes, "Agnosticism as a 'creed' died with Leslie Stephen, in 1904, while the power of agnostic assumptions lived on in the early twentieth century in various forms, sometimes appearing in humanist philosophies, at other times in the shape of positivism or secularism."[96]

In the United States, by contrast, unbelief was comparatively weaker. Although the nation generated its own humanist associations and free-thinking journals, and major tracts on agnosticism eventually appeared on both sides of the Atlantic, the type of conversation—or confrontation—that Britain had experienced and survived was fiercely resisted in many parts of the country. As Alexis de Tocqueville wrote presciently in 1840, addressing the "indirect influence of religious beliefs upon political society in the United States": "America is still the place where the Christian religion has kept the greatest real power over men's souls."[97]

Nevertheless, owing to Asa Gray's and others' earnest attempts to reconcile evolution and Christianity, some U.S. Christians (including, we'll see, a number of Evangelicals) eventually accepted evolution, even as others saw Darwinism as undermining all that they stood for.[98] Summing up the ensuing tension, Harvard professor and philosopher George Santayana declared in *Winds of Doctrine:* "The civilization characteristic of Christendom has not yet disappeared, yet another civilization has begun to take its place. We still understand the value of religious faith; . . . we may even feel an organic need for [it], cling to [it] tenaciously, and dream of rejuvenating [it]. On the other hand the shell of Christendom is broken."[99]

With the psychological price of that break very much in mind, some turned their interest to forms of self-doubt that bordered on pathology. In 1882, for instance, two articles appeared on what the French physician Jean-Pierre Falret had begun to call *la maladie du doute,* or "doubting sickness."[100] *Popular Science Monthly* in New York went on to label the malady "delusions of doubt," but the British magazine *Good Words* insisted, less dramatically, that it was more like "a very common mind-trouble."[101]

The author of the first of these articles, M. B. Bill, offered a sympathetic account of "an extremely curious form of mental alienation."[102] Interestingly, his examples endlessly return to the hazy border between self-doubt and religious doubt. "One patient, for example, will doubt everything, even his own existence, and will not be able to fix himself to any formal conviction" ("DD," 788). Another, "a young collegian," Bill continued, will suddenly be afflicted by an "absurd thought": "If thirteen was an unlucky number, it would be deplorable if God were thirteen, space thirteen, infinity thirteen, and eternity thirteen" (788). Later the man cannot stop himself from bursting out, "'God thirteen!' or else 'Infinity thirteen! Eternity thirteen!'" (789).

It is unclear whether Bill was describing the symptoms of a malady whose eruptions just happen to be tied to religion or whether anxiety about religious tenets drove most of his anxiety about the limits of faith. Bill was fairly confident that religion was merely the form taken by the patient's illness, and he may well have been right. Another of his patients suffered from a type of self-doubt that initially seemed independent of religion. Yet with "the shell of Christendom . . . broken," as Santayana put it, existential questions such as the ones voiced by this patient assumed more urgency than ever.[103]

Bill described the patient as "a young man of about twenty-eight years, of an agreeable and intellectual appearance and a fine physical development" ("DD," 789). "In the month of June, 1874," this man writes, a year before Leslie Stephen's ordeal, "I felt quite suddenly, without any pain or giddiness, a change in the aspect of my vision. Everything seemed to me strange and queer, although the same forms and colors were preserved."

The writer discovers a polyp, or abnormal tissue growth, in his left nostril and has it removed. Unsure whether the growth is an omen or an unrelated medical phenomenon, he says that he "thought the polyp . . . was the cause of the strange appearance of things presented to [him], and that, when it was taken away, [he] would be all right again" (789).

The young man continues: "But nothing of the kind came to pass. . . . No remarkable change occurred till December 1880, more than five years afterward, when I felt myself diminishing, and finally to disappear. Nothing was left of me but an empty body. From that time my personality has wholly vanished, and, in spite of all that I can do to get back that self that has escaped, I can not" ("DD," 789).

This statement is extraordinary, both in its level of self-awareness and in its capacity to convey deep anxiety about one's place in the world. The man is not sure what, if anything, will replace his body. All he seems to experience is a flood of concern and a set of questions that few experts, then or now, could begin to answer: "What am I? What are all these things that are made like me? Why am I? Who am I? I exist, but outside of real life, and in spite of myself" ("DD," 790).

"*Why* am I?" is perhaps the most remarkable of these queries, with religion offering an answer more confident and comforting than science perhaps ever could. But the man finds no solace in theology. He is in one sense suspended between two options, greater faith and firmer uncertainty, yet neither strikes him as possible or appealing.

Simple statistics do not exist for the numbers of people who fell ill owing in part to the gray area between self-doubt and religious doubt. There were, however, enough that psychologists and psychiatrists turned their attention to those who suffered such "delusions of doubt." As the articles above suggest, the experts tended to fold religious doubt, when it did surface, into a broader psychological category of pathological self-doubt.

In January 1890, for instance, the *American Journal of Psychology* published a lengthy, rather dry article on "The Insanity of Doubt," which argued: "In *folie du doute* the want of adjustment is perceived, but not realized;

it is apprehended, but not comprehended."[104] (Some today would view the symptoms as akin to obsessive-compulsive disorder.)[105] In the London-based *Good Words,* however, Dr. J. Mortimer Granville took a slightly different line: "A perpetual state of doubt as to small matters is one of the most distressing of common mind-troubles."[106] Quite intelligently, on this matter he invoked the need for "self-cure": "It is useless, and only exaggerates the trouble, to struggle directly against the impulse to remove a doubt and satisfy the mind. A pressing demand for evidence should be met by the smallest possible concession: but there must be some concession, or the worry, it may be agony, of doubt will ensue, and it is this feeling of uncertainty—not the means to relieve it—that does mental mischief. Better therefore yield than resist, but try to forget the matter as quickly as may be."[107]

Granville was describing the tiny details and rituals that preoccupy obsessive worriers and self-doubters. But he could also be said to have put his finger on some larger religious and metaphysical questions about evidence and proof, and how much of each we need before we can be satisfied.

For individuals still tending to the other extreme, by contrast, any sign of doubt, religious or otherwise, was worrisome. To Professor Jacob Cooper, writing later in the Lancaster, Pennsylvania–based *Reformed Church Review* in 1897, doubt was the sign less of a skeptical mind than of one lacking a childlike capacity to trust. In "Irrationality of Doubt," he declared, "Doubt is used [here] as a generic term, and comprehends all grades of unbelief from the lowest forms of arbitrary distrust to the highest as shown in agnosticism, which distinctly declares that nothing can be known and therefore nothing ought to be believed."[108]

It was something of a tendentious definition of agnosticism, which for Herbert Spencer and many others keeps uncertainty alive—and with it, of course, the possibility (though not the inevitability) of belief. But keeping uncertainty alive turns out to have been precisely Cooper's concern. "We are constantly told," he complained, "that Doubt is the only correct method of procedure in the march after truth" ("ID," 411). Yet doubt, the professor maintained, "is the direct reverse of the state of mind which is nature to man"

(413). The culprits who insist otherwise are a "great crop of philosophers of nescience, who, ignorant of their own paternity, call Hume their father." "In the world of chaos which they create," Cooper continued, "they show that knowledge is impossible, since the cosmos was not designed nor made" (413).

The skepticism that Hume advanced, at considerable personal cost, was not of course to make knowledge "impossible" but to uncouple knowledge from religious belief so that the two could stand on their own legs, to extend Cooper's metaphor. But mischaracterizations abound in Cooper's long essay, during which he calls doubt "a forbidden tree" ("ID," 415), as if the apple that Eve had been tempted to eat, in the Christian allegory, represented doubt rather than knowledge of good and evil. Cooper was also contemptuous of Tennyson's open solution to uncertainty: "So much is said in praise of 'Honest Doubt' and the thralldom of men's minds under hoary errors and superstitions, that we might be led to think the only rational course for the human mind is to believe nothing at all, and, as a consequence, do nothing" (411).

Cooper made several other rash claims for the Evangelical and Reformed Church, which also have not stood up well: "Doubt has no place in the investigation of any science," he insisted quite seriously ("ID," 410). Indeed, "to doubt, to disbelieve, or by whatever name we call that temper of mind which dominates the agnostic . . . has no place in the normal and healthy action of the intellect" (443).

That is one way to try to eliminate uncertainty—to rule it out of bounds, as unhealthy and abnormal. Still, as Dr. Granville insisted quite plausibly in *Good Words,* similar forms of doubt were in fact signs of a "very common mind-trouble" that would persist through two world wars, a Holocaust, and decades' more upheaval and man-made crises. The Victorians' religious doubt had helped make uncertainty a way of life. Yet although such uncertainty struck large numbers of writers and thinkers as an unavoidable consequence of releasing the culture from theology, for many Christians, especially in the United States, there was no way of curbing such open-endedness without leaning more heavily on religious fundamentals.

SIX

Faith-Based Certainty Meets the Gospel of Doubt

Two paragraphs into *Civilization and Its Discontents*, Freud's 1929 treatise on man's "unhappiness in culture," a dilemma surfaced. Having described how a recent book of his treated religious ideas "as an illusion"—indeed, as "fulfillments of the oldest, strongest and most urgent wishes of mankind"—Freud stopped almost dead in his tracks.[1] It was not that he failed to grasp the urgency of such wishes. A sense of their appeal simply was not in him.

When his friend Romain Rolland (author of several religious biographies and a later winner of the Nobel Prize for Literature) insisted that religion gave him a "sensation of 'eternity,' a feeling as of something limitless, unbounded," Freud was frankly puzzled (*CD*, 11). "I cannot discover this 'oceanic' feeling in myself," he wrote bluntly. "From my own experience, I could not convince myself of the primary nature of such a feeling. But this gives me no right to deny that it does in fact occur in other people." The matter, for Freud, boiled down to how we interpret such feelings. As he noted, "It is not easy to deal scientifically" with them (12).

He was certainly right on that score. Setting that matter aside for now, it is a surprising beginning to a now-famous argument about our "unhappiness" in modern society.[2] Having used religion to voice its deepest needs, humanity, Freud argued, found those needs sharply in conflict, at times irreconcilable. While the gods served as "cultural ideals" (*CD*, 38), they helped to solve riddles and settle doubts about the meaning and purpose of life, including the suffering it causes. But the idea that everyone must follow the same illusion—and that others should be converted to it—troubled Freud, who was quick to point out the price of unbelief for skeptics and doubters. "The impossibility of proving the truth of religious doctrines . . . has been felt at all times—undoubtedly, too, by the ancestors who bequeathed us this legacy. Many of them probably nourished the same doubts as ours, but the pressure imposed on them was too strong for them to have dared to utter them." "Since then," Freud concludes, meaning between antiquity and his own generation of Victorian doubters, "countless people have been tormented by similar doubts, and have striven to suppress them because they thought it was their duty to believe."[3]

In the years immediately preceding the Holocaust and the Stalinist gulags, before Freud himself had to flee Vienna for London—aged eighty-two—to escape Nazi persecution, he continued to call religion a man-made response to spiritual and anthropological needs.[4] According to Freud, we cannot divorce one from the other. The individual comfort that friends like Rolland draw from spiritual practices unites wider groups of people in a set of shared beliefs, which mark them as distinct from other groups drawn to different, often conflicting creeds. Antagonism predictably erupts over whose beliefs have greater force, cogency, or priority. As Freud noted with bitter sadness, his historical perspective greatly overdetermined by the surrounding anti-Semitic violence in Austria and Germany:

> The Jewish people, scattered everywhere, have rendered most useful services to the civilizations of the countries that have been their hosts; but unfortunately all the massacres of the Jews in the Mid-

dle Ages did not suffice to make that period more peaceful and secure for their Christian fellows. When once the Apostle Paul had
posited universal love between men as the foundation of his Christian community, extreme intolerance on the part of Christendom
towards those who remained outside it became the inevitable consequence. To the Romans, who had not founded their communal
life as a State upon love, religious intolerance was something foreign, although with them religion was a concern of the State and
the State was permeated by religion. Neither was it an unaccountable chance that the dream of a Germanic world-dominion called
for anti-semitism as its complement; and it is intelligible that the
attempt to establish a new, communist civilization in Russia
should find its psychological support in the persecution of the
bourgeois. One only wonders, with concern, what the Soviets will
do after they have wiped out their bourgeois. (*CD*, 61–62)

The passage is so well known to philosophy freshmen that it serves as a
textbook example of what Freud dubbed the "narcissism of minor differences" (*CD*, 61). The smallest discrepancies in perception and belief assume
outsized importance—are enough, indeed, to create sectarian splits within
all the major faiths. The outcome of those splits depends greatly on the
meaning we give them and the context in which they unfold, but anyone
who has studied recent history will note how quickly they can escalate, to
the point of apparently justifying the eradication of the opposing group
from the very face of the earth.

Freud's passage glosses the fate of many religious doubters, pariahs,
and minorities. Still, as Christopher Hitchens underlines with awful preci-
sion in his survey of religious conflict from Belfast, Belgrade, and Beirut to
Bethlehem, Baghdad, and Bombay, "just to stay within the letter 'B,'" the
fundamental truth of Freud's observation is hard to dispute.[5]

At the same time, that base-level disconnect between Freud and Rolland means that the two friends were still miles apart over the fundamen-

tal question of religious feeling—the sensation of "eternity"—that one of them insisted was real and the other assured him was not.

Whom we take to be right or off-base on that matter says a lot about how we'll react to broader cultural debates about the role that belief and faith should play in society today. To secularists, Freud's admission, "I cannot discover this 'oceanic' feeling in myself," may communicate insight, including into how belief works. To his many detractors, by contrast, including those drawn to Carl Jung's interest in mysticism, it conveys a personal limitation, and even (for orthodox believers) a moral deficiency.

When Jung was asked during a 1959 BBC interview if he believed in the existence of God, he replied a little differently: "I don't believe, I know."[6] The statement conveys such unshakable certainty and, by extension, so little self-doubt, that it seems to end discussion, making belief a bedrock for knowledge.

To Freud, however (and I think he was right here), there were risks, even dangers, in confusing one with the other. Indeed, his own life experience painfully confirmed it, with his daughter, Anna, detained for twelve hours of interrogation by the Gestapo and his four sisters murdered in Nazi concentration camps. His concerns about enmity and intolerance—within and over religion—proved to be tragically well founded. So, too, were his general anxieties about the historically fraught boundary between belief and hostility.

In the wealth of books to appear recently over these ongoing concerns, from *The God Delusion* to *God Is No Delusion,* from *The End of Faith* to *The Reason for God,* and from *Irreligion* to *Answering the New Atheism,* one topic recurs, even to the point of predictability: the wide chasm over how we perceive faith and doubt, including what we think both should mean and accomplish.[7] The chasm is, in a way, quite similar to the mental gulf separating Freud from Rolland. It also reenacts nineteenth-century debates over reason and faith.

The sense of mystery that Michael Novak relishes, for instance, in *No*

One Sees God (his account of the "dark night" that atheists and believers apparently share), is to Richard Dawkins a tiresome obfuscation, when it is not a dangerous "delusion." Novak wants to bring to our attention that both atheists and believers *can* spend "long years in the dark and windswept open spaces between unbelief and belief."[8] As Novak observes, both groups may also experience "the same 'dark night' in which God's presence seems absent, and the conflict between faith and doubt stems not from objective differences but from divergent attitudes toward the unknown."[9]

For Dawkins, by contrast, the aim of encircling belief with reason is to "eviscerate" religious faith, to help bring about its end.[10] Small wonder that Dawkins' approach enrages the devout: it looks to them like an all-out assault on their most cherished beliefs. And in many respects, it is. Numerous questions ensue: Which side permits criticism? Which, a tradition of questioning and doubt? Above all, whose criteria are right?

Dawkins insists that he distinguishes at bottom between the ordinarily "deluded" and the literalists that he once called "faith-heads." Still, one could be forgiven for missing such subtleties in his sweeping denunciations of religious belief, especially after he conflates religious moderates and extremists, and likens faith to a "celestial comfort blanket."[11] It is noticed less often that he reserves particular scorn for agnostics—oddly, even those like Thomas Huxley, "Darwin's bulldog," for stopping a fraction shy of the certainties that Dawkins professes.

To be sure, Dawkins lets a "robust Muscular Christian" preacher from his schooldays condemn agnostics as "namby-pamby, mushy pap, weak-tea, weedy, pallid fence-sitters" before he chimes in: "He was partly right, but for wholly the wrong reason" (*GD*, 46). Still, the term *pap* comes to characterize, for Dawkins, "a deeply inescapable kind of fence-sitting, which I shall call PAP (Permanent Agnosticism in Principle)" (47). So it is not, he writes, a complete accident that the acronym echoes his schoolmaster's ridicule.

"Agnosticism, of a kind, is an appropriate stance on many scientific questions," Dawkins concedes, but in his estimation it is not the right stance to adopt over minor, apparently easily settled matters such as whether God exists (*GD*, 47). "Agnosticism about the existence of God belongs firmly in the temporary or TAP category," he states categorically. Case apparently closed. "Either he exists or he doesn't. It is a scientific question" (48).

So that little conundrum is settled, after all! Concerning Huxley, Dawkins is a fraction more hesitant: "One doesn't criticize T. H. Huxley lightly. But . . . in his concentration upon the absolute impossibility of proving or disproving [the existence of] God, [he] seems to have been ignoring the shading of *probability*. The fact that we can neither prove nor disprove the existence of something does not put existence and non-existence on an even footing" (*GD*, 49). True. But how one establishes consensus there depends greatly on whom one asks in the first place. "Contrary to Huxley," Dawkins continues, "I shall suggest that the existence of God is a scientific hypothesis like any other" (50).

So that minor quandary is settled, too!

Huxley believed that science and religion belong to different realms, an idea that Stephen Jay Gould more recently dubbed a matter of "non-overlapping magisteria": religion is aligned with emotion and feeling, and science tied to facts.[12] But Dawkins replaces what he calls Huxley's "agnostic faith"—the insistence that these fundamentals likely will *never* be answered—with the proposition that they *could* be settled by scientific discovery, though we cannot yet say when. This is, in one respect, where scientific speculation and religious faith share *some* common ground, though Dawkins would never call his expectation a kind of faith. Still, Huxley's firm open-endedness, even as it put the burden of proof on religion, troubles Dawkins. "Why there almost certainly is no God" is his preferred statement, though he cannot quite give up that "almost" (*GD*, 111). Yet he quotes Huxley's famous statement in "Agnosticism" (1889): "I was quite sure I had *not* [solved the problem of existence], and had a pretty strong conviction that the problem was insoluble."[13]

The difference comes down to the gap between Dawkins' "almost certainly" no God and Huxley's "pretty strong conviction" that the problem of existence is insoluble. It isn't quite an example of the "narcissism of minor differences," since a philosopher could still drive a truck between those statements, but it doesn't seem to warrant the breezy dismissal that Dawkins ultimately gives it: "I am agnostic only to the extent that I am agnostic about fairies at the bottom of the garden" (*GD*, 51).

To invoke only John Humphrys' fascinating book *In God We Doubt: Confessions of a Failed Atheist* (which he or his publisher decided to retitle for American audiences as *Confessions of an Angry Agnostic,* as if these things had to be ramped up in the United States before anyone would listen), there is plenty about secular materialism that leaves many people cold and unsatisfied.[14] Indeed, one rather hefty consequence faces those who wrestle with the limits of secularism: Are materialist explanations for the world enough to satisfy, including those longing for a sacred reality?[15] At some point, it needs to be asked whether secularism fails to answer a fundamental need in many for a purpose and reality that surpasses human comprehension.

When the debates become so heated, polarized, and trivialized that pressing ontological matters are likened to belief in "fairies at the bottom of the garden," and even agnosticism is cast as weak-kneed evasion, there's a clear whiff of hubris and hyperbole in the air. As Chris Lehmann noted in *Reason Magazine* of the "new atheists" and their critics, "Each side retreats to its corner, more convinced than ever that the other is trafficking in pure, self-infatuated delusion for the basest of reasons: Believers accuse skeptics and unbelievers of thoughtless hedonism and nihilism; the secular set accuses the believoisie of superstition and antiscientific senselessness."[16]

Dawkins' contempt for agnosticism is in one sense surprising, as doubt tempers extremism, religious and otherwise, while "healthy agnosticism," Bernard Lightman reminds us, "actively questions everything, including itself."[17] For that reason, nineteenth-century agnosticism amounted to neither fence-sitting nor "mushy pap" but a stance advancing a plain and laudable admission: "I don't know." Indeed, "I probably won't ever know." It makes doubt integral to one's position. And in doing so it assumes a level of neutrality in the faith wars that leaves people with the option to change their minds—which seems to be part of what irks absolutists on either side. As Bill Maher puts it in *Religulous,* his light-hearted but probing 2008 film about faith, as he debates a handful of truckers in a North Carolina chapel over whether eternal salvation is possible: "Yeah, you could be right. I don't think it's very *likely.* But yes, you could be right. Because my big thing is, I *don't know.* That's what I 'preach.' I preach the gospel of *I don't know.* I mean, that's what I'm here promoting: *doubt.* It's my product. The other guys are selling certainty. Not me [laughing]. I'm in the corner with doubt."[18]

With its comedy, Maher's perspective is an antidote to extremism, and surely one of its remedies. When certainty seems so necessary that any doubt feels like a catastrophic admission of weakness, it is too easy to group fanatics over there, to represent oneself (and one's group) as under attack, and to miss the elements of strident certainty that mark one's own absolute objections to the absolutism of others. At the same time, it is a convenience —and an error—to continue talking about "The Three Atheists," as Dawkins, Hitchens, and Sam Harris are often dubbed, as if they were the only ones, and as if they did not have large areas of disagreement (just as their critics do).[19] As Hitchens points out early in his book, *God Is Not Great,* "My own annoyance at Professor Dawkins and Daniel Dennett, for their cringe-making proposal that atheists should conceitedly nominate themselves to be called 'brights,' is part of a continuous argument" (*GING,* 5).

Those who can get past the subtitle of Hitchens' book, *How Religion Poisons Everything,* may be surprised to read his admission, concerning his first religious teacher in southwest England, "If I went back to Devon, where Mrs. Watts has her unvisited tomb, I would surely find myself sitting quietly at the back of some old Celtic or Saxon church" (*GING,* 11). It is an appealing image, not because it puts an avowed atheist in a church, but because it so clearly shows his understanding of the history and diversity of religious practice. "If I went back" echoes Hardy's syntax and sentiment, even as Hitchens consciously invokes another Victorian, George Eliot, whose novel *Middlemarch* (1871–72) tries to sum up the secular accomplishments of her idealistic protagonist, Dorothea Brooke. "If I went back" also reminds us, as Dawkins unwittingly made clear in his dealings with "Darwin's bulldog," of the ongoing importance of the Victorians.

One reason for that is because their energetic debates about faith and reason helped to set the terms and parameters of comparable ones today. Yet while they engaged intensively with all facets of religious belief and doubt, Terry Eagleton justly criticizes Dawkins for glossing this cultural and religious history with almost scandalous imprecision, as if none of it really mattered in the first place, no matter how deeply embedded its traditions remain in our lives and shared past.[20] When put that way, Dawkins has comparatively less to say to us than Hardy, Froude, Huxley, Chambers, or Eliot, while they and many other Victorians have a lot more to contribute on religious faith and doubt than we have fully acknowledged.

When I recently flew to Cincinnati to visit the so-called Creation Museum, on the outskirts of the city, that denial of nineteenth-century arguments struck me in full force. At first it seemed easy to dismiss the animatronic versions of Adam and Eve gazing passionately at each other not too far from a hungry-looking dinosaur. It was just cheesy Midwest shtick, I thought, and not to be taken seriously. "Enjoy the first six days of history," I was cheerfully told, before I munched a sandwich in Noah's Café, the organization's restaurant, and listened to a friendly volunteer report that they had had seventy-four thousand visitors in the first few months of opening, with three thousand stopping by on a normal day.

I sat in an auditorium where the seat in front of me sprinkled tiny jets of water in my face as a film tried to impress on me what a global deluge might look and feel like. I read posters explaining, quite seriously, how two

Figure 18. Adam and Eve Prepare for Passion at the Creation Museum, Petersburg, Kentucky, September 2007. Author collection, reproduced with permission.

members of every species, including dinosaurs, *could* conceivably be made to squeeze onto a large wooden ark without eating each other first (a handy to-scale model nearby helped make that seem a fraction more plausible). The "museum" Web site even encouraged visitors to stop by its Dinosaur Den with the tag: "Our dinosaurs cater to groups."[21]

But it was difficult to ignore the distortions that other visitors (including dozens of schoolchildren) were taking very seriously indeed. "What did dinosaurs eat?" asks one of the informational signs. Presumably not Adam and Eve, looking so intently at each other nearby. Though the fangs on the tyrannosaur looked more forbidding than the plastic snake representing Satan, all my Tennysonian thoughts of "Nature, red in tooth and claw" apparently were wrong.[22] Before Adam's fall, every dinosaur was herbivorous! The sign nearby read: "God said, 'To every beast of the earth and to every bird of the air, and to everything that creeps upon the earth, wherein there is life, I have given every green herb for food'" (Genesis 1:30). For the museum "curators," one imagines, the fangs on that tyrannosaur had evolved after the Fall.

Not surprisingly, too, the Creation Museum argues that dinosaurs existed quite recently and may not even be extinct. As Ken Ham puts it in "What Really Happened to the Dinosaurs?" a chapter of his *New Answers Book:* "According to the Bible, dinosaurs first existed around 6,000 years ago. God made the dinosaurs, along with the other land animals, on Day 6 of the Creation Week (Genesis 1:20–25, 31). Adam and Eve were also made on Day 6—so dinosaurs lived at the same time as people, not separated by eons of time."[23] Dinosaurs, continues Ham, president and CEO of Answers in Genesis (USA) and author of *The Lie: Evolution,* "could not have died out before people appeared because dinosaurs had not previously existed; and death, bloodshed, disease, [meat-eating], and suffering are a result of Adam's sin (Genesis 1:29–30; Romans 5:12, 14; 1 Corinthians 15:21–22)."[24]

If we can get past the syllogism that no other land creatures could have preceded man because the Bible dates their origin to the same "day," Ham's assertion might strike us as running together two quite different issues. In-

Figure 19. Girl Playing Near Dinosaurs at the Creation Museum, Petersburg, Kentucky, September 2007. Author collection, reproduced with permission.

deed, one need not jettison the entire concept of sin (or collective guilt) to insist that dinosaurs still preexisted us, and by millions of years. Nor, of course, need one defend Genesis *to the letter* to maintain a faith in God. The secular scholar Keith Thomson, for instance, acknowledges the "glory" of the opening verses of the Bible in ways that grasp their beauty as a meditation on origins: "And the earth was without form, and void; and darkness was upon the face of the deep."[25]

To insist that such lines be burdened with scientific accuracy is to overlook that the Bible was written centuries before the emergence of modern science, under completely different conditions. At the same time, to ignore the poetry of Genesis and to insist that materialism resolve such vast enigmas as why we evolved on this planet is to risk making "science . . . the sacrosanct fetish," as the ambassador cautions in Joseph Conrad's Edwardian novel *The Secret Agent*.[26]

One's immediate question to the founders of the Creation Museum may well be, to paraphrase Bill Maher, "Why does insisting on the coexistence of Adam and Eve with the dinosaurs *matter* so much?" especially when so many other Christians take the Book of Genesis on faith, not as historical truth. What is at stake in arguing so vociferously *against* the teaching of evolution, moreover, when the Roman Catholic Church, encouraged by Pope Pius XII, more or less accommodated itself to that phenomenon in the 1950s?

In the decades since, the Catholic Church has in fact moved from neutrality over the issue to implicit acceptance of it through "theistic evolution," where faith and scientific evidence about human evolution are not in apparent conflict, though humanity is still regarded as a special creation.[27] Even so, it bears repeating that James Hutton struggled to make that argument in 1788, and that Sir Charles Lyell reluctantly abandoned it in 1859 when the full weight of scientific evidence made clear to him that it was no longer tenable, no matter how much he wanted to believe otherwise.

With its fierce commitment to creationism, American fundamentalism and Christian Evangelicalism since the 1920s have largely turned their backs on Republican freethinkers like Robert Ingersoll, who christened doubt "the womb and cradle of progress," and pro-evolutionary Calvinists like Asa Gray, who as early as 1874 argued, "The attitude of theologians toward doctrines of evolution, from the nebular hypothesis down to 'Darwinism,' is no less worthy of consideration, and hardly less diverse, than that of naturalists."[28] With its own forms of unbelief comparatively weaker than those that emerged on the other side of the Atlantic, the United States also tended to reject the looser interpretations of the Bible that transformed 1860s Britain. Those, we have seen, allowed biblical accounts to be cast as metaphorical, a move thought anathema to literalists then and now. Denying the credibility of such readings, literalists denounced as heresy the idea that Christianity might adapt to scientific discovery. They superimposed on scripture a pristine start for Adam and Eve and ignored that the extant version of Genesis is likely only part of a much-longer original story.[29] In doing so, they pushed aside Christians in the 1890s who felt it necessary to concede that "the old belief that the beginning of creation preceded our time by only about six thousand years" has been "shown to be untenable."[30]

In 1925, a law passed in Tennessee preventing any state-funded educational establishment from teaching "any theory that denies the story of divine creation of man as taught in the Bible, and teach instead that man has descended from a lower order of animals."[31] The law effectively made it illegal to *deny* the biblical account of man's creation. Challenging the constitutionality of the ruling, the American Civil Liberties Union approached John T. Scopes, a teacher who was willing to insist that evolutionary theory be part of the curriculum for high-school students in the state. During what would soon be dubbed the Scopes Monkey Trial, the prosecution, led by celebrity lawyer and former secretary of state William Jennings Bryan, lambasted evolutionary theory for contending that the descent of man was "not even from American monkeys, but from old world monkeys." The courtroom response was laughter.[32]

Scopes was found guilty and fined. The Tennessee Supreme Court reversed the conviction on a technicality concerning the fine, but the state legislature did not repeal the 1925 Butler Act until May 17, 1967. And though that ruling became a turning point in the U.S. version of the conflict over evolution and creationism, repeal of the law did not end or resolve the underlying problem of antipathy to evolutionary theory and its scientific argument, based on biblical literalism.

Nor does the Scopes trial appear to be over in some parts of the country. A recent study of religious beliefs in thirty-four industrialized nations found that more people in the United States doubted the existence of evolution (60 percent) than in any other country but Turkey (at 75 percent).[33] The results of a 2007 Gallup poll were even more lopsided, finding that only 14 percent believed in evolution without God (up from 10 percent in 1997) and that the majority of Republicans doubt the theory of evolution.[34] Those numbers came two decades after the U.S. Supreme Court ruled in

1987 that creationism could *not* be taught alongside evolutionary theory on the grounds that creationism is designed explicitly to advance religious interests.[35] Nor are matters substantially better in Britain: in January 2006, *BBC News* reported that "just under half of Britons accept the theory of evolution as the best description for the development of life."[36]

Yet the Christians who supported the Creation Museum with twenty-seven million dollars in donations feel embattled and under attack.[37] One exhibit on display there is a model of an imaginary screeching teacher, dubbed "Miss E. Certainty," whose answer to the question "What if I don't believe?" is, "Then you're in violation of the Constitution." That's not the answer most agnostics and atheists would give to such a question. Nor do most teachers confuse knowledge with belief. To insist that they be the same, after all, is the cause of so much trouble. What the organizers of the "exhibit" obviously meant, and perhaps did not feel the need to spell out, was something more like: "What if I don't believe in secular principles?"

That is not a trivial or easily answered question, given the number of Americans who are currently asking it. But one plausible rejoinder could run, "Well, then you have a serious problem with more or less the entire history of your country, including not only its founding documents, its Constitution, and its Bill of Rights, but also the founders of those principles."

It is often forgotten that one founding father, Thomas Jefferson, decided to remove from the Bible the many parts of it that he considered false, supernatural, and distractingly magical. He did so while in office, it is notable to recall, and excised from the Bible the virgin birth, the miracles, the resurrection, and indeed that God recognized Jesus as part of the divinity. The result, completed in 1820 but published posthumously in 1895, has since become known as *The Jefferson Bible.* Jefferson himself called it *The Life and Morals of Jesus of Nazareth, Extracted Textually from the Gospels in Greek, Latin, French, and English.*[38]

In the United States today, however, the entanglement of religion with politics is far greater than in Jefferson's day or even that of James Madison, the country's fourth president, who railed against "religious bondage" and insisted on a celebrated solution to it: "Religion & Govt. will both exist in greater purity, the less they are mixed together."[39]

During the 2004 presidential campaign, President George W. Bush openly told the American public: "I believe that God wants everybody to be free. That's what I believe. And that's part of my . . . foreign policy."[40] Small wonder that even mainstream *U.S. News and World Report,* characterizing the campaign as one in which "churchgoers and secular voters live in parallel universes," called its report "Separate Worlds."[41] It was uncannily true.

By contrast, most British papers are fairly bullish about the Church of England's disestablishment as the country's official religion. Nor is the archbishop of Canterbury especially troubled by the prospect, saying that it wouldn't be "the end of the world."[42] He comes across as sanguine about the realities facing the Church, which simply doesn't interest large numbers of Britons (though controversy continues to flare over the ordination of women and the openly gay).[43] Indeed, when I was last in England (where I was born and lived the first twenty-four years of my life), Birmingham Cathedral was being pilloried for suggesting that it might open a wine bar and introduce loyalty cards to help fill the empty pews. "Cathedral wine bars," declared the cathedral's first director of hospitality and welcome, "should be seen as a potential commercial operation with profits going into the upkeep of the building and paying for evangelistic work."[44]

What got more press in Britain was a winter 2008 campaign to raise money for a series of advertisements that would appear on thirty London buses. These would bear the message: "There's probably no God. Now stop worrying and enjoy your life."[45] That is quite a statement, after all, and much of its impact hangs on the interesting modifier, "probably." The campaign was a response to the "Jesus Said" ads that had appeared on London buses earlier that summer. Those had published a series of Bible quotations, followed by a link to a Web site, where visitors were told that non-Christians "will be condemned to everlasting separation from God and then [will] spend all eternity in torment in hell. . . . Jesus spoke about this as a lake of fire prepared for the devil."[46]

The counter-campaign to add agnostic posters raised more than enough money (rather quickly, as it happens, after word spread that there had been little enthusiasm for it). Sporadic complaints were heard, along with reports of a driver refusing to drive one of the buses because he opposed the message. The group Christian Voice even grumbled to the Advertising Standards Authority that the second campaign (though not the first) broke the country's regulatory code, that "marketers must hold documentary evidence to prove all claims." Understandably or not, that drew "peals of laughter" from the British Humanist Association, which had organized the counter-response.[47] Its campaign went on to raise enough money to put the posters on eight hundred buses nationwide.

It may be harder to imagine similar advertisements in the United States, even in liberal pockets of the country. Yet in fact the American Humanist Association launched a nearly identical campaign in Washington, D.C., just after the one in Britain. Buses in the capital carried the slogan, "Why believe in a God? Just be good for goodness' sake."[48] And in April 2009, the *New York Times* reported that a group of secular humanists had put up a billboard in Charleston, South Carolina, bearing the words: "Don't Believe in God? You Are Not Alone." Although the group was relatively small, the reporter noted, residents of the state claiming "no religion" had more than tripled, to 10 percent (from 3 percent in 1990).

Across the United States, in fact, that total is now hovering between 15 and 16 percent of the general population (up from 8 percent in 1990), and the trend toward secularism and away from religious affiliation is growing.[49] So much so that a recent op-ed piece on *Fox News* carried the hyperbolic title, "Where Have All the Christians Gone?" "Christianity is plummeting in America," the author Bruce Feiler warned, "while the number of non-believers is skyrocketing." Feiler continued, "The number of Christians has declined 12% since 1990, and is now 76%, the lowest percentage in American history. The growth of non-believers has come largely from men. Twenty percent of men express no religious affiliation; 12% of women. Young people are fleeing faith. Nearly a quarter of Americans in their 20's profess no organized religion." Today, he concluded, "the rise of disaffection is so powerful that different denominations needs [sic] to band together to find a shared language of God that can move beyond the fading divisions of the past and begin moving toward a partnership of different-but-equal traditions. Or risk becoming Europe, where religion is fast becoming an afterthought."[50]

That Feiler spoke of "plummeting" rates of faith, with the number of Christians in America still at 76 percent, indicates how devout the country was before the 1990s and arguably how devout it remains. To equate secularism with a "rise of disaffection" is to betray a characterization of faith comparable in distortion to Richard Dawkins' calling atheists "brights." But while Christians such as Feiler are feeling anxious and embattled, many non-Christians are frankly very worried about the arguments and rhetoric driving religious fanaticism in the United States.

Unlike in nineteenth-century America, today far larger numbers of the country's citizens want to "reclaim America for Christ" and argue that there are really only two types of people in the world: those who will be saved, based on their love of Jesus, and those who will be "left behind," to deal with the aftermath of a religious apocalypse that they, as Christians, are disturbingly keen to instigate. As Hitchens puts it, a weighty—and increasingly obstreperous—aspect of religion "looks forward to the destruction of the world. By this," he adds, "I do not mean it 'looks forward' in the purely eschatological sense of anticipating the end. I mean, rather, that it openly or covertly wishes that end to occur" (*GING*, 56).[51]

Earlier in this book, we saw the Reverend John Cumming writing, in his *Apocalyptic Sketches* (1853), about the coming day of judgment circa 1867, when the "Christian dispensation would come to a glorious end."[52] One wonders how he felt in the final years of his life, before his death from natural causes in 1881. Still, military technology in Cumming's day extended largely to muskets, swords, and sabers, not precision-guided missiles and nuclear weapons designed to wipe out entire populations and make their land uninhabitable for decades.

Almost cheering on that end, "30–40 percent of Americans" (according to one recent estimate)[53] seem as if they cannot wait to test the "egotistical . . . hope that [they] will be personally spared, gathered contentedly to the bosom of the mass exterminator, and from a safe place observe the sufferings of those less fortunate" (*GING*, 57). They have been encouraged— even coached—in this thinking by the *Left Behind* series, coauthored by Christian evangelists Tim LaHaye and Jerry Jenkins, which has sold more than seventy million books worldwide since it debuted in the 1990s, the decade when End Times assumptions were truly reborn.

When *Newsweek* decided to feature the two men on a May 2004 cover, it added in boldface: "The elites may not recognize them, but LaHaye and Jenkins are *America's best-selling authors.* At a time of uncertainty, they have struck a chord with novels that combine *scriptural literalism with a sci-fi sensibility.*"[54]

"Sci-fi sensibility" may not be too far off the mark, but the religious apocalypse that LaHaye and Jenkins fervently describe and anxiously await is far from small bore. They not only welcome but also have strongly tried to promote what they call "a literal interpretation of end-time prophecies."[55] Hitchens quotes a snapshot: "The blood continued to rise. Millions of birds flocked into the area and feasted on the remains . . . and the winepress was trampled outside the city, and blood came out of the winepress, up to the horse's bridles, for one thousand six hundred furlongs" (*GING*, 57). This is "sheer manic relish," Hitchens points out, "larded with half-quotations" (57). To LaHaye and Jenkins, however, "all prophecy should be interpreted literally whenever possible. We have been guided," LaHaye continues, in a notably passive clause, "by the golden rule of interpretation: *When the plain sense of Scripture makes common sense, seek no other sense*" (*TBLB*, 7; emphasis in original).

As but one example of such guided reading, LaHaye and Jenkins turn the period of "tribulation," which Jesus is said to undergo in the Gospel of Matthew, into a 490-year interval (seventy sets of seven-year periods). With a preposterous fantasy of accuracy, they even proclaim that a "divine prophetic clock" began ticking on March 5, 444 BC, "when the Persian king Artaxerxes issue[d] a decree allowing the Jews to return under Nehemiah's leadership to rebuild the city of Jerusalem" (*TBLB*, 99). It is not the first time—and it likely won't be the last—that people have had visions of messianic certainty about the beginning and end of life, even down to the day and minute. The Reverend Cumming, recall, found evidence for the End Times in "everything from the French Revolution to the Irish potato famine to the invention of the telegraph and steamship."[56]

Isaiah, Jeremiah, and especially the Book of Revelation repeatedly mention the ancient city of Babylon. For LaHaye, Jenkins—and, presumably, many of their readers—that means but one thing: "The city of New Babylon [Baghdad] will be rebuilt in Iraq in the last days as a great world political and economic center for the Antichrist's empire" (*TBLB*, 125). Reflexive irony, alas, is missing here. The empire in question—to justify the costly, protracted, and illegal occupation of that land—apparently did not fabricate evidence that it might soon be attacked. If there is cause for marvel, it is surely how quickly the catastrophes of American foreign policy are turned into opportunities for religious prophecy.

If anything, the 2008 American presidential election intensified such fundamentalist anxiety. As Barack Obama's and John McCain's campaigns slogged it out in the final months, the mainstream newsmagazine *Time* found itself needing to ask, quite seriously, whether one advertisement from McCain's increasingly erratic campaign appealed directly to Christian fundamentalist voters and *Left Behind* readers. That was the one, supposedly tongue in cheek, that asked whether candidate Obama was really "The One"—as in, The New Messiah. It was also the ad that led *Time* to wonder, with good reason, whether the Republican nominee was cravenly trying to stoke apocalyptic fear among Evangelicals.

"It should be known that in 2008 the world shall be blessed," the August McCain ad warned portentously. "They will call him 'The One.' And the world will receive his blessings." The ad encouraged viewers to scorn Barack Obama's experience and popularity—normally seen as a plus—by transforming these qualities into disturbing hints of messianism.[57] If the McCain camp "wanted to be funny," one Democratic consultant noted with amazing restraint, "if they really wanted to play up the idea that Obama thinks he's the Second Coming, there [were] better ways to do it. Why use awkward lines like, 'And the world will receive his blessings'?"[58]

Why indeed? It was ominous and disturbing, not funny at all. *Time*—whose article bore the boggling title "An Antichrist Obama in McCain Ad?"—was not alone in noting that the ad, and especially its biblical language, openly invoked the *Left Behind* series.[59] Those books feature a charismatic young political leader, Nicolae Carpathia, who promises to heal the world after a time of deep division. The series finally exposes him as the Antichrist, but not before he tries to end interfaith strife with the ominous, even heretical slogan "We Are God."

Of course, many religious traditions—some of them Christian—come very close to voicing that exact sentiment. Among Evangelicals, however, such ideas as healing the world of religious division must seem as if they come from the devil himself. Hence the dangerous high-wire act that McCain's ad performed. When Rick Davis, McCain's campaign manager, followed up by calling media criticism of vice presidential nominee Sarah Palin "literally an attack on Christianity itself," he revealed the campaign's scorched-earth policy.[60] The McCain camp was playing with fire and clearly knew it.

The disturbing backstory to that moment in McCain's campaign concerns the Evangelical literalism that underwrote it. Soon after candidate Obama began racking up a string of victories in the Democratic primary during the spring of 2008, *Time* noted that a Google search for "Obama and Antichrist" could generate more than seven hundred thousand hits, "including at least one blog dedicated solely to the topic." "A more obscure search for 'Obama' and 'Nicolae Carpathia,'" the columnist continued, "yield[ed] a surprising 200,000 references."[61]

In the teeth of such religious certainty, it is worth noting that there were many other responses to Obama's convincing victory, including by Maira Kalman, who published a series of beautiful paintings about American democracy and the 2008 campaign called "The Inauguration: At Last." At the start of that series, Kalman depicted an angel almost blessing the following text: "Hallelujah. The Angels are Singing on this Glorious Day."[62] The many millions of Americans who swept Obama into power are likely to have felt similarly about his resounding, and very secular, victory.

Long before he won large majorities in the House and Senate, then, President Obama was represented, even by stalwart political rivals, as the enemy incarnate. Most of that animus has been directed at his person and his religious beliefs, which are well documented in his books, but some of the animus came from an early dispute with the influential Evangelical James Dobson, founder of Focus on the Family.

Dobson attracted press attention when he criticized then Senator Obama for "distorting" the Bible and adopting a "fruitcake interpretation" of the Constitution. His comment stemmed from Obama's simple, earlier insistence that it would be "impractical" to govern solely from the word of the Bible and especially the Ten Commandments. Unlawful, too, given the Constitution.[63]

Since Obama would not back down over this fight, he may unwittingly have fueled resentment among influential Evangelicals, particularly since he was chiding them on home turf. "Which passages of Scripture should guide our public policy?" he asked appropriately. "Should we go with Leviticus, which suggests slavery is okay and that eating shellfish is an abomination? Or we could go with Deuteronomy, which suggests stoning your child if he strays from the faith, or should we just stick to the Sermon on the Mount?"[64]

Backed into a corner, Dobson replied that Obama "should not be referencing antiquated dietary codes and passages from the Old Testament that are no longer relevant." But moving the debate to questions of rele-

Figure 20. Maira Kalman, "The Inauguration: At Last," *New York Times*, January 29, 2009. Courtesy Maira Kalman.

vance and hinting at his own selective application of verses was Dobson's immediate undoing. Leviticus is an old standby, not least because it contains a broad range of injunctions—including that eating "all that are in the waters, in the seas and in the rivers" is "an abomination" (11:9–12). The charge is thrice repeated; and Leviticus is no less merciful on those who eat hare, fowl, and pork. So Obama cautioned, to cheers, "Before we get carried away, let's read our Bible"—as worshippers *and* readers, that is, who recognize, without sanctioning, the ancient allusions.[65] Dobson didn't appear to take kindly to the humiliation.

Amid all this religious certainty, what then of doubt and its ongoing importance?

One answer comes from a Pulitzer Prize–winning play, *Doubt: A Parable*, which John Patrick Shanley, its author, has since adapted into a major motion picture. Both the play and the film are set in 1964, at a Catholic church and school in the Bronx. And though the play has nothing to say about scientific uncertainty and the teaching of evolution, the opening scene is a sermon that Father Flynn feels moved to give on the subject of religious doubt amid a growing sense of confusion and collective self-doubt in the United States as a whole.

Only a few months have passed since the Kennedy assassination, and the most common feeling is still "profound disorientation. Despair. 'What now? Which way? What do I say to my kids? What do I tell myself?' [The catastrophe] was a time of people sitting together, bound together by a common feeling of hopelessness. Your *bond* with your fellow beings was your *despair*. It was a public experience, shared by everyone in our society. It was awful, but we were in it together!"[66] From that togetherness over uncertainty, Flynn tells his congregation, in a statement that for some still borders on heresy, "doubt can be a bond as powerful and sustaining as certainty" (*D*, 6).

That Shanley casts his theater audience as the assembled congregation adds something to the atmosphere and tension of the play that the film cannot quite recapture. Willingly or not, the audience is rendered a silent witness to the extraordinary drama that unfolds before them.

Anyone who has seen the play or the film will know that *Doubt* is extremely hard to sum up. One's sense of what takes place, and why, is almost impossible to disentangle from the perspectives and judgments that an audience inevitably brings to the drama. Should we see the play—and its cast—through the lens of certainty or of doubt? There is no single way to read the play, of course, and no one telling us which is the right answer or interpretation. Still, *how* we read it is rather like a Rorschach test of our opinions and convictions, religious and otherwise.

The central conundrum is whether something untoward, perhaps sexual, has occurred between Father Flynn and Donald Muller, the school's "first Negro student," whom Flynn sees as the object of minor bullying (*D*, 21). Having joined the predominantly Irish and Italian school two months earlier, at a time when many U.S. schools were still segregated, Muller "has no friends" and is "thirteenth in class." He does however have "a protector" in Father Flynn, who is described, rather open-endedly, as having "taken an interest" in him (19, 20).

With the Catholic Church making headlines in the late 1990s and early 2000s for lawsuits brought by hundreds of abused pupils over predatory priests, few audience members could fail to imagine the moral dilemma that Sister Aloysius experiences, even briefly, over whether to investigate further. At the same time, as in a Hawthorne novel or *The Crucible*, Arthur Miller's remarkable adaptation of the 1692 Salem witch trials, the "certainty" (her word) with which she pronounces Father Flynn guilty on highly equivocal "evidence" (mostly hearsay) is tinged—even greatly overdetermined—by her own interest in seeing him punished for misdemeanors that may be more in her head than outside it (*D*, 54).

True, Father Flynn resigns abruptly, believing that she has dredged up some professional disgrace from his past. It is never clear whether that infraction was sexual harassment, something far less troubling, or even whether it was trumped up earlier, too. At the same time, Sister Aloysius is deeply disturbed by Flynn's efforts to modernize the church, in part by being more friendly to the pupils and congregation. He gives the boys a talk, for instance, on "how to be a man," which irks her, not least because it includes advice on how to ask girls out on dates (*D*, 18). Far from being treacherous or predatory, it all looks very innocent, even admirable. And of course it may be.

Given all the uncertainties—religious and otherwise—that swirl in Shanley's play, the audience and the reader have to cope with a profound, almost unsettling ambiguity over what they believe happened, and why. As Shanley asks in the play's preface, "Have you ever held a position in an argument past the point of comfort? Have you ever defended a way of life you were on the verge of exhausting? . . . I have. That's an interesting moment" (*D*, vii–viii).

For Shanley, doubt and uncertainty bring to the fore "something silent under every person and under every play." They also manifest, however awkwardly, "something unsaid under any given society" (vii). It is doubt, he says, "(so often experienced initially as weakness) that changes things." Yet doubt that oddly "requires more courage than conviction does, and more energy; because conviction is a resting place and doubt is infinite—it is a passionate exercise" (viii, ix). That may explain why Sister Aloysius breaks down moments before the final curtain, apparently victorious but actually "bent with emotion." One critic called her character "a triumph of hard-won conviction over human indecisiveness," and indeed her exclamations (the play's final words) are meant to seem like a catharsis of self-recognition, though one coming far too late to reassure her or the audience: "I have doubts! I have such doubts!" (*D*, 58).[67]

One of the many lessons of Shanley's play is how little "room or value [is] placed on doubt," a quality, Shanley asserts, that is still "one of the hallmarks of the wise."[68] Another lesson is how firmly, even tenaciously, we hold onto our beliefs. Certainly we do not give them up lightly or willingly! An ability to withstand opposition to, even derision of, one's beliefs and faith is how large numbers of worshippers self-define. That should be a fairly important reminder to those seeking to temper belief with reason, the better to "eviscerate" faith. The sense of assault on belief is precisely what gives it tenacity in the teeth of all opposition. It sends belief into a realm of justification from which it is hard to withdraw.

With beliefs harnessing intense psychological and political power, it should also be clear that while the world wrestles with the near-insupera-ble task of trying to honor everyone's religious tenets, even as they pre-dictably collide with those of others, the experience of losing those beliefs (or tempering them with doubt) can be dramatic, often culminating in a profound reorientation to the world as it is. Similarly life-altering, I hope to have shown, is the sense of uncertainty, creativity, and peculiar freedom that can ensue when one set of explanations gives way, leaving in its wake concerns and dilemmas that faith once seemed to answer. I quoted Leslie Stephen's "Agnostic's Apology" in the previous chapter, including his in-sistence that the central "question is not which system excludes the doubt, but how it expresses the doubt."[69] But it was his daughter Virginia Woolf who captured the full intensity of that insight:

> The mind is full of monstrous, hybrid, unmanageable emotions. That the age of the earth is 3,000,000,000 years; that human life lasts but a second; that the capacity of the human mind is never-theless boundless; that life is infinitely beautiful yet repulsive; that one's fellow creatures are adorable but disgusting; that science and religion have between them destroyed belief; that all bonds of union seem broken, yet some control must exist—it is in this at-mosphere of doubt and conflict that writers have now to create.[70]

If "all bonds of union seem[ed] broken" for Woolf in the late 1920s, what of the "powerful and sustaining . . . bond" of doubt that Father Flynn invokes at the start of Shanley's play almost a century later? The kind of "public experience" of despair following the Kennedy assassination or 9/11, more recently, is not of course the same as the religious crises we have fol-lowed in this book. Nor does the doubt that Sister Aloysius states at the end of the play mean that she's capable of forming a bond with the man whose life she not only has derailed but also might easily have destroyed—and perhaps for no reason at all.

The desire and willingness to voice such doubt is, however, a start. As

Shanley claims, "Doubt is nothing less than an opportunity to reenter the Present," to rethink how it came to exist in this form, and how one assesses the historical difference between our now and our then (*D*, viii). It "stimulates the evaluation of beliefs," Robert Baird emphasizes, including ones that may "be misplaced," and thus is a catalyst for change and moderation.[71] Much of the ability to voice that doubt is due to freethinkers such as William Nicholson dramatizing "The Doubts of Infidels"; to Robert Chambers inquiring into "*the mode* in which the Divine Author proceeded in the organic creation"; to Thomas Huxley standing up to ridicule from the bishop of Oxford; and to James Anthony Froude wondering, among others, "Why is it thought so very wicked to be an unbeliever?"[72]

Through these thinkers and the "passionate exercise" of their doubt, we have an "opportunity to reenter the Present" by questioning what beliefs mean to us and what role we are prepared to assign them (*D*, ix). The rise of religious extremism in many parts of the world makes such questioning more urgent than ever. The process of working through doubt remains one of the best ways to go on thinking, reflecting on choices, and wondering at uncertain outcomes.

Introduction

1. J. Anthony Froude, *The Nemesis of Faith* (London: John Chapman, 1849), 84.
2. Cecil Rhodes, "Confession of Faith" (1877), as quoted in S. G. Millin, *Rhodes* (London: Chatto, 1933), 138.
3. Charles Dickens, *A Tale of Two Cities* (1859; London: Penguin, 2003), 5.
4. John Henry Newman, *Parochial and Plain Sermons in Eight Volumes* (1843; London: Longmans, Green, 1891), 2:215.
5. John Henry Newman, *An Essay in Aid of a Grammar of Assent* (Notre Dame, Ind.: University of Notre Dame Press, 1979), 180.
6. William Hurrell Mallock, *Is Life Worth Living?* (1879; London: Chatto and Windus, 1907).
7. Margaret Maison, *Search Your Soul, Eustace: A Survey of the Religious Novel in the Victorian Age* (London: Sheed and Ward, 1961), 209. See also Martin E. Marty, *Varieties of Unbelief* (New York: Holt, Rinehart and Winston, 1964).
8. Edward Rothstein, "Reason and Faith, Eternally Bound," *New York Times,* December 20, 2003.
9. Leo Bersani, *The Culture of Redemption* (Cambridge, Mass.: Harvard University Press, 1992). My adoption, above, of the phrase "ethical necessity" is from his book *Homos* (Cambridge, Mass.: Harvard University Press, 1995), 151.

10. Owen Chadwick, "Doubt," in *The Victorian Church*, 2 vols. (London: A. and C. Black, 1966–70), 2:120.

11. See, e.g., Newman's thoughts on "notional assent" in his *Essay in Aid of a Grammar of Assent*, 52–76.

12. Thomas Cooper, *The Purgatory of Suicides: A Prison-Rhyme in Ten Books* (1845; London: Chapman and Hall, 1853), 199 (bk. 6, stanza 31); emphasis in original.

13. Josef L. Altholz, "The Warfare of Conscience with Theology," in *The Mind and Art of Victorian England* (Minneapolis: University of Minnesota Press, 1976), 58.

14. Samuel Wilberforce, as quoted in ibid., 63.

15. John Henry Newman, as quoted in ibid., 64.

16. Altholz, "Warfare of Conscience with Theology," 64.

17. For instance, Samuel Wilberforce, bishop of Oxford, *The Revelation of God, the Probation of Man: Two Sermons Preached before the University of Oxford, January 27 and February 3, 1861* (London: John Murray, 1861), and the Reverend George Putnam, "Doubt," *Unitarian Review and Religious Magazine* 19 (May 1883), 442–52.

18. The *Oxford English Dictionary* dates the first use of "benefit of the doubt" to 1848; see also Violet Hunt, "The Benefit of the Doubt," *English Illustrated Magazine* 7 (1895), 23–28. The Rev. G. Frederick Wright, "'Beyond Reasonable Doubt'—A Practical Principle," *Homiletic Review* 36 (October 1898), 291–95; J. S. Erwin, "Reasonable Doubt and Moral Certainty," *Criminal Law Magazine and Reporter* 18 (March 1896), 149–58.

19. James H. Snowden, "The Place of Doubt in Religious Belief," *Biblical World* 47.3 (March 1916), 151.

20. For instance, "Ghosts and the Balance of Doubt," an editorial in the *Spectator*, September 18, 1897, 366–67.

21. W. H. [William Hurrell] Mallock, "Faith and Verification," *Nineteenth Century* (London), rept. in *Littell's Living Age*, November 16, 1878, 411, 410.

22. Mallock, *Is Life Worth Living?* 272. See also the book-length response to Mallock by clergyman John Clifford, *Is Life Worth Living? An Eightfold Answer* (London: Marlborough, 1880), which pleaded with his congregations to make space for Christ in their hearts: "Let us then be trustful and patient, hopeful and brave" (97).

23. Matthew Arnold, "Dover Beach" (1867), in *The Poetical Works of Matthew Arnold*, ed. C. B. Tinker and H. F. Lowry (London: Oxford University Press, 1950), 211 (line 34).

24. Matthew Arnold, *Literature and Dogma: An Essay towards a Better Apprehen-*

sion of the Bible (1873; New York: Macmillan, 1914), x; John Morley, *On Compromise* (1874; London: Macmillan, 1917), 221.

25. Bernard Lightman, *The Origins of Agnosticism: Victorian Unbelief and the Limits of Knowledge* (Baltimore: Johns Hopkins University Press, 1987), 3.

26. John Patrick Shanley, *Doubt: A Parable* (New York: Theatre Communications Group, 2005); David Carr, "'Doubt' and Doubts of a Workingman," *New York Times,* December 4, 2008; Christopher Hitchens, "The Dogmatic Doubter: The Nun's Leading Critic Argues That the Psychic Pain Revealed in a New Book Was a Byproduct of Her Faith," *Newsweek,* September 10, 2007, 41–42, referencing Brian Kolodiejchuk, ed., *Mother Teresa: Come Be My Light: The Private Writings of the "Saint of Calcutta"* (New York: Doubleday, 2007); Antony Flew with Roy Abraham Verghese, *There Is a God: How the World's Most Notorious Atheist Changed His Mind* (New York: HarperOne, 2007).

27. Rebecca Newberger Goldstein, *Thirty-Six Arguments for the Existence of God: A Work of Fiction* (New York: Pantheon, 2010).

28. Vexen Crabtree, "Religion in the United Kingdom: Diversity, Trends and Decline," http://www.vexen.co.uk/UK/religion.html; "Trends in UK Church Attendance," http://www.whychurch.org.uk/trends.php; Phil Lawler, "Sharp Decline in British Mass Attendance," *Catholic World News,* July 6, 2006. See also Stephen Prothero, *Religious Literacy: What Every American Needs to Know—And Doesn't* (New York: HarperCollins, 2007).

29. Laurie Goodstein, "More Atheists Shout It from the Rooftops," *New York Times,* April 27, 2009; Bruce Feiler, "Where Have All the Christians Gone?" *Fox News,* September 25, 2009; Frank Newport, "Majority of Republicans Doubt Theory of Evolution: More Americans Accept Theory of Creationism than Evolution," *Gallup News Service,* June 11, 2007; "Britons Unconvinced on Evolution," *BBC News Online,* January 26, 2006.

30. Charles Lyell to George J. P. Scrope, June 14, 1830, in *The Life, Letters, and Journals of Sir Charles Lyell, Bart.,* ed. Katherine M. Lyell, 2 vols. (London: J. Murray, 1881), 1:268.

31. Charles Darwin, *The Autobiography of Charles Darwin, 1809–1882* (1887), ed. Nora Barlow (New York: Norton, 1958), 87, 72, 78.

32. Robert M. Baird, "The Creative Role of Doubt in Religion," *Journal of Religion and Health* 19.3 (1980), 175.

33. Sam Harris, *The End of Faith: Religion, Terror, and the Future of Reason* (New York: Norton, 2004); Richard Dawkins, *The God Delusion* (Boston: Houghton Mifflin, 2006); Christopher Hitchens, *God Is Not Great: How Religion Poisons Everything* (New York: Twelve, 2007).

34. Thomas Crean, *God Is No Delusion: A Refutation of Richard Dawkins* (San Francisco: Ignatius, 2007); Timothy Keller, *The Reason for God: Belief in an Age of Skepticism* (New York: Dutton, 2008); Scott Hahn and Benjamin Wiker, *Answering the New Atheism: Dismantling Dawkins' Case against God* (Steubenville, Ohio: Emmaus Road, 2008). See also Chris Lehmann's blistering review of *The End of Faith*, "Among the Non-Believers: The Tedium of Dogmatic Atheism," *Reason Magazine* (January 2005), http://reason.com/archives/2005/01/01 /among-the-non-believers.

35. Richard Dawkins, "How Dare You Call Me a Fundamentalist: The Right to Criticise 'Faith-Heads,'" *Times* (London), May 12, 2007.

36. Harris, *End of Faith*, 66: "Faith is an impostor."

37. Dawkins, *God Delusion*, 48.

38. Arthur James Balfour, *A Defence of Philosophic Doubt: Being an Essay on the Foundations of Belief* (London: Macmillan, 1879). See also J. Z. Young, *Doubt and Certainty in Science: A Biologist's Reflections on the Brain* (Oxford: Clarendon, 1951).

ONE *Miracles and Skeptics*

1. *Infidel:* "one without faith," an English word from the Old French, *infidèle,* and Latin, *infidel-is.*

2. John Stuart Mill, *On Liberty* (1859; London: Penguin, 1982), 159, 151, 159.

3. "An Act for Preventing Certain Abuses and Profanations on the Lord's Day, Called Sunday (London, 1781)," as quoted in Robert Cox, *The Literature of the Sabbath Question, in Two Volumes* (Edinburgh: MacLachlan and Stewart, 1865), 2:234.

4. See the Reverend Robert Hodgson, *The Life of the Right Reverend Beilby Porteus, D.D., Late Bishop of London* (London: Cadell and Davies, 1813) (hereafter cited in the text as *LBP*). Hodgson writes: "The following statement I insert exactly as I find it. It marks in the strongest manner his vigilant, firm, and persevering mind, and the unremitting assiduity with which he ever laboured to discharge the high and sacred duties of a Christian Bishop" (70–71).

5. See Edward Royle, *Victorian Infidels: The Origins of the British Secularist Movement, 1791–1866* (Manchester: Manchester University Press, 1974); also Terry Eagleton, *Reason, Faith, and Revolution: Reflections on the God Debate* (New Haven: Yale University Press, 2009), 68.

6. Thomas Bayly Howell, *A Complete Collection of State Trials and Proceedings for High Treason and Other Crimes and Misdemeanors, from the Earliest Period to the Year 1783*, vol. 24 (London: Longman, Rees, 1826), 253.

7. Cox, *Literature of the Sabbath Question,* 2:239.

8. Mark H. Judge, Honorary Secretary, "National Federation of Sunday Societies," instituted in Leeds, May 7, 1894, concerning Statute 21 George III, Chapter 49, *Federation Papers No. 3* (London: Pall Mall, 1894), 1.

9. The Office of Public Sector Information (OPSI), the Sunday Entertainments Act 1932 (chapter 51), part 4, http://www.opsi.gov.uk/RevisedStatutes/Acts /ukpga/1932/cukpga_19320051_en_1, and the Sunday Theatre Act 1972 (chapter 26), part 1, http://www.opsi.gov .uk/RevisedStatutes/Acts/ukpga/1972/cukpga _19720026_en_1.

10. See, among others, Robert Flint, *Agnosticism* (Edinburgh: W. Blackwood, 1903).

11. [William Nicholson], *The Doubts of Infidels; or, Queries Relative to Scriptural Inconsistencies & Contradictions, Submitted for Elucidation to the Bench of Bishops, &c. &c. by a Weak but Sincere Christian* (first published in *The Deist, or, Moral Philosopher,* 1, no. 1, 1781; rept. London: R. Carlile, 1819), v (hereafter cited in the text as *DI*).

12. David O'Connor, *Routledge Philosophy Guidebook to Hume on Religion* (London: Routledge, 2001), 19.

13. David Hume, *The Natural History of Religion* (1757), ed. H. E. Root (Stanford, Calif.: Stanford University Press, 1957), 76.

14. Thomas H. Huxley, "Agnosticism" (1889), in *Science and Christian Tradition* (1894; New York: D. Appleton, 1915), 249. See also Claudia M. Schmidt, *David Hume: Reason in History* (University Park: Pennsylvania State University Press, 2003), 339–40.

15. David Hume, "Of Miracles," in *An Enquiry Concerning Human Understanding and Selections from a Treatise of Human Nature* (Chicago: Open Court, 1907), 116 (hereafter cited in the text as "M").

16. Marcus Tullius Cicero, *De natura deorum: Academica,* trans. H. Rackham (London: Loeb, 1961), 323. Hume's *Dialogues Concerning Natural Religion* were modeled after Cicero's text.

17. Hume, characterizing the "Sum of the Charge" in his *Letter from a Gentleman to His Friend in Edinburgh, Containing Some Observations on a Specimen of the Principles concerning Religion and Morality, Said to Be Maintain'd in a Book Lately Publish'd, Intituled, A Treatise of Human Nature, &c.* (1745), reprinted in Hume, *A Treatise of Human Nature: Texts,* ed. David Fate Norton and Mary J. Norton (Oxford: Oxford University Press, 2007), 425.

18. A. N. Wilson, *God's Funeral: The Decline of Faith in Western Civilization* (New York: Norton, 1999), 25.

19. Hesiod's *Theogony* (c. 700 BC), as referenced by Philo in Hume's *Dialogues Concerning Human Nature* (1779), ed. and intro. Martin Bell (London: Penguin, 1990), 85.

20. Alfred Tennyson, "The Lotus-Eaters" (1833), in *The Poems of Tennyson, 1830–1865* (London: Cassell, 1907), 81 (stanza 6).

21. Robert M. Baird, "The Creative Role of Doubt in Religion," *Journal of Religion and Health* 19.3 (1980), 175.

22. See the "Sum of the Charge" (1745), reprinted in Hume, *Treatise of Human Nature: Texts,* 425.

23. See John Henry Newman, *An Essay in Aid of a Grammar of Assent* (Notre Dame, Ind.: University of Notre Dame Press, 1979), 230–60. Jacques Derrida elaborates on both sides of this argument in "Faith and Knowledge: The Two Sources of 'Religion' at the Limits of Reason Alone," in *Religion*, ed. Jacques Derrida and Gianni Vattimo, trans. Samuel Weber (Stanford, Calif.: Stanford University Press, 1998), 1–78. See also the appendix to Rebecca Newberger Goldstein's *Thirty-Six Arguments for the Existence of God: A Work of Fiction* (New York: Pantheon, 2010), esp. 365–66.

24. Hume, *Natural History of Religion*, 28.

25. Bell, introduction to *Dialogues Concerning Natural Religion*, 8.

26. Baird, "Creative Role of Doubt in Religion," 175.

27. Dennis R. Dean, *James Hutton and the History of Geology* (Ithaca, N.Y.: Cornell University Press, 1992), 22; John C. Greene, *The Death of Adam: Evolution and Its Impact on Western Thought* (Ames: Iowa State University Press, 1959), 76.

28. James Hutton, *System of the Earth, Theory of the Earth, and Observations on Granite*, intro. Victor A. Eyles (1785; New York: Hafner, 1973), 4.

29. James Hutton, *Theory of the Earth; or, An Investigation of the Laws Observable in the Composition, Dissolution, and Restoration of Land upon the Globe* (1788; Sioux Falls, S.Dak.: NuVision Publications, 2007), 11 (hereafter cited in the text as *TE*).

30. For elaboration on Hutton's "deistic geotheory," see Martin J. S. Rudwick, *Bursting the Limits of Time: The Reconstruction of Geohistory in the Age of Revolution* (Chicago: University of Chicago Press, 2007), chap. 3, part 4; Dean, *James Hutton and the History of Geology*, chap. 3; and John Hedley Brooke, *Science and Religion: Some Historical Perspectives* (Cambridge: Cambridge University Press, 1991), 214–15.

31. Hutton, as quoted in Charles Lyell, *Principles of Geology* (1830–33), 3 vols., ed. James A. Secord (London: Penguin, 1997), 8.

32. Richard Kirwan, *Geological Essays* (London: T. Bensley, 1799), 2–3.

33. Ibid., 13.

34. John Williams, *The Natural History of the Mineral Kingdom, in Two Volumes* (Edinburgh: T. Ruddiman, 1789), 1:lvii, lix.

35. Rudwick, *Bursting the Limits of Time,* chap. 3, section 5.

36. Williams, *Natural History of the Mineral Kingdom,* 2:119, 115.

37. John Playfair, "Biographical Account of the Late James Hutton, M.D.," in *The Works of John Playfair, Esq.,* 4 vols. (Edinburgh: A. Constable, 1822), 4:81.

38. See also Nigel Leask, "Mont Blanc's Mysterious Voice: Shelley and Huttonian Earth Science," in *The Third Culture: Literature and Science,* ed. Elinor S. Shaffer (New York: de Gruyter, 1997), 182–203, and Noah Heringman, *Romantic Rocks, Aesthetic Geology* (Ithaca, N.Y.: Cornell University Press, 2004), chap. 2.

39. Percy Bysshe Shelley, "Mont Blanc: Lines Written in the Vale of Chamounix" (1817), in *The Complete Poems of Percy Bysshe Shelley* (New York: Modern Library, 1994), 571 (lines 1–4).

40. Percy Bysshe Shelley, *The Necessity of Atheism and Other Essays* (1811; Loughton, Essex: Prometheus Books, 1993), 35.

41. Shelley, "Mont Blanc," lines 71, 75–79.

42. Michael Erkelenz, "Shelley's Draft of 'Mont Blanc' and the Conflict of 'Faith,'" *Review of English Studies* 40.157 (1989), 100.

T W O *Stunned Victorians Look Backward and Inward*

1. William Tuckwell, *Reminiscences of Oxford* (London: Cassell, 1901), 38.

2. Ibid.

3. The Reverend William Buckland, as quoted in Martin J. S. Rudwick, *Worlds before Adam: The Reconstruction of Geohistory in the Age of Reform* (Chicago: University of Chicago Press, 2008), 75.

4. Keith Thomson, *Before Darwin: Reconciling God and Nature* (New Haven: Yale University Press, 2005), 191–92.

5. John C. Greene, *The Death of Adam: Evolution and Its Impact on Western Thought* (Ames: Iowa State University Press, 1959), 77.

6. The Reverend William Buckland, *Vindiciæ Geologicæ; or, The Connexion of Geology with Religion Explained, in an Inaugural Lecture Delivered before the University of Oxford, May 15, 1819, on the Endowment of a Readership in Geology by His Royal Highness the Prince Regent* (Oxford: University Press, 1820), i (hereafter cited in the text as *VG*).

7. William Henry Fitton in the *Edinburgh Review,* as quoted in Rudwick, *Worlds before Adam,* 84.

8. For those noting the concern with which God commanded Noah to protect

each species, the extinction of species was clearly a theological conundrum. Why would God allow even one species to become extinct? As Robert Plot, an early paleontologist and "Professor of Chymistry" put it in 1677, "If it be said, that possibly these Species may now be lost, I shall leave it to the *Reader* to judge, whether it be likely that *Providence,* which took so much care to secure the *Works* of the *Creation* in *Noah's Flood,* should either then, or since, have been so unmindful of some *Shell-Fish* (and of no other *Animals*) as to suffer any one *Species* to be lost." Plot, *The Natural History of Oxford-Shire, Being an Essay towards the Natural History of England* (1677), 2nd ed. (London: L. Lichfield, 1705), 115.

9. Arthur MacGregor and Abigail Headon, "Re-Inventing the Ashmolean: Natural History and Natural Theology at Oxford in the 1820s to 1850s," *Archives of Natural History* 27.3 (2000), 371.

10. See Thomson, *Before Darwin,* 267.

11. John Ray, *The Wisdom of God Manifested in the Works of the Creation* (London: Samuel Smith, 1691). Paley borrowed heavily from this particular treatise, one of the first of its kind on natural theology in England.

12. John Ray, *The Wisdom of God* (1701 ed.), as quoted in Greene, *Death of Adam,* viii.

13. William Paley, *Natural Theology; or, Evidence of the Existence and Attributes of the Deity, Collected from the Appearances of Nature* (1802; Oxford: Oxford University Press, 2006), 16.

14. Ibid., 10.

15. Wilson, *Charles Lyell, The Years to 1841: The Revolution in Geology* (New Haven: Yale University Press, 1972), 33.

16. Ibid.

17. John Charles Ryle, *Evangelical Religion: What It Is, and What It Is Not* (1867), as quoted in Elisabeth Jay, *Faith and Doubt in Victorian Britain* (London: Macmillan, 1986), 13.

18. Paley, *Natural Theology,* 216.

19. Ibid.

20. Ibid., 15.

21. Charles Lyell to George J. P. Scrope, June 14, 1830, in *The Life, Letters, and Journals of Sir Charles Lyell, Bart.,* ed. Katherine M. Lyell, 2 vols. (London: J. Murray, 1881), 1:268.

22. Roy Porter, "Charles Lyell: The Public and Private Faces of Science," *Janus* 69 (1982), 29–50, esp. his sections "Creating a Public Rôle" and "Lyell and the Strategy of Truth." But see also Rudwick, *Worlds before Adam,* 250.

23. Lyell, *Principles of Geology* (1830–33), 3 vols., ed. James A. Secord (London: Penguin, 1997), 102 (hereafter cited by the abridged edition in the text as *PG*).

24. James Hutton, *Theory of the Earth; or, An Investigation of the Laws Observable in the Composition, Dissolution, and Restoration of Land upon the Globe* (1788) (Sioux Falls, S.Dak.: NuVision, 2007), 75. The term "deep time" is John McPhee's, from his *Basin and Range* (New York: Farrar, Straus and Giroux, 1982), 20. See also Stephen Jay Gould, *Time's Arrow, Time's Cycle: Myth and Metaphor in the Discovery of Geological Time* (Cambridge, Mass.: Harvard University Press, 1987).

25. Greene, *Death of Adam*, 249.

26. Adrian Desmond, *The Politics of Evolution: Morphology, Medicine, and Reform in Radical London* (Chicago: University of Chicago Press, 1989), 4.

27. Lyell, *Principles of Geology*, 3:x–xi, as quoted in Secord's introduction to *Principles*, xxvi.

28. Lyell to Scrope, June 14, 1830, in *Life, Letters, and Journals of Lyell*, 1:268.

29. According to Secord, Lyell abstained from voting to avoid conflict with his father and brothers: "He could not violate his beliefs by voting Tory; but neither could he slight his father by siding with the Whigs, at the height of the Reform Bill agitation and in an open election with less than a hundred voters" (introduction to *Principles*, xiii).

30. Porter, "Charles Lyell," 30. One exception was Darwin's teacher, the botanist and geologist professor the Reverend John Stevens Henslow, who was married when he taught at Cambridge.

31. Secord, introduction to *Principles of Geology*, xxvii.

32. Ibid.

33. Lyell, cited in ibid. I am grateful to Secord's introduction to *Principles* for detailing many of these sources.

34. Lyell to George Ticknor, 1850, in *Life, Letters, and Journals of Lyell*, 2:169.

35. Porter, "Charles Lyell," 30.

36. The separation, that is, of church and state, so that the Church of England would cease to be the country's official religion and the monarch would no longer be supreme governor of both the Church of England and the twenty-six bishops who sit in the House of Lords.

37. Secord, introduction to *Principles of Geology*, xxx.

38. Michael Bartholomew, "Lyell and Evolution: An Account of Lyell's Response to the Prospect of an Evolutionary Ancestry for Man," *British Journal for the History of Science* 6.23 (1973), 267.

39. Lyell to Gideon Mantell, December 29, 1827, in *Life, Letters, and Journals of Lyell*, 1:174.

40. Ibid., 173.

41. Lyell to Thomas S. Spedding, May 19, 1863, in ibid., 2:376.

42. "I re-read his book," Darwin writes, "and remembering when it was written, I felt I had done him injustice." Quoted in Secord, introduction to *Principles of Geology*, xxxvii.

43. Lyell to Mantell, March 2, 1827, in *Life, Letters, and Journals of Lyell*, 1:168.

44. Lyell, *Principles of Geology*, 196; also Secord, introduction to *Principles of Geology*, xxx.

45. Lyell to Mantell, March 2, 1827.

46. Ibid.

47. "Principles of Geology," *Monthly Review* (London), ser. 4 (March 1832), 1:353.

48. Lyell, *Sir Charles Lyell's Scientific Journals on the Species Question*, ed. Leonard G. Wilson (New Haven: Yale University Press, 1970), 280. The entry, "Birth of Man—Progressionists," is dated June 29, 1859. Darwin's *On the Origin of Species* was published in November that year.

49. Ibid., 84–85 (entry dated May 5, 1856).

50. Ibid., 57 ("Origin & Reality of Species"; entry dated April 29, 1856).

51. Ibid., 172 ("Unity of Creation"; entry dated July 11, 1858).

52. Ibid., 86 ("Dignity of Man"; entry dated May 7, 1856).

53. Ibid., 120 ("From the Lower Mammalia to Man"; entry dated July 10, 1856).

54. Ibid., 98 ("Races & Species"; entry dated June 13, 1856).

55. Secord, introduction to *Principles of Geology*, xxxiii–xxxiv.

56. Lyell, *Sir Charles Lyell's Scientific Journals*, 196 (entry dated November 1, 1858).

57. Ibid., 180 ("Species"; entry dated July 2, 1858).

58. Bishop Berkeley, *Verses on the Prospect of Planting Arts and Learning in America* (1726), as quoted in Lyell, *Sir Charles Lyell's Scientific Journals*, 211. Adam Sedgwick, then Woodwardian Professor of Geology at Cambridge, whose criticisms of Robert Chambers will recur in chapter 4, took a line similar to Berkeley in his 1833 *Discourse on the Studies of the University*, intro. Eric Ashby and Mary Anderson (Leicester: Leicester University Press, 1969), 16.

59. Lyell, *Sir Charles Lyell's Scientific Journals*, 182 ("Immortality"; entry dated July 2, 1858); emphasis mine.

60. Ibid., 200 ("Creation"; entry dated December 23, 1858).

61. Wilson, private conversation with the author, November 15, 2008.

62. Ibid.

63. Alfred, Lord Tennyson, *In Memoriam* (1850; New York: Norton, 1973), 3, 35 (prologue and section 56).

64. Ibid., 36, 34–36 (sections 56, 55, 55, 56, 56). See also Michael Tomko, "Varieties

of Geological Experience: Religion, Body, and Spirit in Tennyson's *In Memoriam* and Lyell's *Principles of Geology*," *Victorian Poetry* 42.2 (2004), 113–33.

65. Tennyson, *In Memoriam*, 34 (section 54).

66. George Eliot, *The Mill on the Floss* (1860; London: Penguin, 2003), 543. For more on Eliot's debt to Lyell, see Jonathan Smith, *Fact and Feeling: Baconian Science and the Nineteenth-Century Literary Imagination* (Madison: University of Wisconsin Press, 1994), chap. 4.

67. Thomas Carlyle to Jane W. Carlyle, July 11, 1843, in *The Collected Letters of Thomas and Jane Welsh Carlyle*, ed. Clyde de L. Ryals and Kenneth J. Fielding, 37 vols. (Durham: Duke University Press, 1977–2009), 16:260.

68. Carlyle to MacVey Napier, October 8, 1831, ibid., 6:13.

69. Carlyle, *Sartor Resartus: The Life and Opinions of Herr Teufelsdröckh in Three Books* (1833–34), intro. Rodger L. Tarr, with text established by Mark Engel and Rodger L. Tarr (Berkeley: University of California Press, 2000), 121 (hereafter cited in the text as *SR*).

70. Volume 1 of *Principles* appeared in July 1830. Carlyle began writing the first draft of *Sartor Resartus* in September that year, though it took him several more years to complete it and find a publisher for it.

71. For one of several good essays on Carlyle, science, and doubt, see Carlisle Moore, "Carlyle and the 'Torch of Science,'" in *Lectures on Carlyle and His Era*, ed. Jerry D. James and Charles S. Fineman (Santa Cruz: University of California Press, 1982), 1–25.

72. Carlyle, as quoted in the introduction to *Sartor Resartus*, xliii.

73. Ibid., li.

74. Tarr, introduction to ibid., xxxv.

75. A. L. Le Quesne, "Carlyle," in *Victorian Thinkers*, ed. Keith Thomas (Oxford: Oxford University Press, 1993), 13.

76. Tarr, introduction to *Sartor Resartus*, xxxv.

77. Ibid., xl.

78. Ibid., xxxviii.

79. Ibid., xxvi.

80. John Bunyan, *The Pilgrim's Progress* (1678; New York: P. F. Collier and Son, 1909), 119–23.

THREE *Feeling Doubt, Then Drinking It*

1. John Henry Newman, "My Illness in Sicily" (March 1840), based on travels from December 1832, in *Autobiographical Writings*, ed. Henry Tristram (London: Sheed and Ward), 1957), 125.

2. Ibid., 121; Newman, *Apologia pro Vita Sua* (1864; London: Penguin, 1994), 50.

3. Newman, "My Illness," 125.

4. Newman, *Apologia,* 50.

5. Newman, "My Illness," 121. See also Ian Ker, *John Henry Newman: A Biography* (Oxford: Oxford University Press, 1988), 61–83.

6. Kevin Rawlinson, "Cardinal Newman Moves Step Closer to Sainthood," *Independent* (London), July 3, 2009. Rawlinson begins: "Campaigners for the canonisation of John Paul [sic] Newman are praying for another miracle after the Pope confirmed that the Cardinal was responsible for curing a case of spinal debility more than 100 years after his death."

7. Close friends since 1826, Hurrell and Newman grew centrally involved in its Tractarian Movement, so named because of the "Tracts" that Newman edited and often wrote. Many of these strongly contested the political principle—established since the Reformation—that the Anglican Church was in theory beholden to the British state and monarch and not to the pope (*Apologia,* 32).

8. Newman to John Frederic Christie, March 7, 1833, and Newman to Samuel Rickards, April 14, 1833, both in *The Letters and Diaries of John Henry Newman,* ed. Birmingham Oratory, 29 vols. (Oxford: Oxford University Press, 1970–78), 3:240, 289.

9. Newman, *Apologia,* 50.

10. Newman, "Lead, Kindly Light" (June 16, 1833), in *John Henry Newman: Prose and Poetry,* ed. Geoffrey Tillotson (Cambridge, Mass.: Harvard University Press, 1957), 807.

11. Currer Bell [Charlotte Brontë], "Biographical Notice of Ellis and Acton Bell," reprinted in Emily Brontë, *Wuthering Heights* (1847; London: Penguin, 1995), xlvii.

12. Newman, *Apologia,* 25. See also J. M. Robertson, *History of Freethought in the Nineteenth Century,* 2 vols. (London: Watts, 1929), 1:147.

13. Newman, *Apologia,* 164.

14. Newman had left Oriel College two years earlier, in 1841.

15. Bernard Lightman, *The Origins of Agnosticism: Victorian Unbelief and the Limits of Knowledge* (Baltimore: Johns Hopkins University Press, 1987), 3. See also Frank M. Turner, "The Religious and the Secular in Victorian England," in Turner, *Contesting Cultural Authority: Essays in Victorian Intellectual Life* (Cambridge: Cambridge University Press, 1993), 3–37.

16. Arthur Hugh Clough to J. P. Gell, October 8, 1843, in *The Correspondence of Arthur Hugh Clough,* ed. Frederick L. Mulhauser, 2 vols. (Oxford: Clarendon, 1957), 1:124.

17. Clough to Gell, November 24, 1844, in ibid., 1:140.

18. Anglicans Online, "The Thirty-Nine Articles of Religion" (updated April 15, 2007): http://anglicansonline.org/basics/thirty-nine_articles.html.

19. Susan Budd, *Varieties of Unbelief: Atheists and Agnostics in English Society, 1850–1960* (London: Heinemann, 1977), 105.

20. Robert Lee Wolff offers a comprehensive summary of many of them in *Gains and Losses: Novels of Faith and Doubt in Victorian England* (New York: Garland, 1977); "Victorian Fiction: Novels of Faith and Doubt," his own book series with Garland, encompasses ninety-two novels simply by staying with mostly noncanonical works. See also Lance St. John Butler, *Victorian Doubt: Literary and Cultural Discourses* (London: Harvester Wheatsheaf, 1990), and A. N. Wilson, *God's Funeral: The Decline of Faith in Western Civilization* (New York: Norton, 1999), two works of central importance to mine.

21. John Kucich, "Intellectual Debate in the Victorian Novel: Religion, Science and the Professional," in *The Cambridge Companion to the Victorian Novel,* ed. Deirdre David (Cambridge: Cambridge University Press, 2001), 215.

22. Thomas Hardy, "God's Funeral" (c. 1908), line 21.

23. Winifred Gérin, *Anne Brontë* (London: Allen Lane, 1959; 2nd ed., 1976), 35.

24. Charlotte Brontë, *Jane Eyre: An Autobiography* (1847; London: Penguin, 2006), 76.

25. Ibid., 78, 38.

26. Ibid., 424, 464, 471. Other, unforgettable depictions of Evangelicals include Dickens' Murdstone in *David Copperfield* (1850) and Chadband in *Bleak House* (1853). Samuel Butler's semiautobiographical novel *The Way of All Flesh* (1903; London: Penguin, 1986) is also a riveting account of a stifling Evangelical Victorian childhood. For more on Dickens and religion, see Janet L. Larson, *Dickens and the Broken Scripture* (Athens: University of Georgia Press, 1985).

27. Newman, *Apologia,* 41–42.

28. [William Nicholson], *The Doubts of Infidels; or, Queries Relative to Scriptural Inconsistencies and Contradictions* (London: R. Carlile, 1819), 1.

29. Francis William Newman helps explain why in his own religious autobiography, *Phases of Faith; or, Passages from the History of My Creed* (1850; 1874; Charleston, S.C.: BiblioBazaar, 2008). He later participated in the important debates that formed *Agnosticism: A Symposium* (1884), which included Thomas H. Huxley and appeared in the *Agnostic Annual* (1884). For another, equally fascinating account of agnosticism at Oxford, see Nitram Tradleg [Edmund Martin Geldart], *A Son of Belial: Autobiographical Sketches* (London: Trübner, 1882).

30. "The Church has authority in controversies," Newman later explained; but the articles "do not say *what* authority. They say that it may enforce nothing beyond Scripture, but do not say *where* the remedy lies when it does," and so on. Newman, *Apologia*, 91.

31. Ibid., 57.

32. John Keble, "National Apostasy" (preached at Saint Mary's, Oxford, on July 14, 1833; London: A. R. Mowbray, n.d.).

33. Ibid.

34. Ibid.; emphasis in original.

35. For elaboration on Constable's relation to Salisbury Cathedral, often in his own words, see C. R. Leslie, *Memoirs of the Life of John Constable, Composed Chiefly of His Letters*, 2nd ed. (London: Longman, Brown, 1845), 94, 115.

36. Thomas Arnold to A. P. Stanley, May 24, 1836, in Arthur Penrhyn Stanley, *The Life and Correspondence of Thomas Arnold*, 2 vols. (New York: Scribner's, 1895), 2:46–47. See also Arnold, "The Oxford Malignants and Dr. Hampden," *Edinburgh Review* 63 (April 1836), 225–39.

37. The Rev. Edward Monro, *Reasons for Feeling Secure in the Church of England: A Letter to a Friend, in Answer to Doubts Expressed in Reference to the Claims of the Church of Rome* (London: I. H. Parker, 1850), 3. However hyperbolic the reverend's rhetoric, the issue is still making news. See Rachel Donadio and Laurie Goodstein, "Vatican Bidding to Get Anglicans to Join Its Fold," *New York Times*, October 20, 2009.

38. John Stuart Mill, *On Liberty* (1859; London: Penguin, 1982), 109, 66, 104. See also his *Three Essays on Religion* (1874), in *Essays on Ethics, Religion and Society, Collected Works of John Stuart Mill*, ed. J. M. Robson and F. E. L. Priestley, 33 vols. (Toronto: University of Toronto Press, 1963–91), 10:369–489.

39. David J. DeLaura, *Hebrew and Hellene in Victorian England: Newman, Arnold, and Pater* (Austin: University of Texas Press, 1969), 13.

40. Ibid.

41. Acton Bell [Anne Brontë], "The Doubter's Prayer" (September 1843; published 1846), in *The Poems of Anne Brontë: A New Text and Commentary*, ed. Edward Chitham (Totowa, N.J.: Rowman and Littlefield, 1979), 91 (lines 25–28). Subsequent references to Anne's poetry are to this edition.

42. Gérin, *Anne Brontë*, v.

43. Ibid., 34, 33.

44. Ibid., 33.

45. Marianne Thormählen, *The Brontës and Religion* (Cambridge: Cambridge University Press, 1999), 72.

46. Gérin, *Anne Brontë*, 99.

47. Brontë, "Doubter's Prayer," line 29.

48. Ibid., lines 5, 8, 9, 12; emphasis in original.

49. Edward Chitham, *A Life of Anne Brontë* (Oxford: Blackwell, 1991), 105.

50. Patrick Brontë, as quoted in Michael Baumber, "William Grimshaw, Patrick Brontë, and the Evangelical Revival," *History Today* (November 1992), 29.

51. [Charlotte Brontë], "Biographical Notice of Ellis and Acton Bell," reprinted in Emily Brontë, *Wuthering Heights,* xlvii. The preface dates from September 19, 1850, the year after Anne died of pulmonary tuberculosis and two years after Emily also died of tuberculosis (from influenza).

52. See, e.g., Lucasta Miller, *The Brontë Myth* (New York: Knopf, 2001), esp. chap. 1.

53. May Sinclair, *The Three Brontës* (1912; Charleston, S.C.: Dodo/BiblioBazaar, 2007), 49.

54. [Elizabeth Rigby], "*Vanity Fair* and *Jane Eyre,*" *Quarterly Review* (London) 84, no. 167 (December 1848), 173–74.

55. Charlotte Brontë, preface to the second edition of *Jane Eyre,* 5–6. See also John Maynard's useful complication of Charlotte's and her sisters' position in "The Brontës and Religion," in *The Cambridge Companion to the Brontës,* ed. Heather Glen (Cambridge: Cambridge University Press, 2002), esp. 196.

56. Charlotte Brontë, *Shirley: A Tale* (1849; London: Penguin, 2006), 521.

57. Charlotte Brontë, *Villette* (1853; New York: Modern Library, 2001), 186 and 133. For other uses of the term *heretic,* see 479, 481, 513, 535.

58. Emily Brontë, "No coward soul is mine," in *The Brontë Sisters: Selected Poems,* ed. Stevie Davies (New York: Routledge, 2002), 89.

59. Review of Anne Brontë, *The Tenant of Wildfell Hall, Spectator,* July 8, 1848, rept. in *The Brontës: Critical Heritage,* ed. Miriam Allott (London: Routledge, 1974), 270, 252.

60. Review of Anne Brontë, *The Tenant of Wildfell Hall, Fraser's Magazine* 39 (April 1849), rept. in *The Brontë Sisters: Critical Assessments,* ed. Eleanor McNees, 4 vols. (Mountfield, Sussex: Helm Information, 1996), 2:454.

61. Brontë, preface to the second edition, *The Tenant of Wildfell Hall* (1848; London: Penguin, 1996), 4 (hereafter cited in the text as *WH*).

62. Chitham, *Life of Anne Brontë,* 13.

63. To the sequence of "H" characters that spell out kinship in the *Heights* series (Hindley, Heathcliff, and Hareton), Anne offered a resounding echo, one year later, with Huntingdon, Hargrave, Hattersley, Halford, and of course Helen.

64. Acton Bell [Anne Brontë], "A Word to the 'Elect,'" in *Poems of Anne Brontë,*

89; original emphasis in most other editions, including in the first edition of the Brontës' *Poems* (1846). According to Chitham, *Life of Anne Brontë*, 104, Brontë wrote "A Word to the Calvinists" in May 1843, four months before "The Doubter's Prayer."

65. According to Herman Hanko, "Election is . . . that decree of God which He eternally makes, by which, with sovereign freedom, He chooses to Himself a people, upon whom He determines to set His love, whom He rescues from sin and death through Jesus Christ, unto Himself in everlasting glory." Hanko, with Homer Hoeksema and Gise J. Van Baren, *The Five Points of Calvinism* (Grand Rapids, Mich.: Reformed Free Publishing Association, 1976), 33.

66. Review of Brontë, *Tenant of Wildfell Hall, Fraser's Magazine,* 2:455.

67. For contrasting perspectives on Brontë's suggestion here, see Thormählen, "The Villain of 'Wildfell Hall': Aspects and Prospects of Arthur Huntingdon," *Modern Language Review* 88.4 (1993), 831–41, and Chitham, *Life of Anne Brontë,* on the critical chap. 49 of Brontë's novel: "Helen's arguments from passages in the Bible are toned down as "*mere* suggestions" (175).

68. Review of Brontë, *The Tenant of Wildfell Hall, Fraser's Magazine,* 2:454.

69. Brontë, "A Prayer" (October 1844), in *Poems of Anne Brontë,* 105 (lines 3–4, 13).

70. Brontë, "Despondency" (December 1841), in ibid., 81 (lines 31–32).

71. Brontë, "To Cowper" (November 1842), in ibid., 84 (lines 15, 11, 16, 17, 21–22).

72. Susan R. Bauman, "'How Shall *I* Appear?' The Dialogue of Faith and Doubt in Anne Brontë's Hymns," in *Sublimer Aspects: Interfaces between Literature, Aesthetics, and Theology,* ed. Natasha Duquette (Newcastle: Cambridge Scholars, 2007), 84; and Brontë, "Three Guides" (August 1847), in *Poems of Anne Brontë,* 144 (lines 195, 206, 210).

73. Charlotte Brontë, as quoted in *The Brontës: Their Lives, Friendships, and Correspondence,* ed. Thomas J. Wise and John Alexander Symington, 4 vols. (Oxford: Blackwell, 1932), 2:261.

74. Esther Alice Chadwick, *In the Footsteps of the Brontës* (London: Pitman and Sons, 1914), 85–86.

75. Daphne du Maurier, *The Infernal World of Branwell Brontë* (Garden City, N.Y.: Doubleday, 1961); Joan Rees, *Profligate Son: Branwell Brontë and His Sisters* (London: Robert Hale, 1986); Mary Butterfield, *Brother in the Shadow: Stories and Sketches by Patrick Branwell Brontë,* ed. R. J. Duckett (Bradford: Bradford Libraries and Information Service, 1988).

76. Du Maurier, *Infernal World of Branwell Brontë,* 61. On page 239 she uses the word "schizophrenia" to describe Branwell's dissociative states.

77. Victor A. Neufeldt, introduction to *The Poems of Patrick Branwell Brontë: A New Text and Commentary* (New York: Garland, 1990), xxxvii.

78. Rees, *Profligate Son*, 13.

79. Gérin, *Anne Brontë*, 193.

80. [Patrick] Branwell Brontë, "The Doubter's Hymn" (November 1835), in *The Poems of Patrick Branwell Brontë*, ed. Tom Winnifrith (Oxford: Blackwell/ Shakespeare Head, 1983), 210–11 (lines 21–24).

81. Ibid., lines 1–4.

82. Ibid., lines 17–20.

83. Branwell Brontë, quoted in du Maurier, *Infernal World of Branwell Brontë*, 62.

84. Ibid., 63.

85. Michael Walker, "J. B. Leyland: Sculptor and Friend of Branwell Brontë," *Brontë Studies* 32 (March 2007), 57–70.

86. *Morning Chronicle*, as quoted in ibid., 60.

87. Martin Priestman, *Romantic Atheism: Poetry and Freethought, 1780–1830* (Cambridge: Cambridge University Press, 2000). For a comparable example, see Samuel Taylor Coleridge, "Confessions of an Inquiring Spirit," in *The Collected Works of Samuel Taylor Coleridge*, ed. H. L. Jackson and J. R. de J. Jackson, 16 vols. (Princeton, N.J.: Princeton University Press, 1969–2000), 12:1111–71.

88. Branwell Brontë, "Harriet II" (May 1838), in *Poems of Patrick Branwell Brontë*, ed. Winnifrith, 92 (lines 57–61).

FOUR *Natural History Sparks Honest Doubt*

1. Robert Chambers, *Vestiges of the Natural History of Creation and Other Evolutionary Writings*, ed. and intro. James A. Secord (Chicago: University of Chicago Press, 1994), 153 (hereafter cited in the text as *V*).

2. James A. Secord, *Victorian Sensation: The Extraordinary Publication, Reception, and Secret Authorship of* Vestiges of the Natural History of Creation (Chicago: University of Chicago Press, 2000), 39.

3. *Spectator*, November 9, 1844, 1072–73; [E. Forbes], *Lancet*, November 23, 1844; *Atlas*, November 2, 1844, 746, as cited by Secord in *Victorian Sensation*, 35–36. Here, as elsewhere, I am much indebted to Secord's exhaustive research and meticulous analysis of the book's reception.

4. Erasmus Darwin began to spell out his theory in *Zoönomia; or, The Laws of Inorganic Life* (London: J. Johnson, 1794–96), a work that anticipated Jean-Baptiste Lamarck's developmental theory of evolution.

5. Secord, introduction to *Vestiges*, xxiv.

6. [Lewis Tayler], "Vestiges of the Natural History of Creation," *American Review* 1 (1845), 526, as quoted in Secord, introduction to *Vestiges,* xi–xii.

7. Florence Nightingale to [? P. Nightingale], February 1845, as quoted in Secord, *Victorian Sensation,* 162.

8. Susan Budd, *Varieties of Unbelief: Atheists and Agnostics in English Society 1850–1960* (London: Heinemann, 1977), 104–5. The breadth and depth of Budd's research seems necessary to underscore because Timothy Larsen has since disputed its importance, arguing in *Crisis of Doubt: Honest Faith in Nineteenth-Century England* (Oxford: Oxford University Press, 2006) that Budd failed to account for reconversions to Christianity, which for obvious reasons wouldn't have appeared in such journals. In fact, Budd wrote that deathbed repentance stories "were usually reported anonymously and were sometimes true" (105). On the same page, she also discusses "patterns of conversion to Christianity." While Larsen is right to point out that "reconversions were a major reality in the Secularist movement" (14), he overstates their cultural impact relative to Budd's far greater numbers of secular obituaries, which he largely ignores to focus on the reconversion of seven relatively minor intellectual figures. For more on the spread of secularism, see also Edward Royle's excellent study, *Victorian Infidels: The Origins of the British Secularist Movement, 1791–1866* (Manchester: Manchester University Press, 1974).

9. See, e.g., J. P. Earwaker, "Natural Science at Oxford," *Nature,* December 29, 1870, 170–71.

10. "Deliverance from Doubt," *Universalist Quarterly and General Review* 14 (April 1857), 122–29; W. B. Clarke, "Faith, Doubt, and Reason," *New Englander* 22 (January 1863), 79–103. See also J. F. Spalding, "The Discipline of Doubt," *Boston Review* 6 (1866), 120–28.

11. Clarke, "Faith, Doubt, and Reason," 103; emphasis in original.

12. John Stuart Mill, *On Liberty* (1859; London: Penguin, 1982), 115, 93.

13. See in particular Jeremy Bentham's chief work, *An Introduction to the Principles of Morals and Legislation* (1789; Oxford: Clarendon, 1907), 27, 36, 40.

14. Ludwig Feuerbach, *The Essence of Christianity* (1841; Amherst, N.Y.: Prometheus Books, 1989), x. See also 283–84, 289.

15. Charlotte Brontë, *Jane Eyre: An Autobiography* (1847; London: Penguin, 2006), 396, 468.

16. Robert Flint, *Agnosticism* (Edinburgh: W. Blackwood, 1903), 30.

17. Ayaan Hirsi Ali, "Blind Faiths," *New York Times Book Review,* January 6, 2008. See also Jonathan Israel, *A Revolution of the Mind: Radical Enlightenment and*

the *Intellectual Origins of Modern Democracy* (Princeton, N.J.: Princeton University Press, 2009), esp. chap. 1.

18. William Henry Fitton in the *Edinburgh Review,* as quoted in Martin J. S. Rudwick, *Worlds before Adam: The Reconstruction of Geohistory in the Age of Reform* (Chicago: University of Chicago Press, 2008), 84.

19. Secord, introduction to *Vestiges,* xxii.

20. Ibid.

21. Ibid.

22. Ibid.

23. [Adam Sedgwick], "Vestiges of the Natural History of Creation," *Edinburgh Review* 82 (July 1845), 63–64.

24. Ibid., 3.

25. Ibid., 7.

26. Secord, *Victorian Sensation,* 13, 37.

27. Ibid., 132–34.

28. Ibid., 274, referencing [D. Brewster], "Explanations," *North British Review* (February 1846), 487–504.

29. Ibid., 330, quoting *Nonconformist,* July 9, 1845, 490, and August 13, 1845, 569; and "Vestiges of Creation," *Christian Observer,* n.s., 165 (September 1851), 606, 601; and "Claims of the Animal Creation," ibid., 95 (November 1845), 671.

30. Charles Darwin, "An Historical Sketch of the Progress of Opinion on the Origin of Species," in *On the Origin of Species by Means of Natural Selection* (1859), ed. J. W. Burrow (London: Penguin, 1968), 58.

31. Alfred, Lord Tennyson, diary entry for March 28, 1871, as quoted in Secord, *Victorian Sensation,* 9.

32. Tennyson, *In Memoriam* (1850; New York: Norton, 1973), 34 (section 55, line 5); see also David R. Dean, *Tennyson and Geology* (Lincoln: Tennyson Society, 1985), 1–8.

33. Tennyson, *In Memoriam,* 62 (section 96, lines 9, 11–12, 4).

34. Secord, *Victorian Sensation,* 253.

35. J. Anthony Froude, *The Nemesis of Faith* (London: John Chapman, 1849), 12, 121 (hereafter cited in the text as *NF*).

36. Froude to Charles Kingsley, January 1849, as quoted in Waldo Hilary Dunn, *James Anthony Froude: A Biography,* 2 vols. (Oxford: Clarendon, 1961–63), 1:131. See also Rosemary Ashton, "Doubting Clerics: From James Anthony Froude to *Robert Elsmere* via George Eliot," in *The Critical Spirit and the Will to Believe: Essays in Nineteenth-Century Literature and Religion,* ed. David Jasper and T. R. Wright (Basingstoke: Macmillan, 1989), 74.

37. Julia Markus, *J. Anthony Froude: The Last Undiscovered Great Victorian: A Biography* (New York: Scribner, 2005), 41–42.

38. Froude to Kingsley, January 1849, in Dunn, *Froude,* 1:131.

39. Ibid.

40. Kingsbury Badger, "The Ordeal of Anthony Froude, Protestant Historian," *Modern Language Quarterly* 13.1 (1952), 46. But see also Basil Willey, *More Nineteenth Century Studies: A Group of Honest Doubters* (New York: Columbia University Press, 1956), 121–32, and Daniel Cook, "Froude's Post-Christian Apostate and the Uneven Development of Unbelief," *Religion and Literature* 38.2 (2006), esp. 60–61.

41. The Reverend John Cumming, *The Church before the Flood* (London: Arthur Hall, Virtue, 1853), 47.

42. Robert H. Ellison and Carol Engelhardt, "Prophecy and Anti-Popery in Victorian London: John Cumming Reconsidered," *Victorian Literature and Culture* 31.1 (2003), 379. See also the Rev. John Cumming, *Apocalyptic Sketches; or, Lectures on the Book of Revelation, First Series* (London: Arthur Hall, 1849); *The Romish Church, a Dumb Church* (Arthur Hall, 1853); and *The Destiny of Nations as Indicated in Prophecy* (London: Hurst and Blackett, 1864).

43. The Reverend John Cumming, *Is Christianity from God? or, A Manual of Christian Evidence for Scripture Readers, City Missionaries, Sunday School Teachers, &c.* (London: Arthur Hall and J. F. Shaw, 1847), 144–45; emphasis in original.

44. George Eliot, "Evangelical Teaching: Dr Cumming" (*Westminster Review,* October 1855), in *George Eliot: Selected Essays, Poems and Other Writings,* ed. A. S. Byatt and Nicholas Warren (London: Penguin, 1990), 50.

45. Ibid., 40 (hereafter cited in the text as "ET"). See also Peter Allan Dale, *In Pursuit of a Scientific Culture: Science, Art, and Society in the Victorian Age* (Madison: University of Wisconsin Press, 1989).

46. Lord Byron, "Euthanasia" (1811), as quoted in ibid., 47–48; emphases in original.

47. Lewes was unable to procure a divorce from his wife, Agnes Jervis, because he had countenanced her adultery and agreed to represent himself, on birth certificates, as the father of several of the children that she had had with other men. In the eyes of the law, he thus forfeited his legal right to end the marriage. The price that he and Eliot paid for such open-mindedness was considerable, especially when *Adam Bede* made her a literary celebrity.

48. Thomas Carlyle, *Sartor Resartus: The Life and Opinions of Herr Teufelsdröckh in Three Books* (1833–34), intro. Rodger L. Tarr, with text established by Mark Engel and Rodger L. Tarr (Berkeley: University of California Press, 2000), 34.

49. George Eliot, "Prospectus of the *Westminster and Foreign Quarterly Review*" (January 1852), a revised and expanded version of the draft Eliot cowrote with John Chapman, in *George Eliot: Selected Essays*, 6–7.

50. Gordon S. Haight, *George Eliot: A Biography* (1968; London: Penguin, 1992), 186.

51. Eliot's phrase is, "sunt quibus non credidisse honor est, et fidei futuræ pignus," in *George Eliot: Selected Essays*, 51.

52. Cumming, as quoted in ibid., 51.

53. Ibid.; emphasis mine.

54. Anne Brontë [Acton Bell], "A Word to the 'Elect'" (May 1843; published 1846), in *The Poems of Anne Brontë: A New Text and Commentary,* ed. Edward Chitham (Totowa, N.J.: Rowman and Littlefield, 1979), 90.

55. See Bernard Lightman, "Huxley and Scientific Agnosticism: The Strange History of a Failed Rhetorical Strategy," *British Journal for the History of Science* 35.3 (2002), 271–89, and A. O. J. Cockshut, *The Unbelievers: English Agnostic Thought, 1840–90* (London: Collins, 1964), chap. 3: "George Eliot: The Search for Justice."

56. See, e.g., Bernard J. Paris, "George Eliot's Religion of Humanity," in *George Eliot: A Collection of Critical Essays,* ed. George R. Creeger (Englewood Cliffs, N.J.: Prentice-Hall, 1970), esp. 13. The phrase is Auguste Comte's, from his *System of Positive Polity; or, Treatise on Sociology, Instituting the Religion of Humanity* (Paris: Carilian-Goeury et Dalmont, 1851–54). See also U. C. Knoepflmacher, *Religious Humanism and the Victorian Novel: George Eliot, Walter Pater, and Samuel Butler* (Princeton, N.J.: Princeton University Press, 1965).

57. All that remains of the poem appears in Rosemary Ashton's biography *George Eliot: A Life* (London: Penguin, 1997), 22.

58. John Keble, *The Christian Year: Thoughts in Verse for the Sundays and Holydays throughout the Year,* 2 vols. (Oxford: J. Parker, 1827), 2:131 (84, stanza 12). See also Jude V. Nixon, "Framing Victorian Religious Discourse: An Introduction," in *Victorian Religious Discourse: New Directions in Criticism* (New York: Palgrave, 2004), 3.

59. Thomas à Kempis, *De Imitatione Christi* (The imitation of Christ), as quoted in Eliot, *The Mill on the Floss* (1860; London: Penguin, 2003), 301. "Stern, ascetic views": as quoted in Ashton, *George Eliot,* 25.

60. Charles C. Hennell, *An Inquiry Concerning the Origin of Christianity* (1838), 2nd ed. (London: T. Allman, 1841), 476.

61. Ibid., 72.

62. Arthur James Balfour tackles some of these arguments in *A Defence of Philosophic Doubt: Being an Essay on the Foundations of Belief* (London: Macmillan, 1879), part 2.

63. Ashton, *George Eliot*, 36.

64. Eliot, as quoted in Kathryn Hughes, *George Eliot: The Last Victorian* (New York: Farrar, Straus and Giroux, 1999), 38.

65. Hughes, ibid., 49.

66. "Higher criticism" was meant to distinguish the approach from a long-standing tradition of studying religious manuscripts, dubbed "the lower criticism."

67. Eliot, review of Robert William Mackay's *Progress of the Intellect, as Exemplified in the Religious Development of the Greeks and Hebrews* (London: John Chapman, 1850), *Westminster Review* 54 (January 1851), in *George Eliot: Selected Essays*, 268–69.

68. Feuerbach, *Essence of Christianity*, 63.

69. Ibid., 316; emphasis in original.

70. For elaboration, see my chapter "George Eliot and Enmity" in *Hatred and Civility: The Antisocial Life in Victorian England* (New York: Columbia University Press, 2004), 107–35.

71. George Eliot, *Silas Marner: The Weaver of Raveloe* (1861; London: Penguin, 1996), 14 (hereafter cited in the text as *SM*).

FIVE *Uncertainty Becomes a Way of Life*

1. Among the wettest Junes on record in Britain, June 2007 just beats out June 1860: http://www.metoffice.gov.uk/climate/uk/interesting/june2007/.

2. Baden Powell, "On the Study of the Evidences of Christianity," *Essays and Reviews: The 1860 Text and Its Reading*, ed. Victor Shea and William Whitla (Charlottesville: University of Virginia Press, 2005), 258.

3. See, e.g., John William Draper, *History of the Conflict between Religion and Science* (London: King, 1875).

4. Samuel Wilberforce, as quoted in, among others, John A. Moore, *From Genesis to Genetics: The Case of Evolution* (Berkeley: University of California Press, 2002), 76. See also J. R. Lucas, "Wilberforce and Huxley: A Legendary Encounter," *Historical Journal* 22.2 (1979), 313–30.

5. Thomas H. Huxley, as quoted in Leonardo Huxley, *Life and Letters of Thomas Henry Huxley*, 2 vols. (London: Macmillan, 1990), 1:208.

6. Huxley, as quoted in Adrian Desmond, *Darwin: The Life of a Tormented Evolutionist* (New York: Norton, 1991), 497.

7. Keith Stewart Thomson, "Huxley, Wilberforce, and the Oxford Museum," *American Scientist* 83 (May–June 2000), 210.

8. *Press* (London), July 7, 1860, 656, as quoted in J. Vernon Jensen, "Return to the Wilberforce-Huxley Debate," *British Journal for the History of Science* 21.2 (1988), 161. See also *Athenaeum*, July 7, 1860, 19. The *Guardian* and *Jackson's Oxford Journal* joined the *Athenaeum* in running summary reports of the debate.

9. John Hedley Brooke, *Science and Religion: Some Historical Perspectives* (Cambridge: Cambridge University Press, 1991), 41.

10. John C. Greene, *The Death of Adam: Evolution and Its Impact on Western Thought* (Ames: Iowa State University Press, 1959), 266.

11. Christopher Hitchens, editorial preface to Charles Darwin, *Autobiography* (1887), in *The Portable Atheist: Essential Readings for the Nonbeliever* (New York: Da Capo, 2007), 93.

12. Randal Keynes, "Faith, Cricket and Barnacles," *Annie's Box: Charles Darwin, His Daughter and Human Evolution* (London: Fourth Estate, 2001), esp. 118–21. See also Anthony Barnes, "Darwin's Doubts Revealed in His Letters to Friends," *Independent* (London), April 8, 2007, and Nick Spencer, *Darwin and God* (London: Society for Promoting Christian Knowledge, 2009).

13. Bernard Lightman, *The Origins of Agnosticism: Victorian Unbelief and the Limits of Knowledge* (Baltimore: Johns Hopkins University Press, 1987), 15.

14. For a fascinating, comprehensive overview of them, see Lightman, "Huxley and Scientific Agnosticism: The Strange History of a Failed Rhetorical Strategy," *British Journal for the History of Science* 35.3 (2002), 271–89.

15. Charles Darwin, *The Autobiography of Charles Darwin, 1809–1882* (1887), ed. Nora Barlow (New York: Norton, 1958), 76 (hereafter cited in the text as *A*).

16. For elaboration on the broader implications of Darwin's position, see Brooke, "Evolutionary Theory and Religious Belief," *Science and Religion,* 275–320.

17. See Nigel M. Cameron, *Biblical Higher Criticism and the Defense of Infallibilism in Nineteenth-Century Britain* (Lewiston, N.Y.: E. Mellen, 1987).

18. Henry Longueville Mansel, *The Limits of Religious Thought Examined in Eight Lectures, Preached before the University of Oxford in the Year 1858* (London: J. Murray, 1870) (a fifth edition), vii–viii.

19. Lightman, *Origins of Agnosticism,* 6, 7.

20. Shea and Whitla, "From Clerical Culture to Secularized Anglicanism: Positioning *Essays and Reviews* in Victorian Social Transformation," in *Essays and Reviews,* 25.

21. Mark Pattison, "Tendencies of Religious Thought in England, 1688–1750," in *Essays and Reviews,* 412.

22. William Thomson, Lord Bishop of Gloucester and Bristol, "Preface" to *Aids to Faith: A Series of Theological Essays: Being a Reply to "Essays and Reviews" by Several Writers*, ed. Thomson (New York: D. Appleton, 1862), 3. See also the essays "On Miracles as Evidences of Christianity," by H. L. Mansel, and "The Mosaic Record of Creation," by A. McCaul (9–54 and 219–72, respectively), and Frances Power Cobbe, *Broken Lights: An Inquiry into the Present Condition and Future Prospects of Religious Faith* (London: Trübner, 1864).

23. Benjamin Jowett, "On the Interpretation of Scripture," in *Essays and Reviews*, 501.

24. Ibid., 495, 502. See also his later "Darwinism, and Faith in God," in *Sermons on Faith and Doctrine*, ed. W. H. Fremantle (London: Murray, 1901), 1–22.

25. Jowett, "Interpretation of Scripture," 481, 482, 482. For further elaboration on the implications of Jowett's argument, see Hans W. Frei, *The Eclipse of Biblical Narrative: A Study in Eighteenth- and Nineteenth-Century Hermeneutics* (New Haven: Yale University Press, 1974), and Sue Zemka, *Victorian Testaments: The Bible, Christology, and Literary Authority in Early Nineteenth-Century British Culture* (Stanford, Calif.: Stanford University Press, 1997).

26. The Rev. Charles Wesley Rishell, *The Higher Criticism: An Outline of Modern Biblical Study* (1893; New York: Eaton and Mains, 1896), 35.

27. Ibid.

28. Jude V. Nixon, "'Kill[ing] Our Souls with Literalism': Reading *Essays and Reviews*," *Religion and the Arts* 5.1–2 (2001), 38. See also his excellent edited collection *Victorian Religious Discourse: New Directions in Criticism* (New York: Palgrave, 2004).

29. Nixon, "'Kill[ing] Our Souls with Literalism,'" 40–41; Rowland Williams, "Bunsen's Biblical Researches," in *Essays and Reviews*, 639. Williams here is invoking the research of biblical scholar Baron von Bunsen.

30. C. C. J. Bunsen, *God in History; or, The Progress of Man's Faith in the Moral Order of the World*, trans. Susanna Winkworth, 3 vols. (London: Longmans, Green, 1869–70). For a contemporary version of this argument, see Robert Wright, *The Evolution of God* (New York: Little, Brown, 2009), and for an account of its Victorian implications, see Peter Hinchliff, *God and History: Aspects of British Theology, 1875–1914* (Oxford: Clarendon, 1992).

31. J. Hillis Miller, *The Disappearance of God: Five Nineteenth-Century Writers* (1963; Urbana: University of Illinois Press, 2000), 270–359.

32. See Peter Milward and Raymond Schoder, eds., *Readings of the Wreck: Essays in Commemoration of the Centenary of G. M. Hopkins' "The Wreck of the Deutschland"* (Chicago: Loyola University Press, 1976).

33. Gerard Manley Hopkins, "I wake and feel the fell of dark, not day," in *The Later Poetic Manuscripts of Gerard Manley Hopkins in Facsimile,* ed. Norman H. MacKenzie (New York: Garland, 1991), 271 (lines 9–10).

34. W. H. [William Hurrell] Mallock, "Faith and Verification," *Nineteenth Century* (London), rept. in *Littell's Living Age,* November 16, 1878, 410–11.

35. Friedrich Nietzsche, *The Gay Science* (1882), ed. Bernard Williams (Cambridge: Cambridge University Press, 2001), 120 (section 125).

36. Thomas Carlyle, *Sartor Resartus: The Life and Opinions of Herr Teufelsdröckh in Three Books* (1833–34), intro. Rodger L. Tarr, with text established by Mark Engel and Rodger L. Tarr (Berkeley: University of California Press, 2000), 124.

37. Nietzsche, *Gay Science,* 120.

38. Nietzsche, *Thus Spoke Zarathustra: A Book for All and None* (1883–85), trans. R. J. Hollingdale (London: Penguin, 1961), 23; emphasis in original.

39. Matthew Arnold, "Dover Beach" (1867), in *The Poetical Works of Matthew Arnold,* ed. C. B. Tinker and H. F. Lowry (London: Oxford University Press, 1950), 211, 212.

40. Arnold, *Empedocles on Etna* (1852), in *Poetical Works,* 421.

41. R. W. Dale, "From Doubt to Faith," *Lectures Delivered before the Young Men's Christian Association,* in *Exeter Hall Lectures to Young Men* 20 (1864–65), 119.

42. W. S. Balch, "Modern Doubt and Christian Belief," *Universalist Quarterly and General Review* 13 (July 1876), 239. See also "Victims of Doubt," *Month: A Magazine and Review* (London) 5 (1866), 441–53.

43. The Rev. A. C. Dixon, "How to Talk with Doubters," *Treasury: A Christian Magazine* 15 (May 1897), 184–85, 187. See also James A. Howe, "The Way Out of Doubt," *Treasury* 11 (March 1894), 915; Henry C. King, *The Treatment of Doubts* (Oberlin, Ohio: E. Goodrich, 1887); and R. P. Quadrupani, *Light and Peace: Instructions for Devout Souls to Dispel Their Doubts and Allay Their Fears* (London: B. Herder, 1904).

44. J. M. Howard, "How to Deal with Doubt and Doubters," *Cumberland Presbyterian Quarterly* 4 (July 1883), 296, 297, 312, 311.

45. D. A. Wasson, "Intellectual Doubt," *Radical: A Monthly Magazine Devoted to Religion* (Somerville, Mass.) 3 (1867), 293–99; J. F. Spalding, "The Discipline of Doubt," *Boston Review* 6 (January 1866), 120–28; J. Mortimer Granville, M.D., "A Very Common Mind-Trouble," *Good Words* (London) 23 (1882), 340–43. See also John M'Clintock and James Strong, "Doubt: Mental Uncertainty," *Cyclopaedia of Biblical, Theological, and Ecclesiastical Literature* 2 (1874), 876.

46. Editorial, "The Value of Doubt," *Outlook* (New York), May 29, 1897, 245. See

also W. Raistrick, "The Province and Value of Doubt," *Primitive Methodist Quarterly Review* 33 (July 1891), 438.

47. Aubrey L. Moore, "Darwinism and the Christian Faith," *Science and the Faith: Essays on Apologetic Subjects* (1889; London: Kegan Paul, Trench, Trübner, 1898), 162.

48. *Christian Responses to Charles Darwin, 1870–1900: An Exhibit at the Yale Divinity School Library* (February–June 2009), http://www.library.yale.edu/div/exhibits/Darwin.htm. See also James R. Moore, *The Post-Darwinian Controversies: A Study of the Protestant Struggle to Come to Terms with Darwin in Great Britain and America, 1870–1900* (Cambridge: Cambridge University Press, 1979).

49. Moore, "Darwinism," *Essays Scientific and Philosophical* (London: Kegan Paul, Trench, Trübner, 1890), 30–40.

50. See Asa Gray, *Darwiniana: Essays and Reviews Pertaining to Darwinism* (New York: D. Appleton, 1876); Henry Drummond, *The Lowell Lectures on the Ascent of Man* (London: Hodder and Stoughton, 1894); Arthur James Balfour, *A Defence of Philosophic Doubt: Being an Essay on the Foundations of Belief* (London: Macmillan, 1879). See also L. S. Jacyna, "Science and Social Order in the Thought of A. J. Balfour," *Isis* 71.1 (1980), 16; and David N. Livingstone, *Darwin's Forgotten Defenders: The Encounter between Evangelical Theology and Evolutionary Thought* (Grand Rapids, Mich.: Eerdmans, 1987).

51. Josiah Keep, "Doubts Concerning Evolution," *Overland Monthly, Devoted to the Development of the Country* (San Francisco), n.s., 18 (1891), 191. See also Penelope Frederica Fitzgerald, *A Protest against Agnosticism: The Rationale or Philosophy of Belief* (London: Kegan, Paul, Trench, Trübner, 1890).

52. For instance, H. Carlisle, "Belief and Doubt," *Nineteenth Century* 22 (December 1887), 871–84.

53. Henry van Dyke, *The Gospel for an Age of Doubt* (1896; London: Macmillan, 1904), xvii.

54. Laman Blanchard, "Nothing Certain in Life," *New Monthly Magazine* 57 (1839), 502. For commentary on contemporary forms of uncertainty, see David Brooks, "The God That Fails," *New York Times,* December 31, 2009.

55. Blanchard, "Nothing Certain," 503, 502.

56. William Cowper, "Light Shining out of Darkness" (1774), in *Olney Hymns, in Three Books,* 5th ed. (London: J. Buckland and J. Johnson, 1788), 3:255.

57. Heisenberg's principle states that with certain pairs of physical properties, such as position and momentum, the more precisely one property is known, the less precisely the other can be known. See *Macmillan Encyclopedia of Physics,* ed.

John S. Rigden, 4 vols. (New York: Simon and Schuster Macmillan, 1996), 4:1643–47, and Werner Heisenberg, "Über den anschaulichen Inhalt der quantentheoretischen Kinematik und Mechanik," *Zeitschrift für Physik* 43 (1927), 172–98.

58. For analysis of that discussion in England, see Elaine Freedgood, *Victorian Writing about Risk: Imagining a Safe England in a Dangerous World* (Cambridge: Cambridge University Press, 2000), and, in France, A. Javary, *De la certitude* (Paris: Librairie philosophique de Ladrange, 1847), ix–x.

59. Christopher Herbert, *Victorian Relativity: Radical Thought and Scientific Discovery* (Chicago: University of Chicago Press, 2001).

60. Herbert Spencer, *First Principles* (1862; New York: D. Appleton, 1909), 137, 148 (hereafter cited in the text as *FP*).

61. Frederic W. H. Myers, "Charles Darwin and Agnosticism," *Fortnightly Review,* n.s., January 1, 1888, 99–108; "Agnosticism," *Westminster Review* 132 (August 1889), 148–56; and "Ardent Agnosticism," *Spectator,* March 31, 1888, 299. See also Susan Budd, *Varieties of Unbelief: Atheists and Agnostics in English Society 1850–1960* (London: Heinemann, 1977).

62. Frederick James Gould, *Stepping-Stones to Agnosticism* (London: Watts, 1890), and *The Agnostic Island* (London: Watts, 1891). See also Lightman, "Ideology, Evolution and Late-Victorian Agnostic Popularizers," *History, Humanity and Evolution: Essays for John C. Greene,* ed. James R. Moore (Cambridge: Cambridge University Press, 1989), 285–309.

63. *Temporal agnosticism:* "The view that the existence or nonexistence of any deities is currently unknown but is not necessarily unknowable." *Permanent agnosticism:* "The question of the existence or nonexistence of a deity or deities and the nature of ultimate reality is unknowable by reason of our natural inability to verify any experience with anything but another subjective experience." *Pragmatic agnosticism:* "There is no proof of either the existence or nonexistence of any deity, but since any deity that may exist appears unconcerned for the universe or the welfare of its inhabitants, the question is largely academic." *Agnostic Theism:* "The view of those who do not claim to *know* of the existence of any deity, but do not *believe* in any." See Lightman, "Agnosticism," in *The Continuum Encyclopedia of British Philosophy,* ed. Anthony Grayling, Andrew Pyle, and Naomi Goulder, 4 vols. [London: Thoemmes Continuum International, 2006], 1:48–50; and *Encyclopedic Dictionary of Religion,* ed. Paul Kevin Meagher et al, 3 vols. (Washington, D.C.: Corpus, 1978), 1:77–78; the citations are from *Wikipedia:* "Agnosticism," accessed December 21, 2009. See also Frederic Harrison, "Agnostic Metaphysics," *Nineteenth Cen-*

tury 16 (September 1884), 353–78; H. G. Curteis, "Christian Agnosticism," ibid. 15 (February 1884), 337–44; and Martin E. Marty, *Varieties of Unbelief* (New York: Holt, Rinehart, and Winston, 1964).

64. Thomas H. Huxley, "Agnosticism" (1889), in *Science and Christian Tradition* (1894; New York: D. Appleton, 1915), 238.

65. Ibid., 250.

66. Huxley to Charles Kingsley, September 23, 1860, as quoted in Leonard Huxley, *Life and Letters of Thomas Henry Huxley,* 2 vols. (New York: D. Appleton, 1916), 1:234.

67. Huxley, "Agnosticism," 238.

68. Huxley to F. C. Gould, 1889, as quoted in Edward Clodd, *Thomas Henry Huxley* (Edinburgh: Blackwood, 1905), 220.

69. Huxley, as quoted in ibid., 221.

70. Lightman, "Huxley and Scientific Agnosticism," 287.

71. Huxley, "Agnosticism," 242.

72. Huxley to Gould, 220–21.

73. Lightman, "Huxley and Scientific Agnosticism," 287.

74. Ibid., 289.

75. The first was Spencer, *The Data of Ethics* (London: Williams and Norgate, 1879).

76. Leslie Stephen, as quoted in Frederic William Maitland, *The Life and Letters of Leslie Stephen* (London: Duckworth, 1906), 150–51.

77. Virginia Woolf, as quoted in A. N. Wilson, *God's Funeral: The Decline of Faith in Western Civilization* (New York: Norton, 1999), 10.

78. Noel Annan, *Leslie Stephen: The Godless Victorian* (Chicago: University of Chicago Press, 1984), 70.

79. Wilson, *God's Funeral,* 8.

80. Stephen, "An Agnostic's Apology," *Fortnightly Review* 19 (June 1876), 860 (hereafter cited in the text as "AA").

81. Balfour, *A Defence of Philosophic Doubt;* also Leslie Stephen, "Philosophic Doubt," *Mind* 5 (April 1880), 157–81; and William James, *The Will to Believe* (1897; New York: Dover, 1956).

82. Dickinson S. Miller, "'The Will to Believe' and the Duty to Doubt," *International Journal of Ethics* 9 (January 1899), 169–95; W. L. Sheldon, "The Ethics of Doubt—Cardinal Newman," *International Journal of Ethics* 1 (1891), 224–38; D. W. Simon, "The Idealistic Remedy for Religious Doubt," *Contemporary Review* 62 (July–December 1892), 855–69.

83. Owen Chadwick, "Doubt," in *The Victorian Church,* 2 vols. (London: A. and C. Black, 1966–70), 2:113.

84. Ibid.

85. Clyde de L. Ryals, editor's introduction to Mrs. Humphry Ward, *Robert Elsmere* (1888; Lincoln: University of Nebraska Press, 1967), xii.

86. T. H. Green, *Works,* ed. R. L. Nettleship, 3 vols. (London: Longmans, Green, 1888), 3:233. See also Simon, "Idealistic Remedy for Religious Doubt," 864.

87. Walter Pater, *Guardian,* March 28, 1888.

88. Ward, *Robert Elsmere,* 496.

89. Matthew Arnold, *Literature and Dogma: An Essay towards a Better Apprehension of the Bible* (1873; New York: Macmillan, 1914), x.

90. John Morley, *On Compromise* (1874; London: Macmillan, 1917), 221.

91. Lance St. John Butler, *Victorian Doubt: Literary and Cultural Discourses* (Hemel Hemstead: Harvester Wheatsheaf, 1990), jacket copy.

92. Morley, *On Compromise,* 153–54.

93. Ibid., 154.

94. Butler, *Victorian Doubt,* 108.

95. Other likely models for Watts' *Hope* include paintings by Velázquez, Francisco Pacheco, and Bartolomé Esteban Murillo entitled *The Assumption of the Virgin.*

96. Lightman, *Origins of Agnosticism,* 1–2.

97. Alexis de Tocqueville, *Democracy in America* (1835–40), 2 vols., ed. J. P. Mayer, trans. George Lawrence (New York: Harper and Row, 1969), 2:290, 291.

98. See Gray, *Darwiniana,* esp. Article VII: "Evolution and Theology"; also Moore, *Post-Darwinian Controversies,* esp. chapters 10-12; Susan Jacoby, *Freethinkers: A History of American Secularism* (New York: Holt, 2004), chap. 9; and James Turner, *Without God, Without Creed: The Origins of Unbelief in America* (Baltimore: Johns Hopkins University Press, 1985).

99. George Santayana, "The Intellectual Temper of the Age," in *Winds of Doctrine: Studies in Contemporary Opinion* (London: Dent, 1913), 1.

100. Jean-Pierre Falret, "De la non-existence de la monomanie," in *Des Maladies mentales et des asiles d'aliénés* (Paris: Baillière, 1864), 425–48.

101. M. B. Bill, "Delusions of Doubt," *Popular Science Monthly* (New York) 21 (October 1882), 788–95; J. Mortimer Granville, "A Very Common Mind-Trouble," *Good Words* (London) 23 (1882), 340–43.

102. Bill, "Delusions of Doubt," 788 (hereafter cited in the text as "DD").

103. Santayana, "Intellectual Temper of the Age," 1.

104. Philip Combs Knapp, "The Insanity of Doubt," *American Journal of Psychology* 3 (January 1890), 13.

105. But see Lennard J. Davis's *Obsession: A History* (Chicago: University of Chicago Press, 2008) for an astute account of the fluctuating line between obsession and all that passes in U.S. culture as habit and ritual.

106. Granville, "Very Common Mind-Trouble," 343.

107. Ibid., 342.

108. Jacob Cooper, "Irrationality of Doubt," *Reformed Church Review* (Lancaster, Pa.) 4 (October 1897), 409 (hereafter cited in the text as "ID").

SIX *Faith-Based Certainty Meets the Gospel of Doubt*

1. Sigmund Freud, *Civilization and Its Discontents* (1929, rev. 1930), ed. and trans. James Strachey (New York: Norton, 1961), 10 (hereafter cited in the text as *CD*); Freud, *The Future of an Illusion* (1927; New York: Norton, 1989), 38.

2. Freud's original title for *Civilization and Its Discontents* was "Unhappiness in Civilization," but he later altered the "*Unglück*" to "*Unbehagen*" ("malaise" or "discomfort"). See Strachey's introduction to Freud, *Civilization*, 4.

3. Freud, *Future of an Illusion*, 34.

4. See, e.g., his interesting short commentary "A Religious Experience" (1928), in *The Standard Edition of the Complete Psychological Works of Sigmund Freud*, ed. and trans. James Strachey, 24 vols. (London: Hogarth, 1953–74), 21:167–72. See also Hans Küng, "Freud and the Problem of God," *Wilson Quarterly* 3.4 (1979), 162–71.

5. Christopher Hitchens, *God Is Not Great: How Religion Poisons Everything* (New York: Twelve, 2007), 18 (hereafter cited in the text as *GING*).

6. Carl Jung, "Face to Face," a 1959 BBC interview with John Freeman, as quoted in "Carl Gustav Jung—His Life," http://www.bbc.co.uk/dna/h2g2/A653410.

7. Richard Dawkins, *The God Delusion* (Boston: Houghton Mifflin, 2006); Thomas Crean, *God Is No Delusion: A Refutation of Richard Dawkins* (San Francisco: Ignatius, 2007); Sam Harris, *The End of Faith: Religion, Terror, and the Future of Reason* (New York: Norton, 2004); Timothy Keller, *The Reason for God: Belief in an Age of Skepticism* (New York: Riverhead, 2008); John Allen Paulos, *Irreligion: A Mathematician Explains Why the Arguments for God Just Don't Add Up* (New York: Hill and Wang, 2008); Scott Hahn and Benjamin Wiker, *Answering the New Atheism: Dismantling Dawkins' Case against God* (Steubenville, Ohio: Emmaus Road, 2008). Also John F. Haught, *God and the New Atheism: A Critical Response to Dawkins, Harris, and Hitchens* (Louisville, Ky.: Westminster John Knox, 2008).

8. Michael Novak, *No One Sees God: The Dark Night of Atheists and Believers* (New York: Doubleday, 2008), xxi.

9. Ibid., jacket.

10. Dawkins, *God Delusion,* jacket (hereafter cited in the text as *GD*).

11. Dawkins, "How Dare You Call Me a Fundamentalist: The Right to Criticise 'Faith-Heads,'" *Times* (London), May, 12, 2007.

12. Stephen Jay Gould, "Nonoverlapping Magisteria," *Natural History* 106.2 (1997), 16–22.

13. T. H. Huxley, "Agnosticism" (1889), *Science and Christian Tradition* (1894; New York: D. Appleton, 1915), 238; emphasis added.

14. John Humphrys, *In God We Doubt: Confessions of a Failed Atheist* (London: Hodder and Stoughton, 2007).

15. For more on the limits of secularism, see Karen Armstrong, *The Case for God* (New York: Knopf, 2009); Charles Taylor, *A Secular Age* (Cambridge, Mass.: Harvard University Press, 2007); and William E. Connolly, *Why I Am Not a Secularist* (Minneapolis: University of Minnesota Press, 1999), 6: "Secular models of thinking, discourse, and ethics are too constipated to sustain the diversity they seek to admire, while several theocratic models that do engage the density of culture do so in ways that are too highly centered."

16. Chris Lehmann, "Among the Non-Believers: The Tedium of Dogmatic Atheism," *Reason Magazine* (January 2005), http://reason.com/archives/2005/01/01 /among-the-non-believers.

17. Bernard Lightman, *The Origins of Agnosticism: Victorian Unbelief and the Limits of Knowledge* (Baltimore: Johns Hopkins University Press, 1987), 183.

18. Bill Maher, *Religulous* (LionsGate Films, 2008).

19. Stanley Fish, "The Three Atheists," *New York Times,* June 10, 2007. See also his review "God Talk," ibid., May 3, 2009.

20. Terry Eagleton, "Lunging, Flailing, Mispunching," *London Review of Books,* October 19, 2006, since expanded into the book: *Reason, Faith, and Revolution: Reflections on the God Debate* (New Haven: Yale University Press, 2009).

21. "The Creation Museum": http://creationmuseum.org.

22. Alfred, Lord Tennyson, *In Memoriam* (1850; New York: Norton, 1973), 36 (section 56, line 15).

23. Ken Ham, "What Really Happened to the Dinosaurs?" *The New Answers Book: Over Twenty-Five Questions on Creation/Evolution and the Bible,* ed. Ham (Green Forest, Ark.: Answers in Genesis, 2006), 150.

24. Ibid.

25. Keith Thomson, *Before Darwin: Reconciling God and Nature* (New Haven: Yale University Press, 2005), 281, quoting the King James Bible (Genesis 1:2).

26. Joseph Conrad, *The Secret Agent: A Simple Tale* (1907; Oxford: Oxford World Classics, 2004), 23.

27. For more on "theistic evolution," see Keith B. Miller, ed., *Perspectives on an Evolving Creation* (Grand Rapids, Mich.: Eerdmans, 2003), and Francis S. Collins, *The Language of God: A Scientist Presents Evidence for Belief* (New York: Free Press, 2006).

28. Robert G. Ingersoll, "The Gods" (1872), in *The Works of Robert G. Ingersoll*, 12 vols. (New York: Dresden/C. P. Farrell, 1902), 1:81; Asa Gray, "Evolution and Theology" (first published in the *Nation*, January 15, 1874), in *Darwiniana: Essays and Reviews Pertaining to Darwinism* (New York: D. Appleton, 1876), 252. See also Ingersoll, "Why I Am an Agnostic" (1896), in *Works* 4:esp. 52–53, and David N. Livingstone, *Darwin's Forgotten Defenders: The Encounter between Evangelical Theology and Evolutionary Thought* (Grand Rapids, Mich.: Eerdmans, 1987).

29. James McKeown, *Genesis: Two Horizons Old Testament Commentary* (Grand Rapids, Mich.: Eerdmans, 2008), 48.

30. Josiah Keep, "Doubts Concerning Evolution," *Overland Monthly and Out West Magazine* 18 (August 1891), 197.

31. John Thomas Scopes, *The World's Most Famous Court Trial: Tennessee Evolution Case: A Complete Stenographic Report* (Clark, N.J.: Lawbook Exchange, 1997), 77.

32. William Jennings Bryan, as quoted in ibid., 176.

33. Jon D. Miller, Eugenie C. Scott, and Shinji Okamoto, "Public Acceptance of Evolution," *Science* (Washington, D.C.), August 11, 2006, 765–66.

34. Frank Newport, "Majority of Republicans Doubt Theory of Evolution: More Americans Accept Theory of Creationism than Evolution," *Gallup News Service*, June 11, 2007.

35. *Edwards v. Aguillard*, 482 U.S. 578 (1987). The ruling nonetheless held that "teaching a variety of scientific theories about the origins of humankind to school children might be validly done with the *clear secular intent* of enhancing the effectiveness of science instruction" (emphasis added).

36. "Britons Unconvinced on Evolution," *BBC News Online*, January 26, 2006.

37. Edward Rothstein, "Adam and Eve in the Land of the Dinosaurs," *New York Times*, May 24, 2007.

38. Thomas Jefferson, *The Jefferson Bible: The Life and Morals of Jesus of Nazareth* (New York: Dover, 2006).

39. James Madison to William Bradford, Jr., April 1, 1774, in *Letters and Other Writings of James Madison, 1769–1793,* 4 vols. (Philadelphia: Lippincott, 1865), 1:14, 12; Madison to Edward Livingston, July 10, 1822, in *James Madison: Philosopher, Founder, and Statesman,* ed. John R. Vile, William D. Pederson, and Frank J. Williams (Athens: Ohio University Press, 2008), 128.

40. Kenneth T. Walsh, with Jeff Kass, "Separate Worlds," *U.S. News and World Report,* October 17, 2004.

41. Ibid.

42. Ruth Gledhill, "Archbishop: Disestablishment of Church of England Not 'The End of the World,'" *Times* (London), December 18, 2008.

43. Jerome Taylor, " 'Desperately Difficult' to Keep Church Together Over Women Bishops," *Independent,* July 12, 2010. See also the editorial "Tone-Deaf in Rome," *New York Times,* July 16, 2010, concerning the Vatican's pronouncement earlier that week that the ordination of women would be a "grave crime" as offensive as the scandal of priests who sexually abuse children.

44. Mark Hope-Unwin, as quoted in Jonathan Wynne-Jones, "Cathedral Turns to Wine Bars to Woo New Business," *Daily Telegraph,* August 31, 2008.

45. "'No God' Slogans for City Buses," *BBC News Online,* October 21, 2008.

46. "Jesus Said": as quoted by Ariane Sherine, "The Atheist Bus Journey," *Guardian,* January 6, 2009.

47. "'No God' Campaign Draws Complaint," *BBC News Online,* January 8, 2009.

48. As quoted in Sherine, "Atheist Bus Journey."

49. Laurie Goodstein, "More Atheists Shout It from the Rooftops," *New York Times,* April 27, 2009.

50. Bruce Feiler, "Where Have All the Christians Gone?" *Fox News,* September 25, 2009.

51. See also Kurt Andersen, "The End of the World as They Know It: Why Everyone Has Apocalypse Fever," *New York Magazine,* September 24, 2006.

52. Robert H. Ellison and Carol Engelhardt, "Prophecy and Anti-Popery in Victorian London: John Cumming Reconsidered," *Victorian Literature and Culture* 31 (2003), 379.

53. Chip Berlet of Political Research Associates, a progressive think thank monitoring civil liberties, interviewed on MSNBC's "Rachel Maddow" show, March 29, 2010, http://www.goddiscussion.com/22654/maddow-on-religious-extremism-30-40-percent-of-americans-believe-in-the-end-times/. According to Berlet, "30–40% of the American population religiously believes that the end times are coming, and of those probably 15% . . . think it will happen in their lifetime."

54. Editorial to "The New Prophets of Revelation" cover story, *Newsweek*, May 24, 2004, 3; emphases in original.

55. Tim LaHaye, introduction to Mark Hitchcock and Thomas Ice, *The Truth behind Left Behind: A Biblical View of the End Times* (Sisters, Oreg.: Multnomah, 2004), 6 (hereafter cited in the text as *TBLB*). See also Stephen Prickett, *Narrative, Religion and Science: Fundamentalism versus Irony, 1700–1999* (Cambridge: Cambridge University Press, 2002), chap. 1.

56. Ellison and Engelhardt, "Prophecy and Anti-Popery," 373–89.

57. Others, such as David Gergen, perceived the ad as advancing a different but related message: that Obama was being "uppity."

58. Mara Vanderslice, as quoted in Amy Sullivan, "An Antichrist Obama in McCain Ad?" *Time*, August 8, 2008.

59. Sullivan, "Antichrist Obama?" See also Nicholas D. Kristof, "The Push to 'Otherize' Obama," *New York Times*, September 20, 2008.

60. Rick Davis, appearing on the *Hugh Hewitt Show*, September 11, 2008.

61. Sullivan, "Antichrist Obama?" When Ronald Reagan first ran for office, it is worth adding to put evangelical anxiety in further context, he generated similar concern because each of his three names—Ronald Walker Reagan—contained six letters, resulting in the well-known 666 code for the devil.

62. Maira Kalman, "The Inauguration: At Last—And the Pursuit of Happiness," *New York Times*, January 29, 2009.

63. "Dobson Accuses Obama of 'Distorting' Bible," *CNN* Political Tracker, June 24, 2008. See also Peter Wehner, "Dobson vs. Obama," *Washington Post*, June 28, 2008.

64. Wehner, "Dobson Accuses Obama."

65. Ibid.

66. John Patrick Shanley, *Doubt: A Parable* (New York: Theatre Communications Group, 2005), 5 (hereafter cited in the text as *D*).

67. Ben Brantley, "As a Nun Stands Firm, the Ground Shifts Below," *New York Times*, April 1, 2005.

68. Shanley, as quoted in Alex Witchel, "The Confessions of John Patrick Shanley," *New York Times Magazine*, November 7, 2004. See also Peter Berger and Anton Zijderveld, *In Praise of Doubt: How to Have Convictions Without Becoming a Fanatic* (New York: HarperOne, 2010).

69. Leslie Stephen, "An Agnostic's Apology," *Fortnightly Review* 19 (June 1876), 859.

70. Virginia Woolf, "Poetry, Fiction and the Future" (August 14, 1927), in *Virginia*

Woolf: Selected Essays, ed. David Bradshaw (Oxford: Oxford World Classics, 2008), 75.

71. Robert M. Baird, "The Creative Role of Doubt in Religion," *Journal of Religion and Health* 19.3 (1980), 175.

72. [William Nicholson], *The Doubts of Infidels; or, Queries Relative to Scriptural Inconsistencies & Contradictions, Submitted for Elucidation to the Bench of Bishops, &c. &c. by a Weak but Sincere Christian* (1781; rept. London: R. Carlile, 1819); Robert Chambers, *Vestiges of the Natural History of Creation and Other Evolutionary Writings,* ed. and intro. James A. Secord (Chicago: University of Chicago Press, 1994), 153; J. Anthony Froude, *The Nemesis of Faith* (London: John Chapman, 1849), 84.

ACKNOWLEDGMENTS

It is a pleasure to thank the many people who have helped me finish this book. I am grateful to Leonard Wilson, Lyell's biographer; Julian Reid, archivist of Corpus Christi College, Oxford; and Roderick Gordon, executor of the Reverend William Buckland's estate in England. I am also strongly indebted to several scholars working on nineteenth-century science and religion, including Bernard Lightman, Jude V. Nixon, Martin Rudwick, James Secord, and Keith Stewart Thomson. Books by Lance St. John Butler, Jennifer Michael Hecht, and A. N. Wilson were also frequent touchstones. I was fortunate indeed in the external readers whom Yale asked to evaluate the manuscript, and I greatly appreciate their expert advice.

I owe a debt of thanks to Holly Clayson and Northwestern University's Humanities Institute for giving me a well-timed fellowship to work on the manuscript and to the dean of Weinberg College of Arts and Sciences for a sabbatical leave to complete it. Many thanks also to my colleagues in the English Department at Northwestern, especially fellow Victorianists Chris Herbert, Jules Law, and Tracy Davis. Wendy Wall and Susan Manning, former and current chairs of the department, helped in numerous other ways. Chris Froula, Martin Mueller, Barbara Newman, and our lively cohort of Victorianist graduate students gave different kinds of encouragement. Gretchen Gurujal helped me track down many of the articles cited in this book. I cannot fail to thank the wonderful group of Northwestern seniors who in Spring 2010 took my Humanities seminar, "The Power and History of Religious Doubt." Earlier versions of chapters 3, 4, and 5 were presented respectively at Northwestern's Humanities Institute; as a plenary at the British Association for Victorian Studies conference at the University of Leicester; and as the 2007 Josephine Ferguson Lecture in the English Department at Tulane University. Thanks especially to Gowan Dawson, Molly Rothenberg, and Gaurav Desai for arranging these visits.

Emma Butterfield, a picture librarian at the National Portrait Gallery, London, dealt with a stream of requests with patience and humor. Thanks also to Paul Cox, assistant curator of the gallery's archives and library, for helping me hunt down the owners of several other images. I owe a debt of similar thanks to Auste Mickunaite at the British Library; Daragh Kenny at the National Gallery, London; and to Frances Gandy and Hannah Westall at Girton College, Cambridge. I am grateful to Lybi Ma and the team at *Psychology Today* for their ongoing support. Peter Robertson, editor of the *International Literary Quarterly,* let me reproduce several paragraphs from my essay "On Literalism," issue 5 (November 2008).

Wendy Strothman, Lauren MacLeod, and Dan O'Connell at the Strothman Agency in Boston have been wonderful interlocutors. It's also been a pleasure to work again with Jean Black, my editor at Yale. Sincere thanks to her, to Jaya Chatterjee, her assistant, and to my superb copyeditors Vivian Wheeler and Laura Jones Dooley.

My biggest debt is to Jorge Arce and to our families and friends in England, the States, and Perú. I dedicate this book to him, and to them, with great pleasure, deep thanks, and,"pues, sin duda"—without doubt.